Musical Intimacies and
Indigenous Imaginaries

Musical Intimacies and Indigenous Imaginaries

ABORIGINAL MUSIC AND DANCE IN PUBLIC PERFORMANCE

BYRON DUECK

OXFORD
UNIVERSITY PRESS

OXFORD
UNIVERSITY PRESS

Oxford University Press is a department of the University of Oxford.
It furthers the University's objective of excellence in research, scholarship,
and education by publishing worldwide.

Oxford   New York
Auckland   Cape Town   Dar es Salaam   Hong Kong   Karachi
Kuala Lumpur   Madrid   Melbourne   Mexico City   Nairobi
New Delhi   Shanghai   Taipei   Toronto

With offices in
Argentina   Austria   Brazil   Chile   Czech Republic   France   Greece
Guatemala   Hungary   Italy   Japan   Poland   Portugal   Singapore
South Korea   Switzerland   Thailand   Turkey   Ukraine   Vietnam

Oxford is a registered trademark of Oxford University Press in the UK and certain other
countries.

Published in the United States of America by
Oxford University Press
198 Madison Avenue, New York, NY 10016

© Oxford University Press 2013

Library of Congress Cataloging-in-Publication Data
Dueck, Byron.
Musical intimacies and indigenous imaginaries : aboriginal music and dance in public
performance/Byron Dueck.
   pages cm
Includes bibliographical references and index.
ISBN 978–0–19–974764–1 (hardback : alk. paper)—ISBN 978–0–19–974765–8 (pbk. : alk.
paper)   1. Indians of North America—Manitoba—Music—History and criticism.   2. Folk
music—Manitoba—History and criticism.   3. Indians of North America—Manitoba—Social
life and customs.   4. Music—Social aspects—Manitoba.   I. Title.
ML3563.7.M36D84 2013
781.62'97007127—dc23
    2013005307

Publication of this book was supported by the AMS 75 PAYS Publication Endowment
Fund of the American Musicological Society

A version of chapter 2, "Public and Intimate Sociability in First Nations and Métis Fiddling,"
appeared in *Ethnomusicology* 51/1 (2007): 30–63.
Thanks to the Society for Ethnomusicology for allowing it to be republished here.

9 8 7 6 5 4 3 2 1
Printed in the United States of America
on acid-free paper

Contents

Acknowledgments

This book would not have been possible without the many people who supported, taught, and guided me, invited me to musical gatherings and dances, introduced me to their friends and families, welcomed me into their homes, and allowed me to become part of their lives. Foremost among these are Edward and Audrey Guiboche, Victor and Laureen Courchene, and Chris Beach. It is thanks to them that I learned about many performances and venues and was able to travel to them. I was regularly in the company of one or more of them at a number of weekly events that, in the early 2000s, ran in inner-city venues in Winnipeg: Edward Guiboche's Wednesday night coffeehouse at William Whyte School, Stirling Ranville's Monday night coffeehouse at 215 Selkirk Avenue, and Ivan Spence's Thursday night fiddle dance at the Winnipeg Indian and Metis Friendship Centre.

These gatherings were my central points of entry into urban aboriginal social life, and it was at them that I met many of the people who would play a role in shaping my experience of Manitoban indigenous musical sociability, including Albert Audy, Joey Bird, Reg Blackbird, Rose Boissinot, Billy Hamelin, Dennis and Doreen Johnston, Tommy Knott, Emery Marsden, Nelson Menow, Eugene Moore, Stirling and Yvette Ranville, Kendra and Mary Sinclair, Ivan and Verna Spence, and my dance teacher, Jean Sutherland. These gatherings opened up other opportunities for socializing in turn; it was thanks to the Ranville coffeehouse, for instance, that I became part of a loose-knit group of people who, for a time, met on Monday nights at a North End doughnut shop, including Anne Beach and her children, Caroline, Chris, and Ingrid, as well as Adria Burkhardt, Stan Cook, and Jack Meade.

While the aforementioned venues played an important part in shaping my social activities in Winnipeg, research also took place in other contexts. Others who contributed substantially to my understanding of Manitoban indigenous music, dance, and culture include Cliff Maytwayashing, fiddler; David McLeod, CEO of radio station NCI FM; Mark Morisseau, my fiddle teacher; Ryan Richard, dancer; Roger Roulette, my Ojibwe professor; Gloria Spence, general manager of Manito Ahbee; and Ray Stevenson and Rhonda James, traditional singers and powwow club coordinators. Many of the aforementioned were kind enough to grant me interviews.

I also owe thanks to many others who agreed to be interviewed over the years, including Danny Bulycz; Kyle, Louis, and Orville Councillor; the Dick Brothers; Ness Michaels; Ernest Monias; Morris Moneas; Tash and Alex Moodie; Errol Ranville; Mary Richard; Ray St. Germain; and Percy Tuesday. I am further grateful to those people who gave their permission for their music, lyrics, and writing to appear in this book, including Albert Audy, Chris Beach, Donald Bradburn, Garry Lepine, Juliet Little, Cliff Maytwayashing, Olga McIvor, Nelson Menow, Errol Ranville, Cal Richard, Les Shannacappo, and the family of Emile Spence.

This volume has also benefited from the guidance, support, and critical interventions of fellow researchers and academic colleagues. In Manitoba I had much help from Lewis Stubbs at the University of Manitoba Archives and Special Collections, from Gilbert Comeault and Chris Kotecki at the Archives of Manitoba, and from Gilles Lesage at the Service d'archives de la Société historique de Saint-Boniface. Jennifer Brown, Gerald Friesen, Peter Geller, and Maureen Matthews gave guidance and encouragement as well. I began the fieldwork I draw upon in this book while undertaking a Ph.D. in ethnomusicology at the University of Chicago, and I owe thanks to those who mentored me while I was in that program, including Phil Bohlman, my dissertation advisor, whose dialectical approaches to ethnomusicology have been an inspiration for the explorations of intimacies and imaginaries here, and Rick Cohn, Martin Stokes, and Larry Zbikowski. Their influence is evident throughout the following pages, as is (in obvious and subtle ways) that of students who were pursuing their doctorates at the University of Chicago at the same time I did, including Jayson Beaster-Jones, Vicki Brennan, Jeffers Engelhardt, Luis-Manuel Garcia, Jaime Jones, Josh Pilzer, and Joti Rockwell.

Since I moved to the UK, my work has benefited immensely from discussions and collaborations with the members of the Excursions and Meaning in Music Performance team—Martin Clayton, Laura Leante, Mark Doffman, Glaura Lucas, Andy McGuiness, Nikki Moran, and Adrian Poole—as well as with other UK colleagues, including Mark Banks, Georgina Born, Anna Morcom, Henry Stobart, Catherine Tackley, and Jason Toynbee. I am particularly indebted to Martin Stokes, whose questions and comments continue to provoke insights and point to weaknesses (as they did on the other side of the Atlantic). I have also been fortunate to benefit from conversations and collaborations with other scholars of indigenous music, including Klisala Harrison, Anna Hoefnagels, Sarah Quick, Dylan Robinson, Chris Scales, and Joshua Tucker. I owe special thanks to Beverley Diamond for her encouragement, criticism, and guidance with this book and other projects.

At Oxford University Press, I am indebted to Suzanne Ryan, who provided guidance and encouragement as I worked on this first monograph, to my copy editor, Barbara Norton, and to the anonymous reviewer of early drafts of parts of this volume. In Winnipeg, I owe thanks to Anders Swanson, who provided the maps.

My research would not have been possible without the support of family and friends. One of the benefits of doing fieldwork "at home" was that it allowed me to spend some time closer to my parents, Ernest and Lorraine Dueck, and to a number of old friends, including Glenn Bergen and Mike Koop. I am especially grateful for the companionship of my partner, Brenna Speiser, who, while often physically in a different city or country, has nevertheless been together with me since the very early days of this research.

In closing it is appropriate to extend special thanks to the five people mentioned at the very beginning of these acknowledgments, who became close friends during fieldwork, who were present with me at many of the events described in this book, and who made possible many opportunities and experiences I would not otherwise have had: Chris Beach; Laureen Courchene, who passed away in 2011; her husband, Victor Courchene, who passed away in 2010; Audrey Guiboche; and her husband, Edward Guiboche, who passed away in 2006. It is thanks to them that this book, and my research, range over a variety of musical and choreographic practices rather than focusing on any single one. From the beginning, the aboriginal music they introduced me to included the secular as well as the sacred, the new as well as the old, and the Christian as well as the traditional, and they moved between musical spaces matter-of-factly, in ways that suggested continuities rather than differences between them. Their inclusive understanding of what constituted aboriginal music suggested that neither tradition nor contemporaneity were exclusively bound to the genres and practices most frequently associated with those terms. I am profoundly indebted to them for all they have taught and continue to teach me. This book is dedicated to them.

Maps

Map 1 Manitoba, showing major centers and aboriginal communities. Map by Anders Swanson.

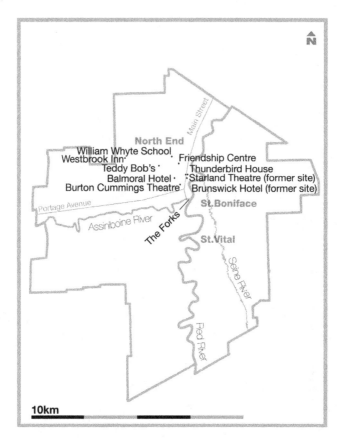

Map 2 Winnipeg, showing venues for aboriginal musical performance discussed in this volume. Map by Anders Swanson.

Musical Intimacies and Indigenous Imaginaries

1

Introduction

Publicity, Counterpublicity, Antipublicity

"Run as One"

Manitoban aboriginal audiences heard C-Weed's "Run as One" countless times on the radio and in live performance during the summer of 2002. Its theme of aboriginal solidarity and integration of elements of traditional song rendered it an ideal vehicle to represent indigenous aspirations, including at several high-profile concerts bringing together First Nations and Métis people from across the Canadian province and further afield. In its recorded form, the song combines two very different idioms. It is in part a rock tune, and throughout much of its length an insistent pentatonic riff is reiterated in the electric guitar as other instruments progress through a series of slow harmonic changes. Bandleader and songwriter Errol C-Weed Ranville sings with passion, but intimately and almost conversationally.[1] This fades up from, and back down into, a second piece in a very different style: an honor song performed by the drum group Red Bull. The mixed-gender ensemble sings with high, tensed voices in unison and octaves to the steady beat of a large drum, beginning each "push-up" or strophe at the very top of the male singers' range.[2]

Thus "Run as One" gradually emerges from drum song and slowly disappears into it. The musical rhetoric seems straightforward: Ranville's contemporary song grows out of something older and more traditionally aboriginal. The juxtaposition of genres furthermore suggests a link between the individual and the communal: Ranville's solitary, reflective voice stands contrasted with powwow song, the iconic sound of North American indigeneity in collective public performance. Still, "Run as One" works well enough without its evocative musical frame, and in live performances in 2002 and 2003 Ranville typically performed it without the members of Red Bull, as a straightforward rock number.

The lyrics reflect on the "Indian summer" of 1990, when Quebec police and Canadian armed forces engaged in an armed standoff with members of the Mohawk community of Kanesatake in southern Quebec. They refer to a legacy of broken treaty promises and intimidation by the state while expressing hope for future aboriginal generations. They are above all a call for unity: referring to the sense of togetherness aboriginal people had experienced a decade earlier, during the Kanesatake crisis—"So strong with pride, side by side / We shared a social changing tide"—they enjoin their audience to a similar accord in the present and future:

> Got to run as one now that it's begun,
> Feel the beat of a different drum,
> And close our ranks and give our thanks to
> The spirit up above.[3]

The identity of the "we" in the lyrics is never explicitly stated, but it seems evident that it refers to the song's indigenous audience. Explaining the song to me in an interview conducted in the autumn of 2002, Ranville remarked:

> The world changed a bit because of Oka [i.e. the Kanesatake crisis]. We came together somewhat as a nation. We joined hands in a lot of ways in spite of our geographical and political differences across the country. In the Maritimes, the Native people there, hey, their reality is fishing, and it's a big issue. It isn't to me on the Prairies. But I'm still Native. And so are they. The logging and the environment...it's a bigger issue down there. Here in northern Manitoba, the [hydroelectric power], the rivers and streams that run through our homeland, reservations, it's a big issue. It's not the same issue as South Dakota, or the swamps in Florida for the Seminoles. But we're all still Native. We're all still aboriginal, we still have roots and characteristics and realities, of human condition. So when I say, "Let's run as one," there's all sorts of things that we can get together and get together on, and in doing so, produce a new level of power, influence.

I heard Ranville (Figure 1.1) perform "Run as One" in a number of contexts during the summer of 2002, two of which stand out. In early August Ranville performed an evening concert on a large outdoor stage at the Forks, a park located at the juncture of the Red and Assiniboine Rivers at the center of Manitoba's capital and largest city, Winnipeg (see Map 2). In official discourses the juncture of the rivers is celebrated as a place of encounter: between indigenous groups, between those indigenous groups and European traders, between anglophone and francophone Winnipeggers, and between these and other groups that together constitute the city and the nation. Performances at the Forks therefore often have a symbolic weight, iconically representing the city, the province, and the nation; the

Figure 1.1 ERROL RANVILLE. Photo by Jerry Flett/NCI FM. Used with permission of NCI FM.

linguistic and cultural constituencies that make up these polities; and meetings between these groups (see Dueck 2005: 122–26).

A similar kind of symbolism was in play at the concert at which Ranville performed. Entitled Canada Night and sponsored by the federal government, it was the last in a series of themed shows held in tandem with the 2002 North American Indigenous Games (NAIG).[4] Canada Night featured indigenous performers from across the country, as well as a high-profile American singer and songwriter, Keith Secola. The musicians performed in front of an immense Canadian flag. But while this backdrop suggested that the evening's festivities celebrated Canada, the lyrics of "Run as One" suggested that rather they affirmed a different—indigenous—national "we." Tellingly, earlier that summer, I had heard an emcee at another event, attended by a largely Native audience, describe Ranville's "Run as One" as "the new aboriginal national anthem." The North American Indigenous Games celebrated a diverse indigenous nation that spanned contemporary political borders, bringing together thousands of young Native women and men from communities across Canada and the United States.

Thus the Games, like Ranville's song, invited simultaneous reflection on both indigenous solidarity and its sociopolitical contexts: that is, on both the continent-wide aboriginal nation and its contemporary Canadian and American locations. Much of the public discussion concerning the Games framed them as an opportunity for aboriginal people to negotiate their relationship to settler society. One NAIG organizer described them as not only a celebration of aboriginal culture, but also an otherwise rare chance for aboriginal voices and aspirations to be at the center of public attention.[5] Articles in the *Winnipeg Free Press* portrayed athletics and the arts, the two main focuses of the Games, as positive forces in the lives of indigenous people.[6] And at least one Native commentator portrayed them as an event that called mainstream stereotypes and prejudices into question: a *Thunder Voice News* editorial remarked at the conclusion of the Games that, perhaps contrary to mainstream expectations, "the large influx of Aboriginal people did not cause the crime rate to soar."[7]

In keeping with the focus on youthful aspiration and success, Ranville took to the stage with a band of young singers, songwriters, and musicians who moved through his material confidently, occasionally stepping to the front with songs or tunes of their own. As one of the final groups to perform at the final NAIG concert, the C-Weed band represented a culmination of sorts, and it is significant that they finished with "Run as One." The song and the performance seemed to capture what the Games were about: the talent, confidence, and aspirations of (young) aboriginal people, Native pride and success, and North American indigenous solidarity.

I saw Ranville perform "Run as One" in a very different venue on a Saturday in September of the same year: the Westbrook Inn, a medium-sized Winnipeg nightclub located west of the city center. In 2002 the Westbrook courted a Native clientele by regularly hosting well-known aboriginal country bands, including Ernest Monias and the Boys, the Dutiaume Brothers, the Dick Brothers, and various incarnations of the C-Weed Band. On Saturday afternoons the music got started at around three. The headlining band typically opened with an hourlong performance that was broadcast live on NCI FM, a radio station with a Manitoba-wide, and primarily aboriginal, audience. A semistructured jam session usually followed during which singers and songwriters came up to perform, accompanied by members of the headlining band. The latter resumed the better part of the musical duties in the evening, typically playing its strongest material just before the bar closed at two in the morning. The Westbrook had a mixed reputation: it had an auspicious association with NCI, one of Manitoba's most successful and widely respected aboriginal institutions, but it was also rumored to be a hangout for members of organized-crime groups.

On the Saturday in question, I went to see C-Weed's afternoon performance and stayed to watch the jam session for a few hours. I went home for a bit to clear my head and returned later in the evening. Upon my return I ran into a friend, Tracy, who had volunteered with me at the North American Indigenous Games—in fact, I had stood with her and her family while watching the C-Weed Band perform at the Forks. She invited me to sit down with her party: her in-law Donna, her uncle, and her uncle's significant other.[8] As the evening progressed we talked, drank, listened to the band, and danced; Donna refused to let us pay for anything. Toward the end of the evening, C-Weed performed some of his best-known songs, to an enthusiastic response. The band of younger players from the NAIG concert was absent; C-Weed performed instead with a group of freelance musicians who regularly worked on the aboriginal country circuit. The performance was perhaps unsurprisingly less polished than the Forks gig—the lead guitar player, I remember, made some obvious blunders—but it got a warm reaction from the audience all the same. People moved onto the dance floor and even formed an impromptu conga line during one number. The band concluded with "Run as One" shortly before closing time as even more patrons crowded the dance floor.[9]

After the show was over, Donna invited us around to her house to continue partying. She paid for several cases of beer at the vendor around the back of the venue, and I loaded these into my car. Plans were somewhat complicated when it was discovered that Donna's estranged husband, Danny (another of Tracy's uncles), was also at the bar and had been hiding from Donna during the show. Amid much laughter, he was roped into coming along too. All in all, eight of us headed over to Donna's house: Tracy; her uncle Danny; his estranged wife, Donna; Tracy's other uncle; his significant other; and three non-intimates (including me) they had invited along from the bar. The party was convivial enough, and there was no shortage of drinks, but Donna controlled much of the conversation and kept bringing it back to how Danny had done wrong by her, and how he should stop fooling around with his current girlfriend and come back to her. Danny protested: he had broken things off with Donna and was now in a new relationship, which was no passing infidelity. He expressed his determination to sleep downstairs rather than in his wife's bed. At one point the two of them disappeared upstairs, and when they came back down, Danny's head was bleeding. They both insisted that he had fallen in the bathroom. As various partygoers succumbed to exhaustion, the socializing wound down, and the party ended around daybreak.

Imagining, Intimacy, and Public Space

IMAGINARIES

The preceding accounts illustrate, among other things, three interrelated and intersecting contexts of musical sociability explored throughout this volume: imaginaries, intimacies, and public spaces. "Imagining" is here understood as an orientation to a public of strangers. It is a relationship, facilitated by mass mediation, between people who, though unknown to one another, understand themselves to have something in common. Such imagining is evident when, for instance, Manitobans speak of "Manitobans" or aboriginal people discuss "the aboriginal community." It is also apparent when Errol Ranville speaks in the first person plural in "Run as One" or when he remarks, in the interview quoted above, that "we came together somewhat as a nation." In that interview Ranville mentions aboriginal people from maritime Canada, Manitoba, South Dakota, and Florida, making it clear that his song speaks about (and to) an aboriginal public that encompasses many more people than one person could ever get to know.

Related to imagining are "imaginaries," social formations that come into being through the circulation of mass-mediated performances and publications. These are similar in some respects to the "imagined communities" described by Benedict Anderson (1991) but should be understood along the lines of the "publics and counterpublics" explored by Michael Warner (2002). They come into existence as people perform and publish for unknown audiences, and especially as they acknowledge the previously circulating performances and publications of others—for instance by training their minds and bodies to make music in ways that respond to those previous performances. Imaginaries emerge as performances, broadcasts, publications, and acts of bodily discipline respond to previous ones, and anticipate others to come (Warner 2002: 90).

The use of terms such as "imagining" should not suggest that publics or imaginaries are unreal. The lyrics of "Run as One," the effort that went into putting together the North American Indigenous Games, and the willingness of men and women to devote their lives to the defense and development of nations evidence the reality and importance of social imaginaries (see Anderson 1991). At the same time, these terms convey some of the indeterminacy and contestedness of publics, for participants construe the imaginaries they address in very different ways. "Imagining" and "imaginaries" should also be distinguished from concepts of the sacred world, although, as will become evident, spiritual practices and sacred songs play important roles in aboriginal public culture (and in key ways shape and even impose limits on indigenous publicness). The terms are used here to describe the social relationships that mass mediation makes possible.[10]

Such relationships are very evident in the case of C-Weed's "Run as One." In its recorded form, the song circulates through radio broadcasts, on compact discs, and on the Internet. It stands in dialogue with other, already disseminated "texts," most clearly news reports and commentary concerning the Kanesatake crisis. And so it can be understood to belong to a network of mutually referential mass-mediated performances, broadcasts, and publications that together enable a public to emerge. But, crucially, the lyrics imagine and address a particular kind of public: an aboriginal "we" whose members felt proud or united by the experience of seeing First Nations people stand up to the government. In enjoining this audience to "run as one," the lyrics not only identify listeners as an aboriginal public, but also encourage them to be one. In doing so the song does explicitly what acts of public address typically do implicitly: it hails a particularized audience (see Berlant 2008; Warner 2002), a listenership whose members share experiences and hopes, a sense of a social transformation in process, and a feeling of solidarity.[11]

INTIMACIES

Standing in contrast to imaginaries—though not exclusive of them, as will become clear—are intimacies. Intimacy, as I will use that term in this volume, is not the same thing as privacy, or loving or tender closeness. It rather describes engagements between known and knowable persons, especially those that involve the "interaction rituals" (see Goffman 1967) of "face-to-face" social and musical contact.[12] Such a definition might perhaps be perceived to strip the term of some of its resonances: for instance, of amity or the expectation of future mutuality.[13] It also orients the term toward somewhat different social practices than those explored by recent theorists of intimate publics and cultural intimacy, as I suggest below. Yet the point of using it in this way is to make it in certain respects more inclusive, especially of real-time musical and choreographic encounters. Intimacy in the broad sense proposed here does not refer only to the relationship Donna wished to reestablish with her estranged husband, or the closeness between the members of Tracy's family. It also refers to the getting-to-know-you conversations between the latter and the strangers they invited to Donna's house, and to the interactions between Ranville, his band members, and the patrons dancing at the Westbrook. It can also be understood to include the personal relationships that people establish or cultivate through telephone or Skype calls and email or Facebook correspondence—but not the general "stranger-sociability" that exists between people who address unknown audiences by means of mass mediation (here compare Berlant 2008: viii).

The idea that some relationships are more intimate than others is retained. People who interact frequently tend to have expectations that are more closely calibrated. This is typically true of kin, friends, and members of small communities, and of musicians and dancers who regularly perform together. Note, however, the variety of potential intimacies: in relationships both tender and adversarial, both "private" and "public," and not only between lovers and spouses, but also between regular sparring partners and bitter rivals.

PUBLIC SPACES

A third context for music making, and the most important for the ethnographic investigations in this volume, is public space. Venues such as the Forks or the Westbrook occupy a middle ground between publicity and intimacy, as Figure 1.2 shows. On the one hand, they are oriented to a public of strangers, extending mass-mediated invitations to unspecified audiences and clienteles. On the other hand, when people show up at the advertised events, the intimacy of interaction ritual commences. Attendees behave in ways that take into account the others around them, whether this involves getting to know them, moving with and around them on the dance floor, or keeping them politely out of frame. The becoming-intimate that is possible in public spaces is particularly evident in the account just related, in which three strangers were invited to a house party, made beneficiaries of a hostess's generosity, and recruited to roles as witnesses and commentators in a family conflict. Public venues thus occupy a kind of civil twilight, being simultaneously oriented to an imagined public and sites of face-to-face engagement.[14]

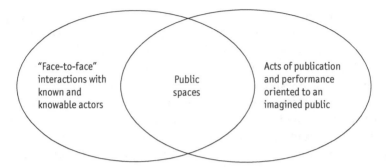

Figure 1.2 PUBLIC SPACE: Bridging intimacy and imagining.

The way the term "intimacy" is deployed here might perhaps be criticized for confusing social and physical proximity. Certainly, as noted above, intimacy can emerge or develop in the course of nonproximate contact—telephone conversations, written correspondence, social networking over the Internet—but the accounts in the pages that follow nevertheless do privilege co-presence and real-time interaction. Whatever the disadvantages, this has at least two benefits. First, it facilitates discussions of how people interact in the shared public venues that are the settings for most of the ethnographic accounts that follow. In such spaces people are often physically close but socially distant—yet they have opportunities to move into more socially proximate states (depending of course on the kinds of social comportment that are deemed normative within these spaces, agents' penchant for transgressing rules, etc.). Second, and perhaps more important, the definition of intimacy used here seems particularly amenable to discussions of musical and choreographic interactions.

Although I distinguish imagining and intimacy, they are nevertheless interrelated, as the in-between phenomenon of public space suggests. Indeed, face-to-face engagement is often intricately entwined with the stranger-sociability that enables public culture. So, for instance, interpersonal interaction in public spaces is frequently an index of what participants perceive to be (or, in cases of activism, believe should be) normative behavior in the public sphere. Patrons at a bar gauge their social and musical behavior and expectations to those of others they imagine might come through the door. Perhaps more obviously, such interactions—including of musicians, audience members, or both—are regularly broadcast outward from specific, emplaced sites to a wider public. Intimacies are continually becoming the very stuff of publicness.

That musical and social interactions can become the material of public culture does not mean they always do so, and this has two important implications for the character of indigenous intimacies and imaginaries. First, certain practices are more common in, and valued by, certain publics. Circulating music and discourse not only constitute imaginaries but also distinguish them from one another.[15] For this reason publics are discussed here in the plural: national publics are differentiated from indigenous ones, and dominant publics from sub-altern ones. Second, certain realms of indigenous cultural practice tend not to take much account of publics and in some cases explicitly avoid public exposure. Practitioners prioritize interpersonal interactions and circumscribe publicness. All cultures place limits on what is or can be oriented to an audience of strangers, of course, but they do so in different ways. Part of what distinguishes indigenous intimacies and imaginaries, then, is how aboriginal people prioritize the former with respect to the latter.[16] Bearing these points in mind, I investigate how indigenous people have made publicness their own with the help of two recurring concepts: counterpublicity and antipublicity.

Counterpublicity

One important difference between C-Weed's performances at the Forks and the Westbrook was that alcohol was unavailable at the former. While this was an exception for concerts at the Forks, it was not at all unusual for high-profile aboriginal events. Many First Nations and Métis people are strongly opposed to the use of intoxicants, and alcohol is frequently unavailable at events celebrating what are considered to be the exemplary elements of aboriginal culture. That more than half of the competitors at the Games had not yet reached the legal drinking age was probably also a consideration, but Manitoban indigenous concerts and gatherings are frequently "dry" even when the average age of attendees is much higher.

It is not only indigenous discourses that characterize aboriginal drinking as problematic, but national ones as well. For decades the Canadian government prohibited Status Indians from purchasing or consuming intoxicating drinks. Perceptions persist to the present day that aboriginal people are particularly prone to alcohol abuse, and drinking is widely held to be a destructive force in Native communities and families (see Thatcher 2004; for a historical survey see MacAndrew and Edgerton 1969: 100–64). The stereotype of the "drunken Indian" is still active and hurtful—indeed, some readers, encountering the above narrative of good-timing at the Westbrook, may have been dismayed to see an apparent recapitulation of the kind there. Aboriginal Canadians are painfully aware of the surveillance of the national public in this area, and this pressure is probably partly responsible for the negative perceptions they have of it themselves (see Dueck 2013a). The delicateness of the question is evident in the following comments by Errol Ranville:

> The whole booze thing and our world and its relation to country music: We've had our problems since day one, I am the first to admit, with booze. And, hey…I've been a nightclub owner for the past ten years, selling booze, to my own people [Ranville opened clubs under the

name "C-Weed's Cabaret" in three western Canadian cities]. So, getting away from the hypocrisy of that...if you really want to get down to the truth, the reality, in your studies, that's a sensitive issue. A very sensitive issue, and...there's shame attached to it, and there's also stereotypical connotations attached to it, so it's hard to deal with, to approach, without offending somebody about it.

Ranville's remarks convey his ambivalent feelings about alcohol as a substance that is at once a source of problems and one of business revenue. But they also point to the national context that has helped to shape aboriginal sensitivities; his use of the word "stereotypes" is telling here. There is a hint, too, that exactly this national context is salient to the interview with me, a nonaboriginal researcher— that he as a spokesman feels called upon to explain why aboriginal people act in ways the national public finds disturbing ("if you really want to get down to the truth, the reality, in your studies...").

It is difficult to explore the subject of aboriginal drinking without reproducing one or both of two well-established national folk discourses: racist stereotypes of "drunken Indians" on the one hand and discourses concerning "the troubling substance abuse of Native peoples" on the other. Proposed here is an analysis that understands aboriginal good-timing to already be in a long-standing relationship with such discourses, as a kind of problematic or "counter" publicness, believed by insiders and outsiders alike to differ from nationally normative forms of civility.

Interaction at bars with a largely working-class aboriginal clientele tends to differ from the middle-class Euro-Canadian habitus (Bourdieu 1977) that plays a significant role in determining what is normative in western Canada. As chapter 3 explores, sociability is generally more convivial, even exuberant, and patrons tend to drink more and over longer periods of time (temporally extended social gatherings are characteristic of both "wet" and "dry" sociability). Musically, jam sessions are common and manifest an egalitarian, participatory spirit. There tends not to be a great concern for getting things exactly right, and if a singer chooses an unfamiliar tune, the accompanying musicians muddle through as best as they can.[17] In some cases, musicians seem to flaunt the rhythmic norms typical in popular music, yet this does not seem to hinder the enjoyment of the audience.

But, as noted, the kinds of comportment that are characteristic in the spaces of the aboriginal public sphere are regarded as problematic in mainstream discourse—and indeed by many members of the aboriginal public themselves. Indigenous venues, behaviors, ways of making music—in short, indigenous ways of being public—are stigmatized. There exist dominant and subaltern forms of publicness, a distinction characterized here, following Michael Warner (2002), as that between publics and counterpublics. As Warner explains, a counterpublic is not simply one whose performances, practices, and behaviors are understood by the larger public to be problematic, but additionally a social formation that understands itself to stand in a problematized relationship to normative ones. (In using the term "counterpublic," I do not seek to imbue it with the romance of political resistance that Berlant identifies in some uses of it (2008: 24). Indeed, overtly political songs such as C-Weed's "Run as One" constitute a minority of the expressive material that circulates in the aboriginal public sphere and that is explored in the pages that follow. The "counter" in my use of "counterpublic" points to disparities in power, and especially to how certain publics, and the practices and performances that constitute them, are problematized and derogated by others.)

In the arena of musical aesthetics, certain indigenous practices can also be understood as a form of counterpublicity. This is not so much the case with those artists who have enjoyed mainstream success or recognition—Errol Ranville or Ray St. Germain, for instance. It is truer of the large constituency of aboriginal singers and instrumentalists who make recordings and give performances on the fringes of the mainstream. Here there is less concern about aligning musical performances with some professional ideal: almost anyone with a voice and a song can contribute. Some of these performances might be deemed unacceptable in national public forums but are entirely appropriate in the venues in which they take place and in which a participatory ethos reigns. Consider again the contrast between the two shows by Errol Ranville described above. The first performance, presented on one of the most visible stages in the city, was supported by a well-rehearsed group of performers; the second, held in the more stigmatized environs of the Westbrook, was backed by a band of pickup players who made some noticeable mistakes. Nobody was complaining at either one.

Mainstream musicians and audiences often perceive infelicities in the music that fills indigenous public spaces. Many hear an absence of professionalism or a failure to live up to dominant aesthetic standards. At a 2008 music convention, for instance, I heard a prominent figure from the Manitoba fiddling scene who regularly works with young Native musicians pillory what he perceived to be a lack of musicianship among aboriginal gospel singers (the worst music he had ever heard, he called it). Certainly not all nonaboriginal musicians feel this way (see below), yet there remains a tendency to dismiss music that does not evidence mainstream standards of competence. Such dismissiveness probably stems in large part from a failure to recognize that distinct priorities are in play: in many aboriginal performance contexts the quality of the presentation is less important than that of the participation, for instance (see Turino 2008). The problem is that the broader public perceives not successes in other registers, but rather failures to attain presentational excellence, and that these failures are sometimes understood to index a broader, racialized abjection.

In summary, then, mainstream publicness and indigenous counterpublicity may be constituted through similar activities, but the former has the benefit of appearing normative and morally or aesthetically superior. This is not to suggest that aboriginal public culture is homogeneous. Many aboriginal people urge drinkers to give up the bottle, just as many indigenous musicians encourage their fellows to adopt mainstream musical standards. Nor is this to deny that various musicians and scholars have sought to rehabilitate distinctive aspects of indigenous musical practice for mainstream appreciation. Anne Lederman and John Arcand have done much to broaden appreciation for the "crooked" rhythms and phrasing of traditional indigenous fiddling. (It is difficult, however, to think of many instances when aboriginal drinking has been presented in a positive light.) The goal in pointing out the distinctions between mainstream publicity and aboriginal counterpublicity is not anything so naive as an unqualified celebration of all that constitutes the latter. All the same, this volume hopes to raise questions about the thoroughly negative mainstream characterizations of indigenous drinking that persist in the postcolonial era, and it attempts to continue the long-standing ethnomusicological interrogation of dominant aesthetic standards. A broader goal, however, is to explore the moral and musical frameworks and the concepts of propriety and good comportment—in short, the powerful structures of thought, feeling, and aesthetics—that distinguish publicity from counterpublicity, and that shape how settler Canadians and aboriginal people conceptualize themselves and one another.

Antipublicity

The opposition between intimacy and imagining introduced above moves away from a more conventional distinction, that between privacy and publicness. In *The Structural Transformation of the Public Sphere*, Jürgen Habermas describes a dialectical relationship between privacy and publicness that began to predominate in eighteenth-century bourgeois life in Western Europe (1989: 27–56). According to Habermas, this bourgeois privateness, far from excluding the public, was in fact oriented to it through plays, novels, published letters, and even domestic architecture. Habermas's private-public dialectic does seem to capture something crucial about Western European public culture, and the central, if often overlooked, role of domesticity within it. More recently, however, Dipesh Chakrabarty has questioned the cross-cultural application of Habermas's theory. Chakrabarty contends that the private-public opposition is in fact a European phenomenon not necessarily replicated in other public cultures, for instance that of India (2000: 34–37). He argues against locating this opposition where it may not be appropriate, and especially against regarding cultures that do not manifest it as somehow lacking or as not having made a full transition to modernity.

The opposition between intimacy and imagining advanced here is an attempt to think about social imaginaries without relying upon the private-public opposition, hopefully in a way that is more amenable to cross-cultural application (this is not to say that it is universalizable). Rather than dividing social life into private and public spheres of activity, it distinguishes between interpersonal interaction and mass-mediated forms of relating. Imagining and intimacy, as conceptualized here, cut across categories that might be vernacularly characterized as "private" or "public." So, for instance, large community gatherings, which in everyday speech might be considered public affairs, are frequently in the following pages discussed in terms of intimacy. On the other hand, instances of small-group rehearsal and music making, which might intuitively be understood as private, are explored as sites of interaction oriented to social imaginaries.[18]

When the private-public binary is set aside, it becomes easier to explore how aboriginal Manitobans limit and inflect mass-mediated imagining. It becomes apparent, for instance, that there exist forms of aboriginal corporateness that, while open and collective (and in some cases even oriented toward strangers), do not seem public, at least not in the sense established above. An ethnographic account may help to illustrate. In 2003 I visited Black Island Days, an annual festival celebrated by people from the Hollow Water First Nation and from the nearby communities of Seymourville and Manigotagan. Each summer, I was told, people from these communities loaded camping supplies into boats and headed to Black Island, where they set up a substantial encampment on the shore. One older resident, Morris Moneas, told me that the people of Hollow Water had a special relationship with the island. Before the signing of Treaty 5 with the Crown in the late nineteenth century, they had resided there. When Moneas was young, members of the band still made frequent use of that land to harvest meat, fish, and berries and to meet with people from other communities. The annual festival, then, continued a long-standing traditional use of the land, although it apparently lay outside the acreage reserved for the Hollow Water Band under the terms of the aforementioned treaty.

The year I attended, the organizers had made extensive entertainment arrangements for the final nights of the festival. Thursday was gospel night and featured performances of gospel songs, hymns, and other devotional music by singers from the community and farther afield, accompanied by a pickup house band. On Friday night a number of country singers performed secular music, again accompanied by a house band. The singing was interspersed with step dancing, fiddle music, and performances by two square-dance troupes. On Saturday, the last night of the festival, singers performed traditional honor songs, accompanied by frame drum, and there was a performance by a local country-rock band.

A number of the singers at Black Island Days were well-known figures who regularly performed for largely aboriginal audiences at public events in Manitoba. But the festival was not a public space like the Forks or the Westbrook: no mass-mediated advertisements had announced it beforehand to the general public. In fact, Moneas told me that the Black Island Days were "not really pushed. It's kind of hushed, by word of mouth." Nor was the event particularly private in the vernacular or Habermasian senses of that term. Attendance did not seem to be restricted to any particular membership or constituency, and, by Moneas's estimate, perhaps a thousand attendees had taken part. So, Black Island Days was an open, collective aboriginal festival, neither straightforwardly "private" nor "public." It was a community celebration that privileged face-to-face interaction and, in certain important respects, eschewed an orientation to social imaginaries.

The disinclination to address one's doings to a public is here referred to as antipublicity. Antipublicity was a common aspect of the Manitoban aboriginal interactions I observed and took part in, particularly within the realm of traditional sacred practice. Sometimes there was explicit acknowledgment of a hesitation to orient activities to an imaginary, as when Moneas spoke about the decision not to advertise Black Island Days. In other cases, ways of doing things—traditional protocols, for instance—had the consequence, intended or otherwise, of limiting the public circulation of information. Thus, on a number of occasions I heard elders ask that video cameras be turned off while they spoke about sacred matters to large audiences in public forums. These elders did not say, as Morris Moneas had, that they liked to keep things "word of mouth," and they did not explicitly state that sacred dreams or prayers should not circulate in mass-mediated form amongst a public of strangers. Nevertheless, their requests had the effect of accomplishing just this.

In still other cases social imaginaries were not entirely occluded, but rather neglected in favor of social intimacy. As I relate in chapter 6, a singer I knew whose independently released song had had considerable success on NCI received a distribution offer from a record company that sells to aboriginal audiences across North America. He declined in part because the economics of the deal would have made it less lucrative to do business as he preferred: by strolling around concert venues, signing and selling copies of his album to people who came up to him. There were a good number of factors that motivated his decision, including his wariness of the company. Yet his choice was in part one to prioritize social intimacy—face-to-face engagement with the people who liked his music—over imagining. It was not that he shut out the public altogether: after all, his song was still broadcast on the radio. But he and other musicians I knew frequently acted in ways that gave precedence to immediate possibilities for acquaintanceship rather than interactions with broader audiences and markets.

Organization of this Volume and Theoretical Foundations

As the diverse catalogue of musical and choreographic genres performed at Black Island Days suggests, indigenous Manitobans engage in a wide variety of musical activities. It was not unusual for me to attend, with the same friends, traditional ceremonies, powwows, Roman Catholic services, evangelical Christian coffeehouses, and fiddle dances. And while not all of my acquaintances enjoyed such a wide range of activities, the array of musical doings at Black Island Days was in many respects a microcosm of the pursuits that constitute Manitoban aboriginal public culture. This volume responds to this diversity by exploring a variety of performance venues and genres. Chapter 2 looks at fiddling and festivity, chapter 3 at country music and the talent competition, chapter 4 at Christian song and the funerary wake, chapter 5 at Christian singing in coffeehouse performance, chapter 6 at step-dancing competitions, and chapter 7 at traditional instruments and the museum. (Thematically, chapters 2 and 3 focus on publicity and counterpublicity, chapters 4 and 5 on musical intimacies, and chapters 6 and 7 on antipublicity.)

The venues and genres addressed here in no way constitute the whole of the musical and choreographic activities that animate indigenous social life. They were, however, among the most widespread at the time I did my fieldwork, with constituencies of practitioners that spanned generations, regions, and aboriginal nations. Urban music, including rap, and heavy metal were also popular, but their communities of practice (Wenger 1998) were narrower than that of country music, and for this reason they are discussed only in passing.[19] Similarly, there are aboriginal musicians and listeners who engage with classical music, jazz, and various boutique forms of popular music, but this volume prioritizes the practices that have broader followings amongst the largely working-class Native population. Even so, a number of very popular genres are considered only in passing: there is unfortunately not enough space to address powwow singing and dancing or square dancing in more detail (for discussions of Manitoban powwow culture and its mass mediation, see Scales 2004, 2007, and 2012; I discuss square dancing in Dueck 2006).

Some readers may be hesitant to consider as indigenous some of the music discussed in the following chapters: much of it is sung in English, rather than Cree or Ojibwe, and performed on Western instruments, rather than traditional aboriginal ones; additionally, much of it is associated with potentially homogenizing forces, including the popular-music industry, and colonialism. It may seem irresponsible to characterize these genres as indigenous, especially at a moment when aboriginal languages are endangered and certain cultural practices are no longer being widely transmitted. These are indeed serious concerns, and it would not be appropriate to proceed without acknowledging them. At the same time, many aboriginal people consider these musical practices to be their own, and the way they collectively deploy them does not suggest any simple kind of assimilation. Aboriginal churches, gospel jamborees, country music events, and bars— and the indigenous public sphere more generally—remain conspicuously distinct from nonaboriginal ones, whether in terms of membership and attendeeship or sociability. In short, the expressive genres considered in this book are significantly implicated in contemporary elaborations of recognizably indigenous intimacies and imaginaries, and for this reason alone merit further investigation. In taking these genres seriously as aboriginal music I follow others who have made forceful arguments along such lines, including Beverley Diamond (2002, 2008), Michael McNally (2000), and David Samuels (2004, 2009).

The theoretical underpinnings of this volume are indebted to work on publics and imaginaries by Habermas and Benedict Anderson and especially to the subsequent elaboration of these ideas by other scholars. Habermas's work on the "structural transformation of the public sphere" examines the historical emergence and metamorphosis of a secularized public sphere in which rational and critical thought guided the pursuit of knowledge, morality, and aesthetics (Habermas 1989; see also Calhoun 1992). Anderson's work on "imagined communities" (1991) describes the historical role played by print media in constituting readerships that understand themselves as national bodies, and emphasizes the crucial role that imagining plays in these social formations.[20] Later authors develop and extend these concepts in productive ways. Arjun Appadurai, in *Modernity at Large* (1996), explores imaginaries rooted in affiliations and aspirations other than nationhood. Michael Warner (2002) and Lauren Berlant (Berlant and Warner 1998, Berlant 2008) move beyond Habermas's focus on rational and critical discourse to consider publics constituted through expressive practices, embodied (including sexual) comportment, and sentimental discourses—explorations continued beyond those authors' generally American purview by Charles Hirschkind (2006) and Martin Stokes (2010). All four of these authors give special consideration to how subaltern publics come into being around problematized or denigrated practices and discourses. Elizabeth Povinelli's work on settler modernity in Australia, meanwhile, examines how dominant national publics form around commonly held ideas of what is shameful or disgusting—and interventions that address these troubling cultural practices (see Povinelli 1998: 575–79).

The present volume follows the precedents of more recent authors in holding that embodied and expressive practices—music and dance especially—play a central role in imaginaries. It similarly understands publics as discrete, yet nested and intersecting. Aboriginal imaginaries, for instance, both transcend and are shaped by national ones: they extend across state boundaries and yet are impacted by national politics and discourses. Like Errol Ranville's performance at the Forks, they express aboriginal aspirations in the shadow of the national flag. My frequent use of the term "Manitoban aboriginal public" is in this spirit. The term "Manitoba" derives from a northern Algonquian term for a sacred site in the midst of the system of rivers and lakes that connect many of the communities discussed in this volume (Bowsfield 1956). At the same time, and more obviously, it refers to a political unit whose boundaries do not necessarily coincide with those of the indigenous nations who inhabit it.

Where this book moves in a somewhat different direction from work by other recent theorists of intimacy and publicity is in its framing of the relationship between the two. Like Warner, Berlant, and Stokes, I understand these forms of sociability to exist in a dialectical relationship: on the one hand, intimacies of various kinds constitute the circulating stuff of social imaginaries, while, on the other hand, this stuff is regularly redeployed in everyday, face-to-face interactions. All the same, intimacy and publicity are here set in a more contrasted relationship than in some other work. Berlant speaks of "intimate publics," explaining, "What makes a public sphere intimate is an expectation that the consumers of its particular stuff *already* share a worldview and emotional knowledge" (2008: viii). I do not contest the idea that members of publics presume that they share with one another certain kinds of emotional knowledge, but I suggest that such connections can be distinguished from forms of acquaintanceship that exist between more immediately knowable and engageable others. Stranger- and intimate-oriented sociabilities differ.

My inclination to juxtapose intimacy and imagining (while acknowledging their interconnectedness) stems from ethnographic experiences and subsequent reflection on them. Work on intimacy and publicness often privileges mass-mediated publications and performances,[21] but I have continually been drawn back to how agents deploy these circulating text-artifacts in everyday contexts of face-to-face music making. Such intimacies seem distinct from the stranger-sociability described by Warner and Berlant, and this merits acknowledgment.[22] Just as important, during fieldwork I continually observed occasions when people privileged intimates rather than imagined others, and when they (knowingly or unknowingly) prevented certain kinds of stuff from circulating amongst a public of strangers. Such experiences also indicated that it was important to acknowledge a distinction between forms of acquaintanceship.

As suggested above, the intimacies explored in the following chapters extend beyond expressions and representations of sentiment to include real-time "interaction rituals" of musical performance and social interaction.[23] My analyses of these are indebted to work by Erving Goffman (1967, 1974) and Michael Silverstein (1997). Defining intimacy as interactive alignment has a number of advantages. It distances the idea of intimacy from the concept of privateness Chakrabarty problematizes. It permits insights into the connections between mundane intimacies and social imaginaries: how, for instance, step dancing patterns or the way a band tunes up involve an orientation to a social imaginary. It also underscores the central place that embodied and expressive interactions have in social imagining, including the musical and choreographic interactions explored in the chapters that follow.

The concept of antipublicity—behavior that curtails an orientation to a stranger-public, often by prioritizing intimate interactions and relationships—might be understood as an elaboration of Arjun Appadurai's concept of the production of locality (1996: 178–99), which suggests that social and cultural distinctions, including locality, are produced, renewed, and reinvented through effortful community practice. In a similar way, antipublicity might be understood as a "production of intimacy," an affirmation or prioritization of face-to-face relationships, sometimes in resistance to pressure to align to the practices that are normative in national publics. Another point of reference is Jennifer Hasty's work on "corruption" in Ghanaian journalism (Hasty 2005), and how social actors work strategically to "re-enchant" the increasingly abstract social relations that hold within the state and civil society. Yet another is Appadurai's work on "the social life of things" (1986), in particular his consideration of the various ways cultures restrict the circulation of commodities. Following his model, it is possible to investigate how communities impose limits on the public circulation of songs, performances, and sacred knowledge.[24]

A fourth theoretical touchstone is Michael Silverstein's metapragmatic work on language and culture (Silverstein 1997, 2004; see also Brennan 2008, Monson 1996). Silverstein's approach to language is particularly amenable to studies of music, dance, and improvisation because of the attention it pays to nondenotational aspects of linguistic interaction (that is, aspects of language that do not refer to, or say things about, things in the world). His research gives close consideration to questions of interactional coherence, strategy, and role, all of which play an important role in social interactions, such as dancing or the performance of instrumental music, where denotation is not always particularly important. Moreover, his work presents a performative understanding of culture that avoids, on the one hand, the stasis of structuralist approaches and, on the other, the insufficiency of certain practice-centered theories when it comes to explaining the endurance of social structures, genres, and cultural categories.[25] Silverstein's approach accounts for culture's "solidity" without occluding negotiation, contestation, and change. It does so by examining social interactions as moments when interactants both draw upon and performatively instantiate culture.

Metapragmatic theory informs the Warnerian idea of publicness, which has a similar model of limited performativity at its core. In that model, as here, contributors to publics both presume and produce imaginaries: publications and performances, however new, engage, however ambivalently, with preexisting expectations, norms, and ideologies. In short, musicians who address a public acknowledge previous performances as they make their contribution to the circulating broadcasts and recordings that together constitute publicness. Insofar as metapragmatic theory attempts to account for both cultural continuity and change, it seems particularly appropriate for discussions of Manitoban indigenous cultures, which, having undergone immense transformations in the last century and a half—for instance, in musical practice and religious observance—seem nevertheless to evidence certain continuities in ways of performing selfhood and collectivity.

A final important concept adopted from Silverstein is that of entextualization (see Silverstein and Urban 1996: 1–17). The metapragmatic tradition is equally concerned with analyzing "texts" (songs, dances, stories, rituals, and so on) and their launchings into context. It is just as interested in the meanings and structures of texts as it is in what people do with them and what they make them mean—or, indeed, how they negotiate over what they mean—on the specific occasions on which they deploy them. Texts, after all, only have their being in some context or other: they are simultaneously entextualized and contextualized (Silverstein and Urban 1996: 1). So, although the chapters that follow undertake some analysis of music, they are just as often concerned with analyzing what might be called "enmusicalizations": namely, particular emplaced performances of music.[26]

Research Context: Manitoban Aboriginal Groups

People claiming indigenous identities as Métis or First Nations make up a substantial portion of the Manitoba population. In 2006 the province had a population of about 1.15 million people, with about 15 percent (175,000) claiming aboriginal identity (Statistics Canada 2007: 11; and Statistics Canada 2008: 11). Winnipeg, the province's largest city and the site of much of my fieldwork, had a population of around 700,000, with around 10 percent (68,000) claiming aboriginal identity (Statistics Canada 2007: 22; Statistics Canada 2008: 13). Métis people have a greater presence in the capital city: around 41 percent of the provincial aboriginal population claimed a Métis identity in 2006, while around 60 percent of Winnipeg's aboriginal population did (Statistics Canada 2008, passim).

Simple vernacular definitions distinguish First Nations and Métis people first and foremost with respect to ancestry. Métis people are often characterized as the descendants of unions between indigenous and nonindigenous people, while First Nations people are frequently held to be more aboriginal and less "mixed," genetically and culturally. The two groups are also frequently juxtaposed with reference to legal status: First Nations people are registered with the federal government as Status Indians while Métis people have an indigenous identity but are not registered. These definitions provide some purchase on how aboriginal identities are perceived, but they are nevertheless problematic. Many First Nations people have as mixed an ancestry as people who identify as Métis, for instance. More confusingly, in 1985 a federal bill registered thousands of people previously considered Métis as Status Indians, and many of them now consider themselves to belong to both categories.[27]

Five First Nations groups make up the registered aboriginal population of Manitoba (none of these groups is contained entirely within the province's boundaries). Three of them speak Algonquian languages and share significant cultural similarities: the Cree, Ojibwe, and Oji-Cree. Of these, the Cree, whose traditional homelands are for the most part located in the north, are most numerous. The Ojibwe, Saulteaux, or Anishinaabeg (sometimes also called the Ojibwa or Ojibway) are the second in size; their traditional homelands are for the most part in the south.[28] The Oji-Cree are a less populous group from the northeast of the province whose members speak a language that mixes elements of Ojibwe and Cree. Members of these northern Algonquian groups comprise the majority of the aboriginal population, and consequently the bulk of what is said about the social lives and expressive culture of aboriginal Manitobans in this volume refers to them. This is a representational bias, but it is a conscious one, and although it has drawbacks it also has a certain appropriateness. On the one hand, it reflects my field experiences in Winnipeg, where northern Algonquian people, particularly Ojibwe, are in the majority, and where most of my significant encounters were with working-class Cree, Ojibwe, and Oji-Cree people and Métis people who affiliated themselves with them. On the other, it reflects the dominance of northern Algonquian elements and populations within Manitoban aboriginal public culture. The two remaining First Nations groups in Manitoba are the Dene, whose traditional homelands are in the far northwest of the province, and the Dakota, in the southwest. Of the two, the Dakota receive more consideration here, in large part because Dakota musicians and dancers have played such an important role in introducing the powwow to Manitoba.

The Métis of Manitoba emerged as a self-identifying group in the late nineteenth century. These early Métis were descendants of unions between European fur traders and aboriginal Canadians. They spoke both European and indigenous languages, and indeed a mixed language called Michif in which the verbs were Cree words and the nouns French (see Bakker 1997: 116–17, 277–79). Particularly dynamic within the Métis-identifying population were French-speaking Catholic Métis, among them Louis Riel, who led two armed movements against the Canadian government. It is important to remember, however, that the nineteenth-century Métis were a diverse body that included descendants of both English- and French-speaking Europeans and of a number of different aboriginal groups (Friesen 1987: 201). And of course, métissage did not end in the nineteenth century: indigenous and nonindigenous people have continued to have children together, and the Métis people I met included descendants of British, Icelandic, Ukrainian, and Chinese Canadians. Many were children or grandchildren of First Nations women who married nonaboriginal men and who were consequently denied status as Indians.

The Métis people I knew best tended to have close ties to First Nations communities: many had grown up in close proximity to reserves, married First Nations partners, and pursued traditional aboriginal vocations, and a good many spoke Cree or Ojibwe. Some differentiated between what they called the "French Métis" and the "Indian Métis." They seemed to be distinguishing between people who came from families where French was the mother tongue and who identified with the broader Franco-Manitoban population, and people who came from families where Cree or Ojibwe was the mother tongue and had closer connections to First Nations communities and political networks. Most of my Métis contacts belonged to the latter group. Indeed, they were more likely than Franco-Manitoban Métis to attend aboriginal gatherings where both First Nations and Métis people were welcome (this is not to suggest anything like a solid dividing line, however).

The term Métis is, again, ambiguous, referring to a group with "many local, regional, and cultural variations," as Joe Sawchuk (2001: 74) says of the Canadian

Métis more generally. Moreover, in everyday interactions, indigenous people often use terms of identity strategically, and in ways that suggest complex ambivalences about their arbitrariness, as Sarah Quick (2012) has shown. In the pages that follow I will generally use the term to designate the Métis-identified and -identifying people I got to know at aboriginal music venues and events. First Nations and Métis people alike, typically of working-class backgrounds, came to such gatherings, where they sang and talked in English, Cree, and Ojibwe and enjoyed the same kinds of music and dance. In these contexts, "Métis" seemed to refer to non-registered (or recently registered) aboriginal people who were closely affiliated with First Nations people and had much in common with them socially, culturally, and musically. Certainly, the sense of the word changed from context to context, and on some occasions it was deployed in much more encompassing ways. Most often, though, it seemed to designate a subgroup of the larger population of Métis-identifying Manitobans.

For this reason, I try to make it clear when the word "Métis" refers to a group other than these First Nations–affiliating people—or to a more encompassing one. I typically use the term "francophone Métis" to distinguish persons or groups who have a close relationship to Franco-Manitoban society, for instance. The idea is not to exclude francophone Métis from consideration, or to suggest that any one group has a better claim to the name than another, but rather to (a) clarify that there is a large, nonfrancophone Métis population with close connections to First Nations groups, (b) identify it as the Métis population I worked with most closely, and (c) suggest that it is this group that tends to be most in evidence within the particular aboriginal public sphere I engaged. The point is certainly not to deny the historical importance or ethnomusicological interest of other Métis groups.

Throughout this volume I refer to "aboriginal," "indigenous," and "Native" people interchangeably. The people I know use all three of these terms to refer to themselves (with First Nations people additionally, and sometimes pointedly, referring to themselves as Cree, Anishinaabe, and so on). In the first decade of the 2000s, "aboriginal" was the most common of the general terms, "indigenous" occurred less frequently, and "Native" was used only occasionally and sounded a little old-fashioned. Métis and First Nations consultants alike referred to themselves as Indians from time to time, but that term was avoided in polite conversation among nonaboriginal people as one with colonialist and even racist associations. In the contexts I frequented, "aboriginal people" typically meant First Nations and Métis people, mostly Ojibwe and Cree. It could be the prevalence of that term in my own fieldwork experience was an index of the cosmopolitan urban environment, and the large Métis population, in Winnipeg. Nevertheless, it was commonly used, not least by prominent aboriginal figures and institutions. If it evidenced a (not uncontested) southern and urban bias, so too did Manitoban aboriginal public culture.

Manitoban Indigenous Music and History

Despite differences of language, cultural practice, homeland, and affiliation, Manitoban Algonquian First Nations and Métis communities share many musical and choreographic practices, including fiddle music, step dancing, square dancing, country music, and powwow singing and dancing. Additionally, the singing of hymns and other Christian sacred songs plays an important role in the ritual practice of many First Nations communities and in that of many First Nations–affiliating Métis. The following discussion of the history of contact between indigenous and nonindigenous people in Manitoba helps to explain why these genres play such an important role in contemporary indigenous expressive culture and ritual observance. It also helps to explain the historical, political, and social factors that have contributed to the emergence of an indigenous counterpublic.

Contrary to some vernacular opinions, the genres studied in this volume are not Métis music but rather aboriginal music more generally. Métis Manitobans do not hold a monopoly on fiddle music, country song, or square dancing, and to hold that they do contradicts historical and contemporary evidence (see for instance Beaudry 2001: 391; Fiddler and Stevens 1985: 30–31; Lederman 1988; Mason 1967: 55; Mishler 1993; Quick 2009; Rodgers 1980 (film); Skinner 1911: 142; Whidden 2007) and does a disservice to the First Nations people who practice them.

Little evidence concerning precontact traditions survives, although research on the songs of Cree people living in the forested areas surrounding Hudson's Bay provides some insight into what early northern Algonquian music might have been like (see for instance Preston 1985, Saindon 1934, or Whidden 2007). Repertoires seem to have consisted entirely of vocal music, often accompanied by drum or rattle (Preston 1985: 22–23; Whidden 2007: 16–20). The songs collected by Lynn Whidden in Chisasibi, Quebec, in the early 1980s were sung in a medium register and tended to have an identifiable main beat, but not a regularized metrical structure (2007: 67–68, 73, 85). The same rhythmic characteristics seem evident in two songs collected by Reverend J. Emile Saindon among the Cree of western James Bay in the early twentieth century (1934: 6–7), and they persist in some cases in contemporary performances in genres northern Algonquians have borrowed from Europeans.

During the precontact period and much of the fur trade era, indigenous musical and choreographic traditions appear to have been closely bound up with sacred life. Of these early traditions, hunting songs have been a particular focus of ethnomusicological attention (e.g., Preston 1985, Whidden 2007). These songs did not simply reflect important aspects of northern Algonquian life but were sung to effect active interventions into it. On some occasions singing exerted a spiritual influence upon animals, the other-than-human persons who controlled them, or other aspects of the environment hunters moved through; at other times it was the means by which hunters sought out and found prey (Preston 1985: 21; Whidden 2007: 15–19, 25–28, 49). Songs were often very personal to the hunters who sang them (Preston 1985: 21; Whidden 2007: 55, 63) and in this respect reflected the individualistic aspects of traditional Cree and Ojibwe religion, which emphasized personal dreams and relationships with the sacred beings who appeared in them (see Brown and Brightman 1988: 138–46; Hallowell 1992: 87–88; see also Hallowell 1955: 360–62).

EARLY ADOPTIONS OF WESTERN MUSICAL PRACTICES

The fur trade brought Europeans into prolonged contact with the inhabitants of the boreal forest in northern and western Canada. Trade began to move into the area north and west of Lake Superior in the late seventeenth century, and by the early eighteenth century it was playing an important part in the economic life of indigenous people in the area that now constitutes Manitoba. The trade was lucrative enough that Ojibwe people followed it, moving westward from their original homes in eastern Canada and arriving in what is now Manitoba and Saskatchewan sometime in the early nineteenth century (Friesen 1987: 23–24). Europeans approached the west by both northern and southern routes. In the north, British traders working with the Hudson's Bay Company sailed from the Orkney Islands to outposts on the shores of Hudson's Bay and James Bay.[29] In the south, French Canadian fur traders moved from Montreal to the Red River Valley via the Great Lakes.

English- and French-speaking fur traders were often on close terms with their indigenous trading partners. In many instances traders entered relationships and had children with aboriginal women. Musical exchanges also took place, although musical styles tended to move from Europeans to the indigenous population rather than the other way round. Two bodies of sociomusical practice seem to have been particularly important over the long term. The first of these involved the fiddle, the dance tunes played on it, and the dances associated with them.[30] The adoption of fiddle music began before the onset of high colonialism (here understood as the period from 1870 to 1945) at a time when relationships between European and indigenous peoples were on more even terms.

A second kind of musical transfer occurred in the realm of religion. Christian missionaries began to make an impact on indigenous musical life in the middle of the nineteenth century. James Evans, a Methodist missionary who worked in Ojibwe and Cree communities, played a particularly important role, inventing a syllabic alphabet for writing in both languages. In 1841, working in the Cree community of Norway House (see Map 1), he printed the first book ever to use these syllabics, the *Cree Syllabic Hymn Book* (Evans 1954: 9). Ojibwe hymnbooks in syllabics followed— for instance, the 1879 *Moosonee Hymnal* by John Horden and John Sanders.

It was thus through sacred music that a Cree-speaking and -reading public was first addressed: hymnbooks were the first mass-produced texts to hail an indigenous imaginary. Christian hymnody and Christianity were taken up in many communities in the northern forests (see Mason 1967, Rogers 1962; compare McNally 2000), in some cases before the state had extended its power in significant ways into them. Of course, the fact that some groups embraced Christianity should not obscure how others resisted it, or how traditional indigenous beliefs persisted, sometimes alongside the new religion. Nor should it allow us to lose sight of how the state vigorously sought to eradicate aboriginal sacred practices and beliefs (see Pettipas 1994: 213–23 and passim).

THE PERIOD OF HIGH COLONIALISM

In the late nineteenth and early twentieth centuries, the federal government undertook a series of initiatives that were to have a profound effect on the indigenous peoples in what is now western Canada. First, Rupert's Land, the vast northwestern area of which present-day Manitoba was part, was transferred into Canadian control. Second, limitations on indigenous title, sovereignty, and freedoms were introduced through treaties and the passing of the Indian Act. Third, the government undertook a program of massive western settlement that fundamentally altered the demographic balance of the region.

Taking each of these in turn, a British royal charter in 1670 had granted the Hudson's Bay Company a monopoly on fur trade in Rupert's Land, the huge northern territory that drains into Hudson's Bay. In the late 1860s, plans were made to transfer that land to the newly formed Canadian government (Friesen 1987: 116–17). The francophone Métis elite in the territory became concerned that the proposed Canadian administration of the area would not accommodate their rights and lifeways, and under the leadership of Louis Riel they seized control of the community of Red River (the site of present-day Winnipeg) (Friesen 1987: 120–22). Riel declared the establishment of a provisional government until such time as Canada would negotiate with Red River residents about the terms on which they would become part of the country (Friesen 1987: 122). In 1870, the government made a number of concessions to the Métis: the Manitoba Act ensured Manitoba would join Canada as a province rather than as a territory and that it would have "responsible government . . . bilingual institutions, denominational schools, and guarantees of land titles and of federal respect for Indian title" (Friesen 1987: 125–26). The government also promised that Métis would continue to keep lands they had customarily used, and it set aside 1.4 million acres of land for their children (Friesen 1987: 126). In later years, however, elements of the Manitoba Act were undermined by unscrupulous practices and provincial legislation. The Manitoba Schools Act, for instance, abolished French as an official language in the province and did away with independent tax-supported Catholic schools (Friesen 1987: 197–201, 215–18).

Following the transfer of Rupert's Land to Canada, the Canadian government set about extinguishing aboriginal title in the area. From 1871 to 1877 it signed Treaties One through Seven with First Nations communities in what are today the provinces of Ontario, Manitoba, Saskatchewan, and Alberta (Dickason 2002: 254; Friesen 1987: 163).[31] The bands that signed ceded ownership of lands to the Crown and promised obedience to the laws of Canada; in return they received guarantees that certain reserved lands would belong to their nations in perpetuity, that they would receive annual gifts (usually of cash, clothing, implements, and supplies), that schools would be built on reserves, and that they would continue to be able to pursue traditional harvesting activities such as fishing and hunting on some of the lands outside the reserves (Canada 1971: passim).

In 1876 the federal government passed the Indian Act to govern the peoples with whom it had entered into treaties. Under this law, a federal department of Indian Affairs supervised Indian governments, and Indians' access to alcohol and freedom of movement was restricted (Dickason 2002: 263–65). The government also attempted to extinguish indigenous religious and economic practices it considered wasteful and uncivilized (Pettipas 1994). An 1884 amendment to the Act prohibited the potlatch, an important ceremonial expression of the gift-based economic systems of the indigenous peoples of the West Coast (Titley 1986: 15). An 1895 amendment prohibited "any Indian festival, dance or other ceremony of which the giving away or paying or giving back of money, goods, or articles of any sort forms a part, or is a feature," as well as ceremonies that involved the "wounding or mutilation" of people or animals. This amendment prohibited sun dances and giveaway traditions (Pettipas 1994: 95–96) that were, like the potlatch, important articulations of indigenous economic and religious principles.

The Indian Act and the treaties thus established strict legal distinctions between indigenous and nonindigenous Canadians. The negative aspects of these distinctions are clear: the government was able to extend restrictive laws targeting the aboriginal population alone and to deny the rights of citizenship to a population it regarded as insufficiently civilized to participate fully in Canadian society.[32] But the treaties also created "nations within a nation," establishing a society in which the federal government had distinct relationships with certain differentiated populations. This has ongoing implications for aboriginal-state relationships, including legal bases for the autonomy of indigenous communities. Nevertheless, the legal distinction between indigenous and nonindigenous Canadians originated in a colonial context and reflected an ideology that understood Euro-Canadians to be radically different from, and superior to, First Peoples.

This ideology was particularly evident in the Euro-Canadian reception of certain genres of music and dance performance: namely, the powwows and Wild West shows that became popular in southwestern Manitoba in the late nineteenth and early twentieth centuries. Such events presented opportunities to comment upon the differences between aboriginal Canadians and Euro-Canadians and how they were being overcome through the civilizing project. For instance, in 1912 the

Winnipeg Free Press delivered a report on the Canadian Industrial Exhibition in Winnipeg:

> Redmen from the outlying districts of Manitoba and their squaws, with little papooses, were much in evidence at the exhibition grounds yesterday.... The Wild West show at the Midway was a favorite spot for the Indians. They never tired [of] watching the antics of their fellow redmen who, arrayed in feathers and all the accoutrements of a western desperado, "murdered" tenderfeet, and white men at will. Every time that the pale face was bested by an Indian loud applause came from the portion of the tent where the redmen were sitting, showing that race feeling has not entirely died out in the breast of the Indian and that he still waxes enthusiastic over the deeds of valor performed by his ancestors ("Redmen Gather at Exhibition," July 12, 1912, 3).

As the excerpt suggests, nonaboriginal commentators of the early twentieth century perceived powwows and Wild West shows to evidence both retentions of aboriginal savagery and a gradual trajectory toward civilization; hence, a "race feeling" that is (not quite) "dying out" (see Dueck 2005: 149–55, 169–72). It is ironic that the author of the excerpt focuses on the "race feeling" of Native fairgoers, for such performances were above all occasions for nonaboriginal people to frame their whiteness in relation to indigenous differences (see the articles in Bird 1996, especially Geller 1996).

The treatment of indigenous societies as partially savage, either needing or in the process of attaining civilization, was particularly evident in the residential schooling system. First Nations communities secured guarantees of education in the negotiations surrounding Treaties One through Seven, and provisions were made in each treaty that a school should be introduced on a reserve whenever it was requested (Miller 1996: 98–100). When education was actually introduced, however, it was often delivered through a system of off-reserve residential schooling. Aboriginal children frequently had to travel to schools that stood at considerable distances from their communities, leaving their families behind them for long periods of time (Miller 1996: 100–120, passim). The government understood these schools as the means by which the emergence of a new generation of ostensibly uncivilized Indians might be arrested and a generation of Canadians produced in its place (see Miller 1996, especially 183–216). Isolated from parents and communities, aboriginal children were discouraged from traditional beliefs and practices and forbidden to speak in their mother tongues (Miller 1996: 183–216; Pettipas 1994: 79–82). The trauma of this cultural interference was often compounded by sexual, physical, and emotional abuse (Miller 1996: 317–42).

The third way in which the federal government transformed Manitoban aboriginal life was by initiating an immense program of settlement, beginning in the late 1870s and continuing into the early twentieth century, that would completely change the demographics of western Canada. When Manitoba joined the country, indigenous and Métis people had been in the majority, French was widely spoken, and Catholicism was widespread, but within a few years immigration had transformed the province into a society where white anglophone Protestants were in the majority (Friesen 1987: 201–2). It was this majority that, in supporting the Manitoba Schools Act described above, overturned key provisions that had been extended to the Métis at the time Manitoba joined Canada. Thus, in the early decades of the existence of the province, settler governments violated the spirit of the two main contracts made between the Crown and indigenous peoples. The Indian Act undermined the numbered treaties, turning sovereign Indian nations into second-class wards under the strict control of a colonial government, while the Manitoba Schools Act took away guarantees that had been granted to the Métis in 1870.

POSTWAR DECOLONIZATION AND RECENT STATE INTERVENTIONS

Following the Second World War, First Nations and Métis people saw changes in laws restricting indigenous liberties. In the 1950s and 1960s the right to vote in federal and provincial elections was extended to Status Indians, restrictions on traditional ceremonies were rescinded, and prohibitions on Native consumption of intoxicants were overturned (cf. Dickason 2002: 392, 312; Pettipas 1994: 209–10). Meanwhile, aboriginal people were increasingly integrated into a wage-labor economy and swept up in a general wave of urbanization, moving to Winnipeg and other cities in increasing numbers. They were increasing exposed to mass-mediated music and images: my oldest consultants, even those who came from isolated rural communities, were familiar with country music and movie westerns before the middle of the century. Aboriginal people used their wages to purchase radios, records, and musical instruments, and country music became a part of community life (cf. Bussidor and Bilgen-Reinart 1997: 38). Country hymned the rural during a century of urbanization; it made use of a harmonic and melodic vocabulary similar to that of fiddle music and hymnody; and it talked about the perils of drinking and good-timing. All of these things helped it speak to aboriginal Manitobans, and they carried it with them as they moved into Manitoba's cities and public houses at the dawn of the postcolonial era.

One of the signal moments of the postcolonial transformation was the aboriginal rejection of the 1969 federal white paper on Indian policy. At the time this policy document was drafted Status Indians had won many of the rights that had been denied them under colonialism but still retained the special rights that they had been accorded under the terms of the treaties. The white paper recommended phasing out the Indian Act and the Department of Indian Affairs and ending the treaties, with the goal of creating a unified national public whose citizens would be equal in all respects (Dickason 2002: 377). Canadian First Nations leaders opposed these proposals, expressing a desire for First Nations to maintain a unique and distinct status based upon terms set forth in the treaties as "citizens plus."[33] The government eventually withdrew them. In effect, First Nations made use of the very legal mechanisms that had subjugated them as a lever with which to assert their special status. They have thus retained rights guaranteed under the treaties, including the right of harvest, the right to self-government, and the inalienable community ownership of certain parcels of land (see chapter 2).

Even as overtly racist legislation was rescinded and bids to end the special status of indigenous Canadians were defeated, however, new forms of governmentality targeted Native people. Many of these had the outward appearance of evenhandedness or colorblindness, yet they affected the indigenous population in disproportionate numbers. For instance, during the 1960s Canadian provinces began to make significant extensions of child welfare services to aboriginal communities (Johnston 1983: 23–24). Many aboriginal children were placed in care or adopted out to nonaboriginal families (Johnston 1983: 1–3, 54–59). The percentage of aboriginal children in care was entirely out of proportion to the population: as Olive Patricia Dickason notes, "30 to 40 per cent of all legal wards were Aboriginal, even though they made up less than 4 per cent of the national population" (Dickason 2002: 320). This massive seizure of children, frequently called the "Sixties Scoop" (Johnston 1983: 23), disrupted the lives of thousands of aboriginal families. Similarly, the rate of Native incarceration climbed during the postcolonial era. The *Report of the Aboriginal Justice Inquiry of Manitoba* states that the percentage of aboriginal people in Manitoban jails appears to have been proportional to the provincial aboriginal population until around 1950, when it took a dramatic upswing (Aboriginal Justice Inquiry 2008: chapter 3). It goes on to estimate "that more than 55% of all jail admissions in 1989 were Aboriginal, whereas the Aboriginal proportion of the provincial population was just under 12%" (Aboriginal Justice Inquiry 2008: chapter 3). And so, even as full citizenship was extended to aboriginal people, and even as the law became ostensibly colorblind, government intervention in indigenous communities remained a constant.

Today serious inequities distinguish the aboriginal population from the nonaboriginal population in the areas of poverty, health, and quality of life. If indigenous Manitobans benefit from special rights as citizens plus, they nevertheless suffer severe disadvantages compared to non-Natives in the realm of life chances.

Given the colonial history and incommensurate contemporary circumstances of aboriginal people, some may find it tempting to interpret the expressive practices explored in this volume as the problematic musical legacy of colonialism: to see the prevalence of Christian devotional music, fiddling, and country music as evidence of the triumph of settler society and the music industry; the frequent absence of explicit political content in music as a retreat from resistance; and the apparent infelicities of amateur performance as an aesthetic analogue of financial poverty. Yet there is much more going on here. The chapters that follow show how aboriginal people have made use of musical materials at hand, including ones associated with contact and colonialism, to express indigenous modalities of selfhood and collectivity, extend responses to their colonial and postcolonial circumstances, and articulate Native intimacies and imaginaries. If these musical practices reflect a history of colonization, they are also a reply to it.

Research Context, Methods, and Consultants

Much of the material in this volume draws upon fifteen months of full-time ethnographic fieldwork and archival research conducted between June 2002 and August 2003; this period of study was partially funded by a Felding Fellowship from the University of Chicago. Since that time I have regularly returned to Manitoba for shorter visits to conduct additional fieldwork; one such trip was funded by faculty research funds from the Open University. Between visits I have consulted with contacts by telephone and email, and I increasingly keep in touch through social networking sites on the Internet. On more recent visits I have contacted consultants to show them drafted sections of the book and get their feedback, and to confirm that I have their permission to include their songs and words, and to relate stories about them.

The province of Manitoba was my home until I began university studies in 1990; my parents and many relatives and longtime friends (including consultants cited in this volume) still live there. All the same, this book is the work of a cultural outsider: I am a nonaboriginal Manitoban who had relatively little contact with Canadian indigenous communities before 2002. In some unhappy ways, though, I am an insider, including to the racial dynamics of Manitoban society, having held when I was younger prejudices that I am now ashamed of, and to the kinds of things nonaboriginal Manitobans continue to say about indigenous people in their absence.

The night at the Westbrook described earlier, which moved from a public space to a context of greater social intimacy, in some ways represents my fieldwork experiences in miniature. My initial encounters with aboriginal musicians were at concerts and festivals aimed at the general public. Over time, I made the acquaintance of people who invited me to community dances and coffeehouses. As still more time passed, friendships formed with people I met at those events: I got to know the families of my acquaintances, I supported and was supported by them, and I spent increasing amounts of time with them. Thus the theory of imaginaries, intimacies, and public spaces elaborated in this volume might be understood to attempt to explain what changed as I moved from initial engagements with aboriginal radio, recordings, and print media to become increasingly involved in the doings and daily lives of my consultants. It is more than that, however. The terms "intimacy" and "imagining" attempt to capture something very particular to the aboriginal public culture I encountered. Aboriginal publicness differed from the forms of publicness I had previously known and considered normative, and this distinctness had to do with the particular ways Manitoban indigenous people qualified it—even curtailed it—through prioritizations of interpersonal engagement. Social imaginaries were important, but were nevertheless regularly suspended or deprioritized in order to honor intimacy.

A brief introduction to some of the people whose names appear frequently in this volume may shed some light on my fieldwork methodology. One of the first musicians I got to know was Chris Beach, an Ojibwe Métis singer, songwriter, and playwright from the Manitoban Interlake community of Vogar. At the time I met him, the summer of 2002, he was a regular performer at festivals across Manitoba. I had attended many such events, taking notes and introducing myself to musicians, but had made few close connections. At the Jammin' in the Jackpine festival, however, held at the end of that summer in the town of Mafeking, I ended up spending a significant amount of time with Beach, learning about his music, life, and family and establishing the foundations of future interactions. Afterward I frequently met up with him at the coffeehouses that ran on weeknights in Winnipeg's North End. Beach would show up to sing country and gospel songs, socialize, and listen to other musicians. Often, when things had wrapped up for the evening, Chris, his mother, his sisters, and other musicians and attendees would meet at a nearby doughnut shop for (even more) coffee and conversation. I joined these friendly sessions as well and got to know a number of other contacts in the process.

The organizer of one of the coffeehouses was a man named Edward Guiboche who grew up in the Cree community of Grand Rapids. Edward and his wife, Audrey Guiboche, from the Métis community of Duck Bay, also became close friends. In addition to running the coffeehouse, Edward called square dances at a weekly community dance in Winnipeg, and he traveled around the province to watch or participate in other dance events. I often gave him rides to and from the more distant ones, since he was without a vehicle for a time. At his invitation, I also accompanied him to the wakes and funerals of friends and acquaintances, where we frequently met up with musicians who performed at his coffeehouse, there to sing and pay their respects.

Through Edward I met a number of elders who became valued consultants and friends. One was Nelson Menow, originally from the Cree community of Norway House—a guitarist, singer, and songwriter and the cornerstone of the house band at Edward's coffeehouse. The others were Victor and Laureen Courchene (Figure 1.3), a retired married couple, both Ojibwe, he from the Sagkeeng First Nation (also called Fort Alexander), she from the community of Bacon Ridge near the Ebb and Flow First Nation. With Victor and Laureen, who were also without a car of their own from time to time, I traveled to powwows, church services, traditional ceremonies, dances, and coffeehouses.

In addition to fieldwork, I did archival research at the University of Manitoba Archives and the Provincial Archives of Manitoba (now Archives of Manitoba).

Figure 1.3 Victor and Laureen Courchene at a dance at the Winnipeg Indian and Metis Friendship Centre. Photo by the author.

I enrolled in Ojibwe language courses at the University of Manitoba and took lessons in fiddling and powwow dancing. I conducted interviews with the consultants introduced above and with other musicians. I documented the activities I observed by making audio and video recordings of performances at coffeehouses, dance competitions, social dances, and festivals. Somewhat more often than I recorded, I took notes on repertoire, performers, and performance styles while I socialized. I was open about my research with everyone I encountered, although I did not coordinate my work with any specific indigenous political bodies (for instance, particular First Nations or the Manitoba Metis Federation).

My consultants comprised a heterogeneous group of Métis, Cree, and Ojibwe people, yet shared a number of similarities. All of them had heard, performed, or danced to fiddle music and country songs from an early age. All had grown up in rural areas and moved to the city; the three older men (Victor, Nelson, and Edward) had trapped in their younger years. Most of them were working-class people, but a number had moved into middle-class occupations, taking up jobs in education or bureaucracy (working for provincial, federal, or aboriginal institutions). The older ones had grown up during the years of legislated discrimination; all of them had experienced racism.

Readers familiar with Manitoban aboriginal music may wonder why so little of this volume concerns those musicians who have had the greatest success on Canadian and international stages and who have been most responsible for mediating Native music to wider audiences: Ray St. Germain, Errol Ranville, or Andy De Jarlis, for instance. My focus is rather on amateur and semiprofessional musicians, known to mostly indigenous audiences, who perform at aboriginal coffeehouses, bars, fiddle dances, concerts, and singing and dancing competitions. Prioritizing these "hidden musicians" follows in the footsteps of Ruth Finnegan (2007 [1989]) and Howard Becker and Robert Faulkner (Faulkner and Becker 2009), of course, but it also highlights certain distinctive aspects of indigenous musical publicness. Aboriginal venues and the musical interactions within them open up space for the performance of participatory and inclusive collectivity, on the one hand, and sharply defined individualities, on the other. Accordingly, performances regularly transgress norms that would hold in other, typically nonaboriginal, public spaces—in part because anybody who wants to can get up on stage, and in part because those who do so do not care to sound like others. The musical sociability characteristic of these performers, performances, and venues often differs significantly from what is normative elsewhere in Manitoba, and these musically mediated manifestations of personhood and collectivity help to constitute an indigenous publicness that is both distinctive and marked.

Change and Continuity

On a 2008 trip to Winnipeg, I asked a singer about two other musicians with whom he had once regularly performed. "Things have changed," he said, and I gathered there had been a falling-out. Indeed, quite a lot of things have changed since I began my fieldwork. Dance troupes and bands have broken up, and some musicians have stopped performing altogether. Edward Guiboche, Victor Courchene, and Laureen Courchene passed away in 2006, 2011, and 2012, respectively. I now interact with consultants and friends via online venues for social networking that are opening up new possibilities for aboriginal intimacies and imagining—virtual analogues of the public spaces discussed in the following chapters.

In a broader, music-historical sense, the practices considered in these chapters—country music, fiddle tunes, and gospel music—may gradually be losing a characteristic approach to rhythm. Simultaneously, and conversely, attitudes toward this "crookedness" have been modulating, and efforts have been undertaken to preserve it. Of course, aboriginal musical practices have been in a state of flux for decades. In the 1930s and '40s country music swept through Manitoba; young aboriginal men moving into a wage-labor economy spent their earnings in part on guitars and western wear, and gospel musicians started singing traditional hymns in a country style. In the 1960s younger musicians began to perform rock; more recently it has been rap.

These ongoing transformations make it difficult to talk about continuity in cultural practice, yet this book makes a case for it. It is not simply continuity in the materials of music—for instance, in unique approaches to rhythm, but especially in how aboriginal Manitobans interact, rhythmically and otherwise, in musical contexts. And it is not so much that musical structures reflect, in an abstracted form, northern Algonquian modes of sociability, but rather that musical interactions are sites in which these modes of sociability are enacted and experienced with particular intensity (see Stokes 1994:2). Even if certain musical practices fall out of favor, then, aboriginal people may well find ways to perform through music similar modes of selfhood and collectivity.

Continuity in cultural practice is also evident in how aboriginal Manitobans have engaged with mass mediation and the imagining acquaintanceship it enables. Indigenous imaginaries do not simply extend or ratify some homogeneous, modern form of sociability, but rather reshape it. The circulating "contents" of aboriginal public culture—the performances, broadcasts, publications, and behaviors that make it up—differ; but so too does the "form"—the orientation to strangers—which is in various ways qualified by the privileging of intimacy. In both respects there is potential for tension between aboriginal publics and dominant national ones. Participatory musical practices may be dismissed as aesthetically dubious, good-timing characterized as troubled and troubling, and the privileging of intimacy regarded as parochialism or nepotism. In short, exactly what distinguishes indigenous imaginaries from national ones may render them broken from the latter's perspective. Perhaps here, too, is evident a kind of continuity: in the way a national public, even in the postcolonial era, scrutinizes aboriginal social formations and cultural practices and problematizes indigenous modernities.

2

Public and Intimate Sociability in First Nations and Métis Fiddling

In chapter 1, two kinds of sociability were differentiated. One was intimacy, an orientation to known and knowable others; the other was imagining, a bearing toward an unknown public of strangers, enabled by mass mediation. This chapter draws upon fieldwork conducted with aboriginal fiddlers and dancers to explore these modes of acquaintanceship further. First, musical sociability is explored as something that emerges as musicians train their minds and bodies to interact with other musicians, known and unknown. Both intimacy and imagining come into being as aboriginal musicians coordinate their practices with those of others through disciplines that enable them to play "the same" tune and "in time" with one another, and through performances that affirm a shared affective orientation to rural homelands. Second, intimacy and imagining are shown to stand in a dynamic, dialogical relationship. Intimacies slip the bonds of face-to-face interaction and are mediated to imaginaries through recordings, broadcasts, and publications. They become the stuff of public culture. Meanwhile, this mass-mediated stuff does not remain "out there" in the socially imaginary but rather is continually redeployed and enmusicalized in intimate contexts. Third, publicness is revealed to be plural: there are multiple publics rather than a single unified one, distinguished by the circulation of different musical practices and discourses. Particular though they may be, these publics are not entirely isolated from one another. They frequently overlap: First Nations public culture is constituted around traditions of fiddling and dancing that are similar to those in Franco-Manitoban society, for instance. Perhaps more important, they have a sense of their status in relation to one another—an idea of their "highness" or "lowness," of their centrality or peripherality.

Imaginaries emerge through socially entailing acts of publication, as musicians sing, play, dance, and speak for unknown audiences, responding to the performances of others and responded to in turn. They also come into being through acts of self-discipline, as musicians train their minds and bodies to produce certain patterns of sound and motion, and as they bring these practices into line with those of unknown others. Although publics have often been conceived in terms of the circulation of rational and critical discourses, the examples that follow suggest significant links to the corporeal, the aesthetic, and the affective as well (compare Hirschkind 2006: 13–18, 30–31). Social imaginaries do not emerge solely from the circulation of linguistically mediated concepts, then, but also from the cultivation of embodied and affective practices. And it is not simply as circulating, published "texts" that music helps to constitute public culture, but also as a bodily and mental discipline.

Aboriginal Fiddle Music at Festival du Voyageur

In February 2003 the Frontier Fiddlers, a group of young First Nations and Métis musicians, performed at Winnipeg's annual Festival du Voyageur. At that event, the Frontier Fiddlers were made up of around forty boys and girls from the Frontier School Division, the largest and northernmost such division in the province of Manitoba. The young musicians represented a range of aboriginal communities, many located considerable distances from one another: Wanipigow School, serving the Ojibwe First Nation of Hollow Water and the Métis communities nearby; Grand Rapids School, serving the Cree First Nation of Grand Rapids and the Métis community, also called Grand Rapids, bordering it; Waterhen School, serving the Métis community of Waterhen; Duck Bay School, serving the Métis community of Duck Bay; and Norway House High School, serving the Cree First Nation of Norway House and the Métis communities nearby. Figure 2.1 gives some idea of the distances between these communities.

At the beginning of the program the Frontier Fiddlers lined up alongside their instructors in rows facing the audience. Most of the young musicians wore dark trousers, white T-shirts, and the *ceinture fléchée*, the multicolored sash that typically denotes Métis and Franco-Manitoban heritage. At the cue of their director, who fiddled and conducted at the front of the group, they launched into "Flaming Arrow," a tune popularized in Manitoba by the Métis fiddler Andy De Jarlis and by the Ojibwe fiddler Clifford Maytwayashing.[1] They soon segued into another favorite, "Whiskey before Breakfast." Afterward came the "Frontier Fiddler Jig," a tune written specifically for the group by Calvin Vollrath, and the well-known "Red Wing." Most of this repertoire would have been familiar to anyone who regularly attended public events geared toward aboriginal audiences. The musicians played in unison and without notation, accompanied by a small combo on the stage behind them.[2]

Festival du Voyageur is a celebration of Franco-Manitoban music and culture held each winter in Winnipeg.[3] The ten-day event presents a series of performances of music and dance at a number of venues, many in the largely Franco-Manitoban ward of St. Boniface. An array of musical and cultural difference is on offer, including aboriginal, popular, and traditional musics—to use some

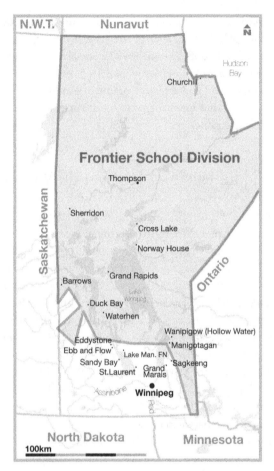

Figure 2.1 THE FRONTIER SCHOOL DIVISION. The Frontier Fiddlers group at Festival du Voyageur 2003 included performers from Wanipigow, Grand Rapids, Waterhen, Duck Bay, and Norway House. Map content appears with the kind permission of Frontier School Division; map by Anders Swanson.

of the categories from the 2003 festival guide.[4] The varied events draw similarly divergent audiences—the general public (that is, an audience with a large proportion of middle-class anglophones) in some cases and a more Franco-Manitoban one in others. The event at which the Frontier Fiddlers performed, a jigging and fiddling competition, stood apart from all of the others I attended in 2003 in that a very substantial contingent of First Nations and nonfrancophone Métis were present. A good number of them seemed to have come to watch or participate in the early-afternoon jigging contest. And as it turned out, they dominated those proceedings, with Ryan Richard, a young Ojibwe man from the Sandy Bay First Nation, winning the open competition.

The extensive participation of aboriginal people at the jigging competition evidences two aspects of Manitoban indigenous life mentioned in chapter 1: the ambiguity of the term "Métis" and the popularity of fiddling and step dancing across a variety of communities. Manitobans who identify as Métis come from a wide range of backgrounds. Festival du Voyageur 2003 explicitly celebrated the music and culture of the francophone Métis, many of whom are descended from the population Louis Riel rallied in the Red River Rebellion of 1869–70. But also present at the competition were speakers of English, Ojibwe, and Cree who identified as Métis but did not have a strong connection to the Franco-Manitoban public or to the French language.[5] Many of the members of the Frontier Fiddlers would have belonged to the latter group: they came from largely nonfrancophone Métis communities located on the outskirts of First Nations reserves, had First Nations ancestors but not necessarily Franco-Manitoban ones, and would have been more likely to identify as "aboriginal" than "Franco-Manitoban."

Moreover, as already remarked, many of those present were First Nations people. First Nations and Métis people alike practice fiddling, jigging, and square dancing in Manitoba.[6] These traditions differ from community to community but remain vital across a number of cultural and linguistic divisions. Accordingly it was not surprising that a significantly aboriginal fiddle troupe made an appearance on the day of the Festival du Voyageur jigging competition, or that that contest was dominated by First Nations and nonfrancophone Métis.

So, while fiddling, jigging, and square dancing are important components of Franco-Manitoban festivity, they play just as important a role in Manitoban aboriginal public culture. Despite these similarities, Franco-Manitoban and aboriginal events have historically been distinct, and as a Franco-Manitoban event attended by a significant contingent of nonfrancophone Métis and First Nations people, the 2003 Festival du Voyageur jigging contest was something of an anomaly. In fact, the sheer number of indigenous attendees, many of whom I recognized from the Winnipeg aboriginal square-dancing scene and from treaty-day jigging contests, rendered the Franco-Manitoban event a node in a network of (largely nonfrancophone) indigenous festivity.

During a break in the Frontier Fiddlers' performance, their director, Cameron Baggins, related the history of the ensemble to the audience. He explained that when he realized just how popular fiddling was with young people from the north, he set up Frontier Fiddlers programs in the communities of Duck Bay and Barrows, working together with the Frontier School Division. (In its very earliest incarnation the program was the idea of Blaine Klippenstein, who taught the fiddle to students in Sherridon, a small northern Métis community, in 1995.)[7] Soon other communities wanted to get in on the program, and more instructors were required. At the time Baggins spoke, at least five other fiddle teachers were coordinating fiddle programs in northern schools; in 2009, according to his fellow founder Blaine Klippenstein, there were seven full-time instructors.

In 2003 the Frontier Fiddlers program comprised several groups of students from mutually distant communities who learned and rehearsed under the guidance of instructors (the latter often from outside the community). Their performance at Festival du Voyageur was a special—though not unprecedented—event insofar as it brought together several groups from distant communities. The instructors and students synchronized this performance and others like it in advance by learning set versions of tunes codified through violin tablature, recordings, and discussions between instructors. In preparing, then, students entered into a kind of long-distance sociability, coordinating musical interactions with as-yet-unknown strangers. When I asked Klippenstein about the relationships between fiddlers from different communities, he told me:

> The [Frontier School] Division probably covers one of the largest geographic areas in Canada, if not in the world. It runs schools from Southern Manitoba to Churchill...so it is difficult to get students together from different communities. Many of the communities are isolated fly-in [communities] so [larger jamborees are probably] the first time that students are getting together.[8]

In the present day similar events go on, but on a much larger scale. When I spoke to a senior Frontier School Division staff member in 2012, he informed me that some 500 students and 150 chaperones from a range of communities were shortly about to take part in a musical get-together at Norway House.

The Frontier Fiddlers' performance evidences in a number of ways the connection between imagining and intimacy. Most obviously, the event was oriented to a public: with the help of advertisements and a website, festival organizers had extended an open invitation to a public of strangers to attend or participate in the afternoon's proceedings. But what was being oriented to this public was intimacy, or rather intimacies. First and foremost it was musical and choreographic intimacy: mutually oriented musicians and dancers engaged in entrained, attentive, real-time interaction (on entrainment see Clayton, Sager, and Will 2004). It was secondly a nostalgic, historical intimacy: the afternoon performances and competitions, as glossed by the event's emcees, revisited the convivial house parties and rural merrymaking of the voyageur past. More broadly, the afternoon was a site for fledgling intimacies. The various performers who made up the Frontier Fiddlers had come together from communities hundreds of miles apart, many probably having never made music together before. Such sudden intimacies were also on display at the fiddle competition that followed the Fiddlers' performance, as musician after musician got up on stage to perform with unfamiliar accompanists.

Thus intimacy was the stuff of festive imagining. This relationship, as a number of authors have suggested (see Berlant 2000 and 2008, Stokes 2010, Warner 2002), is characteristic of many and perhaps most public cultures. (Indeed, one need look no further than John and Yoko, Ike and Tina, or the Carter family to see the important role that conjugal, familial, and musical intimacies have played in Western popular culture.)

Irregular and Minimal Metricality in Aboriginal Music

Fairly early during my fieldwork I began to take lessons with Mark Morisseau, a Métis fiddler who taught privately and worked with the St. Laurent chapter of the Frontier Fiddlers. I met him once a week in the music studios on the upper floor of Martineau Strings, a shop in Winnipeg's St. Vital ward, and over the next few months I learned a few basic tunes, in many cases from the same sheets of violin tabulature the Frontier Fiddlers used. Most of these tunes, like the majority of the pieces that group played at Festival du Voyageur, were regular with respect to both meter and form. One night I managed to get invited to the monthly jam session at the shop. Many of the attendees were francophone Métis, and conversation and singing were in both French and English. My fiddling was extremely rudimentary and I embarrassed myself badly playing in front of the others, so it was a relief when one musician allowed me to accompany the players on the keyboard she had brought (an instrument on which I am much more comfortable). Most of the fiddlers stuck to tunes that everybody seemed to know and that held no surprises in terms of form or rhythm: "Big John McNeil," "Irishman's Heart to the Ladies," "Rubber Dolly," and "The Irish Washerwoman." There was one exception: Mel Bedard, a well-respected fiddler who had released some recordings on the Sunshine label and who played a few tunes that the other fiddlers in the room found difficult to follow. Even those of us chording along on piano and guitar had a hard time of it, since the harmonic changes never seemed to fall where we expected them to. Bedard was playing in what is sometimes now called the "crooked Métis" style (in fact historically practiced by First Nations and Métis musicians alike). As he repeated the tunes, I got a better sense of their twists and turns and was better able to anticipate where to place the chord changes. Nevertheless, a number of particularly difficult spots in one tune continually eluded me, and when Bedard winked at me following its conclusion it seemed clear that he knew he had left me in the dust.

At around the same time, in the autumn of 2002, I was starting to attend the gospel coffeehouses and social dances that would become an important part of my social and musical life during the coming year. At one coffeehouse I was frequently recruited to play the bass, and as a backing musician I became familiar with a similar rhythmic approach in the singing of hymns and gospel songs. Many of the performers had what struck me as an extremely free sense of timing. It was not simply that they sang melodies using rhythms different from those I was used to, but that they tended not to gauge their singing in any rigorous way to an underlying metrical structure. One such musician was the singer and guitarist Johnny Hodgson,[9] who would stretch out the notes of vocal melodies, leave thoughtful pauses between lines, and change chords at unpredictable moments, transforming completely the normative rhythmic structure of well-known songs such as "I Saw the Light" and "Working on a Building." Complicating matters, he varied the rhythm from verse to verse and chorus to chorus, and he tended not to demonstrate great interest in whether his fellow musicians played in time with him. Whereas Bedard appeared to enjoy "losing" the backing musicians who struggled to keep up with him, Hodgson paid little attention to his co-performers. He seemed aloof in performance and almost entirely unconcerned about musical ensemble, characteristics he shared with a number of other singers and instrumentalists at the coffeehouses.

A metrical structure is one in which several layers of pulsation stand in a stable, nested relationship (see Clayton 2007, Lerdahl and Jackendoff 1983, London 2004, Rockwell 2009a). In most such structures, the tactus—Lerdahl and Jackendoff use this technical term to differentiate the beat that is most commonly tapped or danced to—stands in a regularized relationship with one or more slower layers of pulsation. So the metrical structure in Figure 2.2 emerges because beats in the slower layers line up with beats in the faster ones at consistent intervals, each slower layer progressing at a rate one-half or one-third as slow as the next fastest one.[10]

Metrical structures are not always manifest in sounding music: they are rather internalized temporal patterns with which performers, dancers, composers, and listeners coordinate musical activity, physical movement, expectation, and attention. Kolinski calls meter a "framework" and Clayton describes it as an "abstract temporal scheme" (Clayton 2007: 16–17; Kolinski 1973: 499–501; see also Lerdahl and Jackendoff 1983: 17–18). London understands it as the patterned, entrained "attentional behavior" of listeners in the course of engagement with music (London 2004: 9–26). As conceptualized here meter is by no means a universal phenomenon; it is, however, widespread, and recent work on metrical theory seems to be useful for explaining what goes on in Manitoban aboriginal musical performances of various "Western" genres.

The aboriginal musicians I listened to and made music with tended to perform with a steady and even driving pulse. However, in many cases this tactus was not

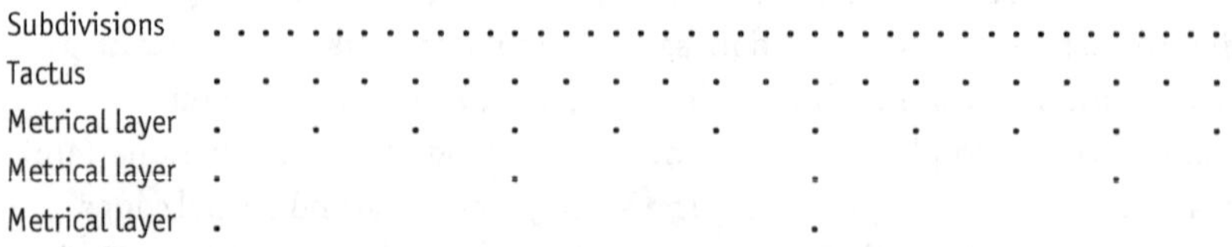

Subdivisions	. . . .
Tactus	. . . .
Metrical layer	. . . .
Metrical layer	. . . . . .
Metrical layer	. . . .

Figure 2.2 METRICAL STRUCTURE. After Lerdahl and Jackendoff 1983.

structured in regularly recurring metrical units. At least three gradations of metrical freedom were evident in performances (see Smith 2007 for a related discussion of metrical irregularity in Newfoundland fiddling). In the first, musicians seemed to synchronize what they performed to some sort of metrical structure, which they occasionally lost track of during long notes and pauses and at the ends of phrases. Metrically attuned musicians listening to such performances would perceive "added" or "dropped" beats. A second group of musicians moved back and forth: sometimes they played without reference to metrical schemes, while at others they were clearly "in" some meter or other. Clifford Maytwayashing's performances of the Red River Jig, transcribed in chapter 6 (pp. 170–71 and 174–75), exemplify this approach: the A section of the tune is not metrically regular, but a clear sense of a two-beat bar emerges in the B section. In listening to these first two groups of musicians, metrically attuned listeners might hear the meter "thickening" and "thinning" from moment to moment or section to section (see Rockwell 2009b). During certain parts of a performance the only regular beat strata are the tactus and its subdivisions, while during others, deeper, slower metrical layers are present.

A third group of musicians performed in a manner that seems best described as "minimally metrical." While they maintained a regular tactus and a consistent relationship between it and its subdivisions, their playing did not suggest the presence of higher metrical layers. Moreover, some musicians varied the rhythms when they repeated material, even within the same performance.[11] Such music can sound disorienting to metrically attuned listeners, for while it maintains familiar aspects of the songs and tunes being performed—melodies, song structures, antecedent-consequent phrasing, and common-practice harmonization— it appears not to be guided by meter at all. This minimally metrical approach is evident in Joe and Juliet Little's "Oh 'Twas Love of God to Me," transcribed in chapter 5 (see pp. 156–57). Readers may also wish to consult Bill Hamelin's *Warriors in Chains* album on the Sunshine label.

Importantly, the presence of irregular or minimal metricality never lined up consistently with musical ability. It is true that relatively unskilled musicians were more likely than gifted ones to perform in an irregular or minimally metrical style and to vary rhythms from iteration to iteration. But so did some highly skilled musicians. Some of the most adept, for instance Mel Bedard, tended to be aware of when their performances were transgressing normative Western metrical structures and the expectations of nonintimate collaborators and listeners.

Thus, musicians approached rhythm in a number of ways. Some played in a metrically regular fashion, some allowed metricality to "thin" during caesuras and at phrase endings, some seemed to move between sections where meter was regulated and sections where it was largely absent, and some seemed not to engage deeper metrical structures very much at all. Such variation was evident across a wide spectrum of musical ability and with varying degrees of apparent self-consciousness. It was also evident in a variety of genres: fiddle music, hymn singing, popular country songs, and contemporary gospel music. It is entirely possible, it should be added, that some of the musicians who played metrical-sounding music were not in fact synchronizing their performances to internalized metrical structures. In other words, while I or other "metricalizing" listeners might have perceived meter in the sounding surface of the music, it might not have been a salient psychological reality for the performers. When I spoke to the fiddler Ivan Spence in 2012, he remarked that during his years as a guitarist he had never noticed that the tunes he accompanied moved in and out of rhythmic regularity (his father, Emile Spence, discussed below, had played in the free style). It was only when he began to play the fiddle, Spence told me, that he had become aware of transgressions of rhythmic regularities.[12]

Certainly behavior at dances suggested that participants can do metrically organized things while remaining relatively unaffected by other, co-present, metrically organized stimuli (compare Smith 2007: 156–59). At many dances I observed participants employing patterns that were inherently metrical, using steps such as those in Figures 2.3 and 2.4 while dancing to a reel. As can easily be verified by following the dot notation at the bottom of each example, the dance patterns have a quadruple metrical structure. On every beat of the tactus (represented in the transcription by the quarter note) the full weight of the body is placed on one foot or the other; on every third beat the pattern of footwork switches over and is mirrored on the opposite side of the body; and on every fifth beat the entire pattern begins again. Yet this metrically regular choreographic patterning did not extend to the fiddle playing that accompanied it, nor was it coordinated between the musicians and the dancers. At social dances, dancers began the dance patterns shown in Figures 2.3 and 2.4 whenever they felt like it, without necessarily coordinating them to a corresponding metrical moment in a fiddle tune—say, the beginning of an eight-bar phrase. Moreover, they were just as likely to use these metrically regular patterns for crooked tunes as for straight ones (compare Smith 2007: 156–59). For instance, I attended a square-dancing competition at which the fiddler Clifford Maytwayashing was in charge of the music. He played his own slightly irregular version of "Big John McNeil" (a Scottish reel popularized in Canada by Don Messer), adding an "extra" beat each time the A section

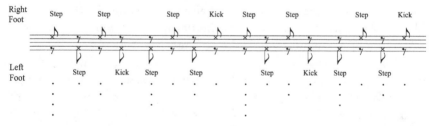

Figure 2.3 BASIC REEL STEP. Notated time values are approximate. Weight transfer occurs at moments marked "step."

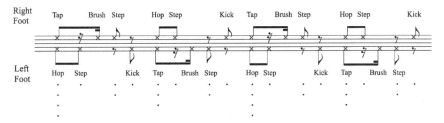

Figure 2.4 MORE ELABORATE REEL STEP. Notated time values are approximate. The hopping or stepping leg is the weight-bearing leg.

repeated, effectively turning a sixty-four-beat tune into a sixty-five-beat one. It did not confuse the dancers in the least. In my experience, this was typical: dancers "devoured" a continual succession of pulses, Pac-Man style, not worrying too much whether they were grouped two by two, three by three, or in some irregular combination.

Thus, the musical practices I observed while doing fieldwork were varied and divergent; nevertheless, they permit some generalizations. A range of rhythmic approaches were in evidence, from the rigorously regularized (evident in the majority of the tunes played by the Frontier Fiddlers) to the minimally metrical. Rhythmically irregular approaches were common in both instrumental and vocal music, as well as in contexts of social and competitive dance. Such music could be heard in venues where francophone Métis gathered to hear traditional music, but especially at events where heterogeneous groups of Métis, Cree, and Ojibwe people met. Older musicians were more likely to play or sing in these styles than young ones. And some musicians were clearly aware that they played in "crooked" styles, while others seemed not to be.

Ethnicity, class, and prestige coincided with the variations just summarized in significant ways. When metrically irregular music was performed in auspicious venues, there tended to be a larger contingent of middle-class, nonaboriginal listeners in the audience, the "crooked" music they heard tended to be fiddle music, there were few opportunities for participation by attendees, and performers often seemed more reflexively aware of the rhythmic irregularities in the music they played. When such music was performed in less prestigious spaces, there tended to be more working-class aboriginal people in the audience, the rhythmically irregular music they heard was more likely to be song, events were more amenable to spontaneous participation by attendees, and musicians seemed less reflexively aware of the "crookedness" of their performances.[13]

How to interpret the widespread rhythmic irregularities evident in Manitoban aboriginal music, but also their apparent recent decline, and their greater prevalence in certain social and musical contexts than in others? As I suggest in the pages that follow, aboriginal musicians have experienced significant shifts in social orientation since the early decades of the twentieth century. One consequence of this is that metrically regular singing and playing have become more common. Another is that the metrically irregular playing that endures is increasingly addressing new kinds of audiences and being implicated in new kinds of relationships between performers.

Fiddle Music and Social Intimacy

Anne Lederman, doing research in western Manitoba in the 1980s, identified a number of characteristic elements of First Nations and Métis fiddling from that area, including metrical irregularity (Lederman 1988: 207–11). In a 1988 article she suggested that this approach to meter was also evident in traditional Ojibwe vocal music: "Native song and Native fiddling reflect a kind of 'one-beat' approach to rhythm, in which the music is felt as a continuous series of steady beats without setting up any expectations in terms of grouping the beats into longer units" (Lederman 1988: 216). In short, fiddling preserved the rhythmic aesthetic of traditional Ojibwe drum song. (The rhythmic approach she describes can probably be understood to correspond to the third, "minimally metrical," category of rhythmic irregularity distinguished above.) Lederman further noted that Native fiddlers from western Manitoba departed in significant ways from the formal structures that are typical in North American fiddle music.[14]

My own fieldwork and listening suggest that similar traits have been evident in places some remove from Lederman's original study area: for instance, in the communities of Manigotagan and Hollow Water in southeastern Manitoba and in Cree communities such as Norway House and Cross Lake in the north. They can also be found in the present day in a variety of vocal genres, including hymn singing and country music, practiced by aboriginal people across Manitoba. As an example of a traditional approach to rhythm and form in fiddle music, I will use a tune by Emile Spence (Figure 2.5), one of the western Manitoban musicians Lederman herself discusses. Spence was a Métis fiddler from the town of Eddystone in western Manitoba; his son Ivan, who accompanies him on the original recording of the tune, was in 2002 and 2003 the regular fiddler at a weekly social dance I frequented at Winnipeg's Indian and Metis Friendship Centre.[15]

Figure 2.6 is a transcription of Spence's performance of his "McAuley's Creek Breakdown" (Spence 2001). The tune appears to be in dialogue with a well-established formal structure. Much North American fiddle music has a binary form in which both sections are repeated: AABB, in alphabetic shorthand. It is possible to hear the four parts of this form beginning respectively in the pickups to measures 1, 7, 13, and 26. It is also possible to hear an AABB'BB' form articulated, the six sections beginning respectively in the pickups to measures 1, 7, 13, 20, 26, and 33.

But while the tune makes use of what can be heard as a conventional formal structure (as well as common-practice harmony and antecedent-consequent

Figure 2.5 EMILE SPENCE. Detail from album cover courtesy of the Spence family. Photographer unknown.

phrase pairings) it departs from at least two conventions of North American fiddle music. First, it is not metrically regular. As the barlines in the transcription suggest, Spence's tune presents a series of musical gestures of uneven length. Certain moments in the piece seem to be in duple meter, for example mm. 2–6 and 13–24. But at other times, the melody falls into longer groupings—such as the five-beat runs that begin in mm. 1 and 7, or the three-beat cadential caesuras that mark the end of the B sections in mm. 25 and 38—and the duple feel disappears (I notate the main beat as a quarter note). Second, the phrase lengths differ from what would be typical in a North American fiddle tune. Whereas a typical reel or breakdown would have a repeated A section that was sixteen beats in length and a repeated B section that was sixteen beats in length, totaling sixty-four beats (16 + 16 + 16 + 16) for a single statement of a tune, Spence's A section is fifteen beats long and his B section is twenty-seven beats long, totaling eighty-four beats (15 + 15 + 27 + 27). This raises some interesting questions about rhythmic organization. Did the players perceive it to move in and out of duple meter, or is it simply "metricalizing" listeners who hear it thus? I have included dotted barlines in my transcription, but mostly for the purposes of identifying sections of the tune. It could very well be that the fiddler heard this as "one-beat" music in which the tactus did not fall into groups at higher levels.

Accompanying musicians would probably find it difficult to play along with a tune such as this one unless they were already familiar with it, and accordingly, such recordings can be understood as documents of musical intimacy. The

Figure 2.6 EMILE SPENCE, "MCAULEY'S CREEK BREAKDOWN." Transcription by the author, with assistance from Sarah Quick. Dotted barlines and measure numbers have been included in part to help identify moments discussed in the text and in part to suggest how the music seems to move in and out of duple meter. At the same time, the lines are left dotted out of recognition that the metrical structure they imply may not reflect the psychological experiences of the musicians playing. Transcription appears courtesy of the Spence family.

traditional style of fiddling thrived in close-knit rural communities where fiddlers were often accompanied by relatives or old friends. (Note, however, that guitarists seem to have begun to accompany fiddlers around the middle of the twentieth century; before this time, harmonic accompaniment was rarer. See Lederman 2001: 407.) It seems reasonable to suggest that in situations of frequent and sometimes lifelong musical collaboration, accompanists were able to learn to accommodate rhythmically complex tunes such as the one above. It also seems reasonable to propose that, in the years before the widespread availability of recordings, particularly in poor communities, fiddlers were much more closely oriented to immediate musical collaborators than to mass-mediated tunes and styles.[16]

When I was doing fieldwork, many performers still made music in family groups: Cliff Maytwayashing (d. 2009), a Saulteaux fiddler from Lake Manitoba First Nation, regularly performed with his son Pat, who accompanied him on guitar; and the fiddler Tommy Knott, who grew up in the Métis community of Grand Marais, performed with his siblings, the guitarist Beryl Knott Bouvette and the pianist Fern Knott Wood. The same was true in the country music scene, where members of the Monias, Ranville, Dutiaume, and Dick families frequently performed together. Close attention to the many family connections mentioned in Anne Lederman's liner notes to the *Old Native and Métis Fiddling in Western Manitoba* collection suggest that such relationships were just as important (and probably more so) in the past. Thus the complex metrical approach evident in traditional indigenous fiddle styles thrived in contexts where performers were longtime collaborators, united by bonds of kinship and, in many cases, economic interdependence. Frequent collaboration allowed accompanists to anticipate and accommodate fiddlers' highly individualized rhythms, and confident musical interaction evidenced the close bonds between intimates.

Irregularly or minimally metrical fiddling was not only an index of closeness, however, but also a marker of personal distinction. Performances of tunes in this style individuated musicians, setting them apart from one another. Lederman writes, "According to conversations I had with several players, there seems to be a fairly widely-held belief that every fiddler should have his own version of a tune which is different from that of the other players" (1988: 215; see also n. 13). A similar attitude toward the singing of country and gospel songs is evident among present-day aboriginal musicians, as is related in chapter 4. Thus, traditionally, musical performances were also performances of singularity. It is nevertheless possible to understand them to be enmeshed in intimate forms of corporateness, for when fiddlers and singers distinguished themselves, it was primarily with respect to other known musicians. Music making may have been competitive or socially individuating—but these rivalries and distinctions were intimate ones.

The metrical characteristics discussed here have been observed in a number of northern North American aboriginal groups and contexts (see, for instance, Chrétien 1996: 125–30; Gabriel Dumont Institute 2002: 20–21; Gibbons 1980: 42–44; Lederman 1988, 2001, 2003; Mishler 1993: 147–50, 175–78; Quick 2009; Whidden 1985: 33; Whidden 2007: 67–68, 73–74, 85–86, 94–95), and it is tempting to propose the existence of a belt of metrically irregular instrumental and vocal traditions that corresponds to areas that were historically part of the fur trade. Metrical irregularity is not universal among aboriginal people in these areas (see Chrétien 1996), but it certainly seems widespread,[17] and it could be that some sort of "Native aesthetic," in Lederman's words, has had a broad impact on rhythmic practice in appropriated genres. There may be other, more general, reasons for such metrical irregularities, however. After all, "crookedness" is evident in an array of nonindigenous fiddling styles, including those from Appalachia, Quebec, and Newfoundland, and in many early recordings of folk and popular music (see Labbé 1997, McCulloh 1967, Neal 2009, Pappas 2007, Rockwell 2011, Smith 2007).

Moreover, in a variety of vernacular musical styles practiced by aboriginal and nonaboriginal communities alike, similar musical changes occur after the early decades of the twentieth century. There has been, on the one hand, a general move toward metrical regularity, and, contrarily, an interest in preserving the crooked. (Indeed, the relatively recent spread of the term "crooked" amongst Manitoban aboriginal fiddlers suggests a rather new realization that formerly unproblematized rhythmic practices might be regarded as unusual by a wider public.) I suggest that, for Manitoban aboriginal music makers, and probably other musical communities as well, these changes are related to important shifts in social orientation.

Metrical Regularity and Musical Publicness

The irregular and even minimal metricality characteristic of older Manitoban aboriginal performers stands in contrast to a much more metrically and formally regular approach in the playing of younger musicians. Most of the aboriginal fiddlers I heard while doing fieldwork, including Emile Lavallee, Tom Dutiaume, Clint Dutiaume, Ivan Spence, and Garry Lepine, tended to perform tunes that fell in line with the dominant conventions that structure rhythm and form in North American fiddling—even when they were familiar with older, more metrically irregular styles.[18] This growth in regularity suggests that performers have increasingly been orienting their musical practice to social imaginaries, bringing their playing into line with that of other, unknown, members of fiddling publics, and in doing so, extending these publics. Thus the greater prevalence of metrical and formal regularity I observed can be understood as an index of social imagining, just as the rhythmic and formal irregularities of older practices pointed to social intimacy. This point needs to be made carefully, lest an exclusive association be understood to exist between the older styles and social intimacy. In the present day, some metrically irregular music is just as implicated as metrically regular music in "imagining" forms of sociability. Nevertheless, it is in the increasing regularization of musical practice that an increasing orientation to a public is most immediately apparent, and accordingly I turn here to consider again the Frontier Fiddlers and the events at Festival du Voyageur. I will subsequently explore how new mediations of older styles also evidence this shift in social orientation.

As explained above, the Frontier Fiddlers program consists of numerous local chapters spread out across a vast school division. Students join local ensembles and, as members of these groups, engage in musical activities coordinated with those of other communities. Their instructors convey techniques of musical self-discipline that allow them to perform the same musical patterns as other, distant students—as well as a broader fiddling public. The basic units enabling this coordination are tunes—which of course also help to transmit more abstract melodic, harmonic, and metrical patterns. Two aspects of the tunes played by the Frontier Fiddlers merit special attention: their relative stability, and the absence of certain characteristics of an older First Nations and Métis style. To begin with the first point, at the 2003 performance described above, students and instructors from communities distant from one another played versions of tunes that were similar enough that a coherent performance could emerge. Their repertoire had been correlated ahead of time through tablature and music notation and through discussions and agreements between instructors. Mark Morisseau told me around this time that fiddle instructors got together annually at Frontier Fiddlers jamborees to discuss, record, and distribute copies of the tunes that would be learned and performed by the various local student chapters.[19] The meetings were an opportunity to get the basics of the tunes down, as well as some finer points such as the bowing.

Second, although the Frontier Fiddlers were explicitly celebrated as an organization that preserved older Métis and First Nations fiddle traditions, their music differed from those traditions in significant ways. Rather than "crooked" tunes with irregular or minimal meter and inventive formal structures, the group played metrical tunes in thirty-two-bar AABA form for the most part. Moreover, whereas the traditional fiddling aesthetic seems to have been highly individuated, with musicians playing unique, idiosyncratic versions of the same tunes, the Frontier Fiddlers played tunes that had been standardized in ways that facilitated collective performance. In fact, when I asked Blaine Klippenstein whether "crooked" rhythmic styles, or old-fashioned tunes by Native fiddlers, were incorporated in the Frontier Fiddlers repertoire, he replied, "The [crooked] style is not taught simply because it is such an individualist style of music and we are always teaching students in groups and it simply wouldn't work. It is the hope that the instructors teach the students and then the students will explore the music and instrument on their own" (email, August 8, 2009). In short, the traditional style was not perceived as one that would suit group learning and performance.

So, dispersed groups come to comprise the larger body of Frontier Fiddlers as they separately engage the same artifacts, synchronizing their musical activities to those of musicians whom they do not yet know. A common repertoire of tunes plays an important role in this process, as do a set of ideas concerning pitch, tuning, tempo, form, and meter. Notably, the disciplinary process turns away from some distinctive aspects of traditional Native fiddling.

The Frontier Fiddlers present a miniature and emplaced model of how other musical publics or imaginaries come into being, including the broader Manitoban aboriginal publics explored in this volume. They emerge performatively, as participants orient their bodies and minds toward shared practices and repertories, disciplining them in order to facilitate coherent collaboration with strangers (compare Elias 1994: 365–79). Perceived in this light, the growing metricalization of Manitoban aboriginal music making can be understood as an index of an emerging bearing toward imagined others.

A more general theoretical point can also be remarked here: Warner's concept of a public as a network of circulating texts, in which mass-mediated performances and publications continually respond to previous ones and are responded to in turn, can be broadened. Publics also emerge as participants train and discipline their minds and bodies to bring them into synchrony with those of imagined others.[20]

An increasing bearing toward social imaginaries does not mean a pulling away from intimacies; on the contrary, this bearing intersects with and informs face-to-face encounters, as the example of the Frontier Fiddlers suggests. For instance, increasing rhythmic and formal regularity facilitate encounters of a kind that has become more and more common over the last six decades. Since the 1950s, a widening transportation infrastructure and growing aboriginal articulation to a wage-labor economy have increased the likelihood that people who grew up hundreds of miles apart will make music together—at competitions, jam sessions, coffeehouses, and bar gigs. Many of these musical collaborations take place in cosmopolitan contexts such as the city of Winnipeg, where tens of thousands of aboriginal people from different backgrounds and communities make their home. A disposition toward conventions that circulate in mass-mediated form coincides not only with the expansion of imagining forms of sociability, then, but also with greater mobility and growing urbanization. In these contexts, musicians have increasingly performed with people they have not previously met, and a musical vernacular has facilitated these sudden intimacies.[21]

Intimacy and imagining thus intersect and overlap, and stranger-sociability enables the emergence of new intimacies. This much was evident at the fiddling competition that followed the Frontier Fiddlers' performance at Festival du Voyageur 2003. Festival organizers had arranged for two pianists to accompany a seemingly unending stream of competitors, each playing a waltz, a jig, and a reel. The fiddlers played a wide variety of tunes, many of which I did not know and some of which I suspected were unfamiliar to the accompanists. Nevertheless, the music making was by and large successful: there were few moments of poor ensemble and even fewer occasions when the players had to stop. Had more competitors employed the traditional aboriginal style of playing, with its irregular meter, ebullient melodic phrasing, and individual variations on well-known tunes, the accompanists might have had much more difficulty.

Trajectories between Intimacy and Publicness

As the preceding account indicates, intimacy and publicness stand in complexly intertwined relationships: publicly circulating formulas (such as those employed by fiddlers and accompanists alike in the fiddling competition) enable musical intimacies to come into being, while musical intimacies (for instance, performances by fiddlers and their accompanists) are oriented to publics through recordings and broadcasts.

I suggested earlier that older examples of (what is now perceived to be) rhythmic and formal irregularity in fiddle music could be understood as manifestations of musical intimacy, while the increasing tendency toward metrical regularity in performance coincided with the growth of imagining forms of sociability. But I also indicated that social imagining has become so widespread that, even where metrically irregular practices endure, they are increasingly bound up in this newer form of affiliation. In short, "crooked" singing and playing now too circulate in mass-mediated form and have been incorporated in listening and practicing publics.

"Intimate" styles of performance have circulated for decades. Fiddlers such as Emile Spence, Lawrence "Teddy Boy" Houle, Cliff Maytwayashing, Nichol Ross, and John Arcand have made recordings, appeared on broadcasts, and given public concerts of metrically irregular music.[22] The fiddler and scholar Anne Lederman has brought traditional fiddling styles to the attention of a wider public through the release of *Old Native and Métis Fiddling in Manitoba*, a set of recordings of musicians whose work might otherwise have gone undocumented (1987; rereleased on CD in 2003). And John Arcand advertises recordings, workshops, and an annual festival publicly via a website.[23] In other words, musicians who play in traditional styles, and their advocates, have sought to constitute a listening public around these styles.

Musicians have also, in recent decades, taught themselves to play circulating versions of certain "crooked" tunes, learning metrically and formally irregular music to perform with other, as yet unknown musicians and dancers. In recent years Anne Lederman and Teddy Boy Houle, working together with the Nunavut fiddler Colin Adjun, have introduced a number of younger aboriginal fiddlers to tunes in the older style. John Arcand has presented workshops offering to teach "crooked Métis" playing. The Gabriel Dumont Institute has published a volume incorporating transcriptions of a number of tunes in the traditional style (Gabriel Dumont Institute 2002). And in 2002 and 2003 the Frontier Fiddlers incorporated a metrically irregular tune, the "Gravel Road Jig," as part of their repertoire.

By far the best example of the mass mediation of the "crooked" style, however, is the late twentieth-century dissemination of the version of the Red River Jig recorded by the francophone Métis fiddler Andy De Jarlis. The tune, which accompanies a step dance of the same name, is first mentioned in nineteenth-century sources (see Begg 1871: 279; Bolton 1961; on the origins of the tune as "La grande gigue simple," see Gibbons 1980). As the name suggests, the dance and tune were originally closely associated with Red River, the area around present-day Winnipeg, and with the Métis people who lived there, but they eventually spread to communities across northwestern North America (see Lederman 1987: 17).[24] The first recording of the Red River Jig was made in 1940 by Frederick Genthon (Gabriel Dumont Institute 2002: 33); two versions of the tune were published in sheet music form, probably around the same time (Johnston and Genthon n.d.). Despite these early publications, transmission of the tune seems to have been largely aural until the second half of the twentieth century (see Gibbons 1980), when De Jarlis made his recording of it (De Jarlis [1961]). It is transcribed in Figure 2.7.

As the transcription shows, the Red River Jig is in a number of respects emblematic of the traditional aboriginal fiddle style. Although a good part of the B section of the tune appears to be in duple meter, the A section is irregular and, arguably, minimally metrical (interestingly, dancers typically dance a four-beat pattern during this section). The form, too, is irregular—the second half of the tune is slightly longer than the first.

Despite these irregularities, De Jarlis's performance has been widely copied in Manitoba and further afield, as Roy Gibbons observed in 1980 (Gibbons 1980) and as was still the case when I was doing fieldwork. For instance, at the Festival du Voyageur jigging competition mentioned above, the fiddler Randy Westlak's version of the tune was clearly based upon the De Jarlis model. Even more dramatically, the opening ceremonies for the 2002 North American Indigenous Games featured, during one medley, a group of aboriginal fiddlers who performed the De Jarlis version of the tune in unison. Thus, growing numbers of aboriginal fiddlers are preparing themselves for public-sphere encounters by learning the same versions of irregular tunes, especially De Jarlis's Red River Jig. Music that stands in

Figure 2.7 ANDY DE JARLIS, RED RIVER JIG (TRADITIONAL). As on the Sunshine Records compilation *Fiddle Legends* (SSCD 506, 2000). Transcription by the author. Dotted barlines reflect melodic groupings; solid barlines indicate apparent metrical groupings. Tuning is ADAE.

keeping with dominant stylistic norms is not the only basis for aboriginal musical publicness.

A transformation is evident, however. As remarked earlier, traditional fiddling appears often to have been highly individuated, with musicians playing significantly different versions of the same tunes (see, for instance, the variants of the Red River Jig included in the *Drops of Brandy* collection). Moreover, while ensemble playing did exist, it was relatively rare for two or more fiddlers to play together (see the recordings and commentary in Lederman 2003). Now, however, tunes tend to be standardized, and it is not uncommon for groups of fiddlers to play them in unison. Preservation of the older style of playing has tended to emphasize the maintenance of specific tunes rather than a cultivation of the tradition of individuation. (Nonetheless, highly personalized performances are still evident in certain contexts of aboriginal music making—namely in the singing of sacred and secular song (see chapters 4 and 5). Significantly, however, such performances do not receive much attention or approbation from the mainstream public.)

If "intimate" styles originally associated with rural communities have been oriented to a wider public, a reverse trajectory is also evident: mass-mediated music is being integrated in quotidian community life and socially intimate contexts. This happens dramatically in the case of the Frontier Fiddlers program, which has introduced fiddles and fiddling to hundreds of homes in northern aboriginal communities. By Blaine Klippenstein's estimation there were seven full-time instructors and fifteen hundred students enrolled in Frontier Fiddler programs in September 2009 (email correspondence, September 8, 2009). Students encounter fiddling on a weekly basis in schools across northern Manitoba; tunes and musical practice are embedded in the habits, routines, and periodicities of everyday life (compare Appadurai 1996: 66–70); and mass-mediated pieces and styles become the basis for and focus of intimate encounters. It is worthwhile to ask to what extent students experience such encounters, and the styles of playing they learn, in terms of social imaginaries. Is it a relationship to a public that is being prioritized here, or is it connections with immediate collaborators, instructors, and fellow community members? It could be that mass-mediated tunes and styles are simply the materials closest to hand for building local relationships. Whatever the case, instructors do situate this musical activity in relation to a broader public culture and in this way connect everyday practice to musical imagining.

Overlapping and Differentiated Publics

Thus, both traditional and mainstream fiddling styles are implicated in intimate and imagining forms of sociability and indeed move in complex trajectories between the two. The remainder of this chapter explores this relationship further and considers how aboriginal imaginaries stand apart from others, even in cases where music is shared between them. As will become evident, some forms of musical intimacy circulate widely, in a variety of imaginaries, while others seem to move within more bounded spheres.

Fiddling has a high profile at many events that bring large aboriginal audiences together in Manitoba. Several First Nations host annual festivals and treaty-day celebrations where jigging, square dancing, and fiddling are headline events; Métis organizations—chiefly the Manitoba Metis Federation—sponsor similar undertakings. Fiddle music also animates social dances. During the main period of my fieldwork weekly square dances were held at Winnipeg's Indian and Metis Friendship Centre; others occurred on a less regular basis in outlying communities. Fiddling is further an important part of the popular music scene: a number of aboriginal country bands feature a fiddler, and it is not unusual to hear a few traditional tunes played as part of a Friday or Saturday night set, or to see people dancing a few changes of the Red River Jig at a nightclub (see chapter 6). Fiddling continues to be mediated through recordings and broadcasts, as well: many aboriginal fiddlers have albums, and selections from these are heard regularly on NCI FM (again, a radio station with an aboriginal directorate serving a largely indigenous clientele across Manitoba; see chapters 1 and 3).

The prominence of fiddling within the aboriginal public sphere can be understood as an elaboration of traditional musical intimacies. A number of my older consultants grew up in communities where square dancing and step dancing were a significant part of social and musical life until well into the second half of the twentieth century. For instance, Victor Courchene told me that his home community, the Sagkeeng First Nation, had had a tradition of "breaking in" a house for newlyweds. Following a wedding, there was typically a well-attended dance at the couple's house. All of the furniture was taken outside and left on the lawn to make room for the dance, which went on until the sun came up. His wife, Loreen Courchene, also Ojibwe, grew up in western Manitoba near the Ebb and Flow First Nation and remembered similar events there. It seems reasonable to suggest that contemporary public culture celebrates such experiences while also extending them in new directions.

PUBLICS AND PERMEABILITY: DISTINGUISHING ABORIGINAL AND FRANCO-MANITOBAN IMAGINARIES

As a number of examples in this chapter—Festival du Voyageur, the upstairs jam session at Martineau Strings, the De Jarlis recording of the Red River Jig—indicate, aboriginal public culture does not have a monopoly on fiddle music and related dance styles: they also play a significant part in Franco-Manitoban imaginaries. The violin is one of the symbols of the Festival du Voyageur, and the Ensemble folklorique de la Rivière-Rouge, an iconic Franco-Manitoban troupe, performs complex choreographies that draw upon step- and square-dancing patterns. As remarked in chapter 1, many Franco-Manitobans identify as Métis people, and no definite line separates the aboriginal and Franco-Manitoban populations.

Nevertheless, the aboriginal and Franco-Manitoban publics seem distinguishable. This is probably in large part because the broadcasts, recordings, and print publications that, in circulating, establish these spheres of affiliation differ from one another. Franco-Manitoban public culture privileges the French language, whereas aboriginal public culture favors English, followed by Cree and Ojibwe. By way of illustration, the two most important Métis political organizations in Manitoba are the Manitoba Metis Federation, an organization for which English serves as the lingua franca, and the Union nationale métisse Saint-Joseph du Manitoba, which addresses its constituency in French. Insofar as language differentiates the two publics, it is interesting that words are not particularly important in the areas where they overlap most significantly, namely in instrumental music and choreography. So, the two imaginaries are at once permeable (as might be expected, given that one typically addresses a public as though anyone could be listening; see Warner 2002) and differentiated. Nor does it appear that language is the only thing that separates them. Social class also seems to be a factor: Festival du Voyageur, the most prestigious event in the Franco-Manitoban calendar, attracts a largely middle-class audience, whereas aboriginal festivals tend to draw mostly working-class attendees.

MUSICAL AND INTERACTIVE AESTHETICS: DISTINGUISHING MAINSTREAM AND INDIGENOUS PUBLICS

Native fiddlers and dancers also take part in performances that hail the broader national public: folk festivals, for instance, and events celebrating the multicultural and indigenous heritage of Canada and North America. In Winnipeg, First Nations and Métis fiddlers and dancers are regular participants at the annual Folklorama and Voyageur festivals, the largest cultural events of the summer and winter, respectively. They are also invited further afield: in 2004 a group of fiddlers from the town of Saint Laurent represented Canadian Métis traditions at the opening of the National Museum of the American Indian in Washington, D.C.[25] Recordings, films, and broadcasts of aboriginal fiddle music similarly hail national or international audiences. Anne Lederman's recorded collection can be mentioned here again, alongside the Smithsonian Folkways recording *Wood That Sings* and two films, Bob Rodgers's *Fiddlers of James Bay* and Michael Loukinen's *Medicine Fiddle*.

Given this overlap, is it in fact possible to distinguish a national or international public from a more specifically indigenous one? It is, in part because certain kinds of music seem less acceptable to mainstream aesthetic preferences, and in part because aboriginal public culture tends to place more value on participation and on idiosyncrasy in musical performance. As already remarked, aboriginal fiddling and related dance styles have received increasing interest and attention in the broader public sphere. Nevertheless, there seem to be some barriers to their circulation. While doing fieldwork I encountered listeners and musicians who disliked elements of the traditional style (compare Diamond 2008: 117–18). Some complained about the "bad timing" of musicians who played with irregular meter, and one instructor who worked with the Frontier Fiddlers told me he did not like the sound of the older traditional fiddlers because it sounded scratchy and weak. Just as important, the aboriginal musicians who have had the most success with wider audiences tend to play in ways that do not offend certain dominant expectations. While some fiddlers maintain the rhythmic and formal ebullience of the traditional style (sometimes with a self-conscious awareness of its "crookedness"), they tend not to play with the soft sound and inexact or nonstandard tuning of older musicians.[26] Even when the rhythmic elements of their playing subvert musical expectations, in other words, other aspects accord with dominant stylistic norms. Whether intentionally or not, the most widely successful exponents of the traditional style tend to acknowledge and affirm the less flexible elements of mainstream aesthetic preferences.

I did encounter the older, softer, scratchier, and less intonationally normative style of playing while doing fieldwork, but typically in places where working-class aboriginal people were in the majority. In other words, timbral and intonational differences had some correspondence with, or rather helped to render as racially and socially other, venues of aboriginal assembly. At least two other things helped to distinguish musical sociability in these spaces—and here I speak of instrumental and vocal music alike. Music making tended to be more egalitarian and participatory, while at the same time musical and personal idiosyncrasy were more readily accommodated. It was held that anyone who wanted should be allowed to perform, but also that individuals would sing songs or play tunes in their own unique way.

To elaborate this last point briefly, there are differences of opinion among Métis and First Nations musicians concerning fiddling and (especially) singing that is metrically irregular, with some of them performing in a less regulated manner and others vocally critical of what they regard as an incorrect approach. Nevertheless, all manner of vocalists and instrumentalists frequently perform with and for one another in certain public spaces where aboriginal attendees are in the majority. Musicians who sing and play in a metrically regular style share the stage with others who do not, and the exclusion of willing contributors, no matter the style of music they play or sing, is regarded as problematic (in many respects these can be understood as the participatory performance spaces described in Turino 2008). Some participants are very idiosyncratic indeed, contravening all kinds of norms and expectations and making the task of accompanying difficult. I have seen them, too, made welcome. To sum up, then, indigenous performers do appear on civic and national stages and contribute to the articulation of general forms of publicness, but distinctly indigenous spheres of musical sociability are also evident. These are differentiated by not only their participatory inclusiveness but also their openness to the prickly and sometimes difficult-to-accommodate individuality of certain performers. These especial kinds of intimacy are explored in chapters 4 and 5.

FIDDLE MUSIC AND RURAL IMAGINARIES

The Franco-Manitoban hosts at Festival du Voyageur, in their banter between items on the program, characterized fiddling and step dancing as traditions from a voyageur past. In their framing, the music and dance on display were a representation less of contemporary practice than of something Franco-Manitobans used to do (they are both, of course). Such practices are also represented nostalgically in the aboriginal public sphere, but in the latter case it seems more common to characterize them as both old-timey and contemporary. For instance, in the early 2000s NCI FM aired a weekly program called *Kitchen Country Music*. The hosts played fiddle tunes and country songs, interspersing commercial recordings with minidisc recordings they had made at live concerts and in performers' homes. The program and its title summoned images of community music making, rural house parties, and dancing and singing in the kitchen—but these musical intimacies had a sense of immediacy and presentness to them. I had seen people break out guitars and make music in their homes. And when I went to square-dance exhibitions and competitions, there were inevitably youth troupes competing, most with an equal complement of female and male dancers, the latter somehow managing to give their country and western costumes a hint of hip-hop.

In the aboriginal public sphere, then, "country" and "rural" seem to have a particularly current character, whatever part nostalgia also plays. Moreover, this contemporaneity is evident in how indigenous people represent themselves, not only to themselves, but also to the wider public. Why should this be so? A simple answer is that these representations reflect the importance, both historically and in the present day, of fiddling, step dancing, and square dancing in many aboriginal communities. But another, complementary explanation also seems possible. These practices have a broader political significance when understood as a celebration of the homes, communities, and lands where the unique economic and political rights of First Nations and Métis people are most commonly vested. As noted in chapter 1, treaties, laws, and the Canadian constitution continue to guarantee special rights to aboriginal people, including the inalienable right to certain territories, the sovereignty of indigenous governments, and the right to harvest. Most of these rights, at least as currently interpreted, pertain to rural lands and occupations. In celebrating country homes, traditional music and dance (and the discourses that accompany them) affirm the places most frequently considered to be the bases of indigenous political autonomy and economic right. However nostalgic indigenous fiddle music is, it also an expression of hope for vital rural presents and futures and a celebration of the good life in the places where indigenous political and economic claims are strongest.

It is often thought that the public sphere is a space for the circulation of rational and critical discourse (Habermas 1989; see also Calhoun 1992: 2), but the work of world making is also accomplished through expressive, embodied, and aesthetic practices (Berlant 2008, Hirschkind 2006, Stokes 2010, Warner 2002), including musical and choreographic intimacies. Indigenous fiddle music acknowledges and constitutes an audience with strong ties to the sounds, motions, and feelings of rural musical life; for whom "kitchen country music" and fiddle dances play an important role in sociability; for whom the thin tone and rhythmic ebullience of traditional fiddling are familiar and pleasurable; and for whom the Frontier Fiddlers represent a new rural generation. And thus aboriginal public culture emerges not only when its participants engage in verbal discourse about treaties, rights, and well-being, but also when they move, feel, dance, make music, and imagine others doing so.[27]

Musical Imaginaries

Drawing upon the foregoing accounts of aboriginal fiddling and the publics it addresses, a number of characteristics of social imaginaries—and, more specifically, musical ones—can be elaborated, loosely following but also expanding on points made in Michael Warner's *Publics and Counterpublics*. First, a public is a social formation that is continually being performed into being. Social imaginaries emerge as new performances, publications, and broadcasts, oriented to imagined audiences, respond to older ones and anticipate still others (see Warner 2002: 67–69, 90–92). They also come into being as musicians discipline their minds and bodies in ways that acknowledge and extend the embodied practices of other, imagined musicians and dancers. So, for instance, they are established as musicians learn to replicate regular metrical patterns and the thirty-two-bar AABB form—or as they teach themselves to reproduce Andy De Jarlis or Frederick Genthon's irregular versions of the Red River Jig—with an eye to future public performances and collaborations with as-yet-unknown partners.

Second, a social imaginary is a contested space constituted through competing practices, performances, and publications. Each effective instance of performance, broadcast, or publication confirms or challenges the state of things, supporting currently dominant practices or advancing alternatives.[28] Exactly this dynamic is evident in contemporary performances, recordings, and broadcasts of aboriginal fiddling, which evidence a variety of approaches to meter and form. These differing styles compete for the attention, recognition, and affirmation of fiddling publics. Thus the differing attitudes to irregular meter or tuning described earlier and in the following chapters might be better characterized as diverging ways of extending publicness. Judging a competition, choosing the repertoire for a group like the Frontier Fiddlers, releasing CDs of traditional performances, and advertising workshops dedicated to teaching music in a traditional style—all of these can be understood as acts of potential consequence within a contested social space.

Third, publicness is not simply internally heterogeneous: at a certain level it is possible to recognize different publics. Thus a Franco-Manitoban public can be distinguished from an aboriginal public, and both can be distinguished from a broader national one. The first two have much in common: both are partially constituted through fiddle music, jigging, and square dancing. Yet in other respects they are discrete: for instance, historically, communities identifying as Franco-Manitoban and Métis have sponsored completely separate pavilions at Folklorama, the annual festival celebrating Winnipeg's ethnic cultures.

Fourth, and related to the foregoing, publics are constituted through communicative acts that presume and address *particular* audiences. Public address may seem to be oriented to an unspecified "radioland" or audience of "dear readers"— but it nevertheless subtly identifies its addressees: "[A public] appears to be open to indefinite strangers but in fact selects participants.... Reaching strangers is public discourse's primary orientation, but to make those unknown strangers into a public it must locate them as a social entity" (Warner 2002: 106). Put another way, different performances, publications, and acts of self-discipline presume and extend different social imaginaries—and the greater the differences, the greater the exclusivity of these networks of circulation.

Moreover, as the situation in Manitoba suggests, these multiple publics are not necessarily on equal or even amicable terms: some stand in subordinate or oppositional relationships to other, more dominant ones. The Franco-Manitoban and aboriginal publics are subordinate to a broader provincial and national public, for example, and for a variety of reasons (see chapter 1) understand themselves to have—or to have had—a troubled relationship with them. Warner refers to such formations as "counterpublics" and suggests that dominant publics often regard the discourses and practices that generate them with "hostility or a sense of indecorousness" (2002: 119).

The indigenous musical public can in some respects be understood as a manifestation of counterpublicity. In part because the musical practices constituting it frequently diverge from what is judged to be normative, and in part because of the prominent participation of nonprofessionals and idiosyncratic performers, the fiddling, singing, and dancing that fill aboriginal venues and airwaves are sometimes liable to be regarded as indecorous by mainstream standards.[29] I wonder how much things have changed since my boyhood, when performances on aboriginal television programs such as *The Western Hour* were subject to derision because they evidenced what appeared to be bad musicianship, distance from cosmopolitan musical standards and modes of self-presentation, and failure to be "properly" aboriginal (i.e., by performing "real" Native music such as drum songs). It is true that traditional fiddling has been welcomed by some listeners and that reception of it seems to be changing, thanks in part to vigorous advocacy; yet certain other elements of indigenous expressive culture are still regarded with dubiety by mainstream arbiters—not because they demonstrate a failure to be modern, I would argue, but insofar as they succeed at being differently so.

Conclusion

In traditional aboriginal communities, close social relationships between musicians seem to have facilitated collaborative performances of a repertoire of fiddle music that was metrically and formally irregular. In the second half of the twentieth century, aboriginal fiddlers began adopting a metrically and formally regular style, a change that reflected the increasing importance of "imagining" social orientations to as-yet-unknown musical collaborators. In fact, these new social orientations have become so much a part of indigenous musical life that even those "crooked" musical forms that seem most closely connected to social intimacies have also become the basis for emerging forms of musical publicness. Aboriginal fiddle music, regular and irregular, now moves in a variety of trajectories between stranger-oriented practice and intimate music making. Musical and choreographic practices associated with rural community, domesticity, kinship, and friendship circulate within and help to constitute social imaginaries. Conversely, publicly circulating material is continually regrounded in indigenous homes and communities, where it shapes encounters between intimates and provides the materials for new, inventive forms of musical bricolage.

Focusing on the dialectic between intimacy and publicness offers a framework for examining musical interactions in communities that, however articulated to larger social imaginaries, are nevertheless what Appadurai (1996: 178–99) might call "neighborhoods": intimate groups of known and knowable persons. It also provides a way to study the particular and emplaced practices that circulate within, and help to produce, translocal imaginaries. Scholars of music have often sought to characterize the relationships between local communities and mass mediation by applying theories of global flows, "scapes" (Appadurai 1996), and indigenization. Such intersections can now also be examined by placing the emphasis on interrelated modes of musical sociability: face-to-face interactions between intimates, and imagining relationships between strangers.[30] Considering the connections between musical intimacy and imagining usefully complicate simple oppositions between what is intimate and what is public. After all, expressive practices play a key role in constituting publics and in the political work of world making. The focus on musical practice is important, too, for social imaginaries come into being not only through the circulation of texts, but also through embodied processes of mutually oriented musical discipline.

3

"#1 on NCI"

Country Music and the Aboriginal Public

How Country Jam became the NCI Jam

COUNTRY JAM

On November 2, 2002, NCI FM hosted its annual Country Jam at the Burton Cummings Theatre for the Performing Arts, a soft-seat venue in downtown Winnipeg. Country Jam was a number of events rolled into one—a variety show featuring performances by prominent aboriginal musicians and an awards program recognizing the performers of the year's most popular aboriginal recordings—but above all it was a talent show. Thirty aboriginal singers, chosen from seventy who had submitted tapes to the radio station, came from across the province of Manitoba to compete. For the winners there would be money and exposure: the top three would receive cash prizes, and recordings of their performances would be broadcast on the radio station throughout the coming year.

Country Jam hailed an aboriginal public in a number of ways. NCI had advertised the show extensively to attract competitors and a live audience. And on the night of the competition the radio station transmitted the event from one end of the province to the other, relaying the proceedings from the Burton Cummings Theatre to a broader listening public. But the concert also benefited from specifically musical modes of publicness. As the evening progressed, a succession of singers came up to perform with the house band, a group of experienced musicians who were regulars on the aboriginal bar and festival scene. Although the singers had submitted tapes of the songs they planned to perform before the event, and although they had had a chance to rehearse them with the band during the afternoon, the performances were relatively unprepared. Their success depended in no small part upon a mutual musical orientation that preceded the competition. Singers and backing musicians alike had cultivated a common fund of stylistic knowledge and expectations, thereby preparing themselves for encounters with as-yet-unknown musical others.

And yet not all participants had attuned themselves to country music in the same way, and the evening did not consist of a series of performances straightforwardly exemplifying a cosmopolitan country style. While the members of the house band appeared to prefer performing in a metrically regular fashion, several singers did not. Les Shannacappo, singing Philip Sinclair's "Never Be a Cheatin' Heart," for instance, occasionally left an "extra" two or four beats between the lines of the song. While these rhythmic liberties conveyed the conversational intimacy of the lyrics, they also had implications for musical ensemble, contravening the default rhythmic orientation of the band.

This simplifies the matter a little too much, perhaps: the band did not seem particularly thrown by "extra" or "missing" beats. Musical collaboration at Country Jam 2002 was possible because all of the participants were attuned to the stylistic specificities of contemporary country music, but also because the members of the house band expected, and were able to accommodate, certain contraventions of this style. If Country Jam affirmed a country-music aesthetic, it also acknowledged a certain Manitoban aboriginal qualification of it: an openness to metrical irregularity and, behind this, a performance aesthetic that valued participation over perfection. In this sense the interactions at Country Jam were enabled not simply by country-music publicness, but by an indigenous inflection of it. Aboriginal imagining was shaped by the particularities of musical intimacy.

IDENTITY AND REPRESENTATION

The performers at Country Jam 2002 included Ojibwe, Métis, and Cree musicians, both men and women, from across the province of Manitoba and beyond. Table 3.1 provides a breakdown of the contestants by region of origin, presumed aboriginal group, and gender, drawing upon information presented on the NCI website and announced on the radio during the competition. Additional information concerning the vocations and pastimes of competitors, also announced, provides clues about social class. Many performers appeared to hold blue-collar jobs; a number mentioned traditional vocations. Some of the assumptions I have made about the identities of competitors may be inaccurate (for instance, some of the Winnipeg competitors—listed in the table as "Métis (?)"—may have been First Nations people). The breakdown is nevertheless useful as an indication of the identities NCI listeners might have ascribed to singers upon hearing the names of the communities they claimed as their homes.

Although the assembled performers presented a picture of a diverse aboriginal Manitoba, it was not an entirely representative one. First, there were more male than female performers, a discrepancy also characteristic of the aboriginal music scene. Second, although performers came from far and wide, northern Manitoba was underrepresented and the south overrepresented. Third, there appeared to be fewer Cree competitors than either Métis or Ojibwe, even though Cree people comprise the largest aboriginal group in Manitoba. The last two points are in fact

Table 3.1 **Aboriginal groups (presumed), regions, and occupations of 2002 NCI Jam competitors**

Presumed abor. group[†]	Region	M/F	Occupations/pastimes at time of Country Jam 2002
Métis	West	M	Works for railway
Métis (?)	Wpg	M	Construction worker
Métis (?)	Wpg	F	School secretary
Cree	North	M	In training program at Keewatin Community College
Métis (?)	Wpg	M	Works at Medical Arts Building
Métis (?)	West	F	Works at Swan River Friendship Centre; attends school during day
Métis (?)	Wpg	M	Works part-time; writes songs part-time
Ojibwe	North	M	Security officer at Berens River Health Centre; DJ on reserve radio station
Ojibwe	East	F	High school student at Port Arthur Collegiate
Ojibwe	Wpg Reg	M	Disc jockey
Cree	North	F	Paramedic; student in BS program at University of Manitoba
Ojibwe	Inter	M	Hunts, smokes fish, cans berries
Métis (?)	Inter	F	Enjoys volleyball, basketball, baseball, and golf
Ojibwe	West	M	Enjoys weightlifting and playing guitar; jams around the city
Métis (?)	West	M	Educational assistant at local middle school
Métis (?)	North	M	Operator in logging industry
Cree	North	M	Fisherman
Métis (?)	Wpg	F	Student at Academy of Broadcasting
Ojibwe	West	M	Band council member
Ojibwe	East	M	Youth coordinator
Ojibwe	Inter	F	Assistant manager for Northern Wolf
Ojibwe	Inter	M	Laborer in Lake Manitoba First Nation
Métis (?)	Wpg	F	Works with troubled youth, advocates on behalf of Sixties Scoop children
Métis (?)	Wpg	M	Machine attendant at plastics company, enjoys playing guitar
Métis (?)	Wpg	F	Stays at home to concentrate on music; writes songs
Métis (?)	Wpg	M	Upholsterer for Winnipeg Transit, has a pilot's license
Cree	North	M	Enjoys hunting, fishing, and playing with his band Ravenhawk

(Continued)

Table 3.1 (Continued)

Presumed abor. group[†]	Region	M/F	Occupations/pastimes at time of Country Jam 2002
Ojibwe	West	F	Student at Erickson Collegiate
Cree	North	M	Self-employed; enjoys performing with local band Moonlight Drift
Métis (?)	West	F	Works at A&W; second-year university student; will be a teacher

†*Note*: Presumed aboriginal group

The aboriginal group listed is that of the home reserve, unless the home reserve is unstated. In such cases "Métis (?)" is listed. This stance is adopted as one that NCI listeners might take, given the same information.

Summary: Gender of Participants

Male	19
Female	11

Summary: Presumed Aboriginal Group of Participants

Métis or unstated:	15
Ojibwe:	10
Cree:	5

Summary: Region of Participants

Winnipeg	9	From the city of Winnipeg
Wpg Reg	1	Within 100 km radius of Winnipeg (First Nations here are generally Ojibwe)
East	2	East of Winnipeg and extending north to Bloodvein and east into Ontario (First Nations are Ojibwe)
West	7	West of Winnipeg and extending north to Barrows and Shoal River (First Nations generally Ojibwe with some Dakota)
Interlake	4	North of Winnipeg in the Interlake, extending north to Dauphin River and Skownan (First Nations are generally Ojibwe)
North	7	Northern Manitoba, including Berens River in the east, Grand Rapids in the Interlake, and The Pas in the west (First Nations are generally Cree, with some Ojibwe, Oji-Cree and Dene communities)

More complete information on the 2002 competition, including the names and home communities of performers, can be requested from the author.

related, since Ojibwe and Métis people dominate the south and Cree the north. Almost certainly contributing to the low number of Cree and northern competitors was that Country Jam was held in Winnipeg. For some northern competitors, taking part would have entailed a drive of more than eight hours. For others living in "fly-in" communities, attending might have required the purchase of a prohibitively expensive airplane ticket.

Keeping track of who performed at the competition may seem like petty bean counting, but exactly such account keeping is central to the self-definition and self-representation of the aboriginal public. When I interviewed the NCI station manager, David McLeod, a few years later in 2006, his remarks about that year's competition suggested exactly such concerns:

> On average we receive anywhere between ninety to a hundred applicants. We pick twenty-five singers. Our first thing is try to make fifty-fifty female-male. We try to make community representation, so there's as many singers from as many different communities, and we try to represent singers from the north. What we've done to remedy [the underrepresentation of aboriginal people from northern communities] is we're looking at the judging, the scoring system, and we're looking at the top scores from the north and ensuring that at least six or seven singers are definitely from the north.
>
> We want the talent show to represent Manitoba as best as we can, and that's still our goal. So if somebody walks through the door, they're going to see people from different regions in Manitoba singing...and also from First Nation, Métis backgrounds....But in terms of the talent...we are still looking for the best talent we can find.

The broadcasts, recordings, and performances that constitute aboriginal public culture are oriented as though to an unknown audience of strangers, but they nevertheless specify their attendees in terms of identity, experience, and aesthetics. And although a public is not the same as a population, broadcasters take demographics into account as they attempt to capture the attention of an audience. As Michael Warner writes, "All discourse or performance addressed to a public must characterize the world in which it attempts to circulate and it must attempt to realize that world through address" (Warner 2002: 113–14). It is for this reason that station managers and listeners alike keep track of who is represented and how often: constituencies want to hear themselves addressed and see themselves represented, and broadcasters try to avoid alienating or offending them. McLeod remarked of the NCI Jam: "Within the aboriginal community, which is a pretty diverse word in itself, we have to try to represent...the definition of the word 'aboriginal' in our talent showcase." This is difficult to do.

As McLeod's comments seem to suggest, individual instances of public performance and address never construe their audience entirely accurately or successfully; rather, they hail "icons" or "stereotypes" of their listenerships (cf. Herzfeld 1997). Inaccuracy being inevitable, publics exist in a continual state of negotiation. Indeed, many performances and publications have the character of strategic interpositions to correct ostensibly faulty ways of characterizing their publics (others, conversely, can be understood as conservative or reactionary attempts to maintain imaginaries as they have traditionally been understood). Public addresses, then, continually recharacterize their audiences, and as these recharacterizations are ratified or challenged, publics gradually change, although never into anything completely stable.

The shifting and contested character of public culture also has implications for scholarly representation. As chapter 1 suggests, this book probably privileges southern Manitoba, culturally cosmopolitan Winnipeg, and Ojibwe and Métis contributions to indigenous public culture. In this respect it reflects how "aboriginal Manitoba" has often represented itself to itself. At the same time, and, like its subject, it is open to strategic and potentially transformative challenges, being an inevitably inaccurate representation of (representations of) an aboriginal Manitoba that can be portrayed in other ways.

IS "PURPLE RAIN" REALLY A COUNTRY SONG?

The singing competition at the heart of Country Jam 2002 exemplified how performers differently construe their publics and how imaginaries take shape through negotiation and even explicit debate. At issue was musical taste. Competitors evidenced both "conservative" and "progressive" interpretations of the audience's aesthetics at the competition, but during and afterward, it was the latter that made significant headway, with a number of dramatic events and decisions acknowledging change and heterogeneity in aboriginal musical preference.

Although the performers at Country Jam 2002—special guests as well as competitors—performed in genres as diverse as traditional drum song, blues, rap, and folk, the overwhelming majority of them performed country music. In doing so, they acknowledged the historical significance of that genre for the Manitoban aboriginal public. Nevertheless, country music was itself contested territory, with two styles vying for prominence. The first of these my consultants referred to as the "classic" or "traditional" country style. It was acoustic-guitar based, tended toward simple harmonies (I, IV, V, and V/V) and straightforward antecedent-consequent phrase structure, and lent itself to homemade music making. The aforementioned "Never Be a Cheatin' Heart" was a good example, with its simple harmonic palette and lightly swinging foxtrot rhythm. The second was a style my informants called "new country." Falling into this category were songs that employed more complicated harmonic patterns, including modal harmony and chords built on roots other than scale degrees 1, 2, 4, and 5 (one of my consultants referred to this as music with "minor chords"). The new style drew upon resources from other genres, especially rock and pop, and placed particular emphasis on virtuosic singing. Additionally, it tended to require singers to have a more extensive range and greater facility with melismatic passagework.[1]

The distinction people identified between traditional and new country resembled binaries discussed in other writing on country music: music that courts a core country audience versus music that attempts to garner a pop listenership as well (see Neal 2009: 255–62), or, to a lesser extent, the difference between "hard" and "mainstream" country (Ching 2001). "Classic country" probably also overlapped with the "REAL country music" Aaron Fox explores in *Real Country*, especially in its association with working-class identity and a rural hinterland (2004). To me, it seemed that the distinction hinged in large part on how easy the music was to integrate in everyday contexts of amateur music making. Classic country was music that was more amenable to vernacular appropriation: it made use of a musical vocabulary that facilitated democratic, participatory music making. David McLeod was probably thinking of classic country music, rather than new country, when he remarked to me in a 2003 interview:

> [Another] reason country music's popular is...technically, it's not jazz....[You] can learn the basic chording, you can learn some basic scales and you're a country singer. So...it's something that people can learn on their own by ear in a community....If you look at a northern community, somebody gets a guitar, they learn to tune a guitar, they can learn to play a few chords and learn songs, and learn to play by ear a lot...easier.

As the chapters that follow suggest, straightforward country songs, fiddle tunes, hymns, and "country gospel" songs have thrived among Manitoba aboriginal people in part because these genres are agreeable to learning and redeployment. They consequently facilitate musical sociability in the venues of the aboriginal public sphere (jam sessions, coffeehouses, jamborees, and talent shows) and make it easy to put something together on the spur of the moment. My point is not to deny the musicianship and virtuosity that are also evident in country music, but rather to emphasize the way so much of it is singable and playable by everyday musicians.

Table 3.2 lists Country Jam performances again, this time including the titles and themes of songs and making an attempt to identify genre. My genre categorizations may seem problematic to some readers, but I think the two broader groupings that emerge from them—indicated in the chart by the use of bold and regular font—identify a useful and defensible distinction. Those songs where the genre is identified, in bold, as "traditional country," "country rock," or "blues" make use of simple, predictable harmonic structures that are easily navigable in the context of the kinds of participatory jam sessions in which I regularly took part. Those labeled, in a regular font, as "new country," "rock," or "folk" are less harmonically formulaic. It is this contrast—between a predictable "common practice" and a less obvious "new" one—that was a salient musical boundary for the amateur musicians I played with.

As Table 3.2 indicates, songs that used a basic harmonic grammar were more prominent than those that did not—eighteen compared to twelve—and country music in traditional styles was more common than new country. Nevertheless, new country was gaining increasing prominence amongst amateur singers in

Table 3.2 **Songs performed at NCI's 2002 singing competition, showing genres and themes**

Song title	Orig†	Genre	Theme
Jammin' in the Jackpine	O	**Trad. country**	Rural home: Mafeking. Good-timing.
Family Tree	O	**Trad. country**	Drinking and good-timing.
Every Little Thing	C	New country/rock	Love song: positive.
Sing Me Back Home	C	**Trad. country**	Crime and punishment.
1,000 Miles of Misery	C	**Trad. country**	Love song: breakup.
Barrows All-Stars	O	**Country rock**	Rural home: Barrows. Drinking and good-timing.
Here I Am, Down and Out Again	O	**Blues**	Drinking and good-timing.
I'm From the Country	C	**Trad. country**	Rural home.
Purple Rain	C	New country	Love song: breakup.
For a Change	O	**Trad. country**	Love song: hopeful.
I'll Still Be Loving You	O	New country/ country rock	Love song: breakup.
Wild and Free	O	**Country rock**	Self-realization.
Don't Waste Your Heart	C	New country	Love song: breakup.
The Blues Man: A Tribute to Hank Williams Jr.	C	**Trad. country**	Love song: positive. Drinking.
Hot Rod Heart	C	**Country rock**	Adventure and excitement.
Should've Been an Angel	O	Folk/country	Love song: positive.
Southern Streamline	C	**Country rock**	Love song: positive.
Love You Darling	O	New country	Love song: breakup.
Never Be a Cheatin' Heart	A	**Trad. country**	Love song: hopeful.
Such Lonely Nights and Days	O	**Trad. country**	Love song: breakup. Drinking and heartache.
Two More Bottles of Wine	C	**Trad. country**	Love song: breakup. Drinking and heartache.
Who Were You Thinkin' Of?	C	**Trad. country**	Love song: potential breakup.
The First Place to Go	O	New country	Love song: breakup.
Always More	O	Folk/new country	Love song: breakup.
But You Wouldn't Let Me	O	Rock/country rock	Love song: breakup.
Killin' Time	C	**Trad. country**	Love song: breakup. Drinking and heartache.
Where Were You (When the World Stopped Turning)	C	New country	September 11, 2001 bombings.

(Continued)

Table 3.2 (Continued)

Song title	Orig†	Genre	Theme
It's My Time	C	New country	Love song: breakup. Self-realization.
My Town	O	**Trad. country/ country rock**	Rural home: Norway House.
Better Things to Do	C	New country/ country rock	Love song: breakup. Self-realization.

†*Note*: Orig.

"O" indicates an original composition by the singer. "A" indicates a song written by another Manitoban aboriginal performer, but not the singer. "C" indicates a cover song.

Summary: Genre

Traditional country, including with elements of country rock (1)	13
Country rock	4
Blues	1
Total: Harmonically "Predictable" Songs	**18**
New country, including with elements of country rock (2) and rock (1)	9
Folk, including with elements of country (1) and new country (1)	2
Rock, including with elements of country rock (1)	1
Total: Harmonically Less "Predictable" Songs	**12**

Summary of Song Themes

Love songs:	20
Breakup:	14
Positive feelings:	4
Tentative hope:	2
Drinking	7
Drinking and heartache	3
Drinking and good-timing	3
Good-timing	4
Rural home	4
Specific Manitoba communities	3
Self-realization	3
Crime and punishment	1
Attacks of September 11, 2001	1
Adventure and excitement	1

More complete information about the 2002 competition, including the names and home communities of performers, can be requested from the author.

2002 and 2003. This was thanks in part, I suspect, to the increasing presence of karaoke, which allowed performances of songs that would otherwise have been difficult to accompany.

Although traditional country and songs using a basic harmonic grammar dominated statistically, it was new-country performances that took home the big prizes. The top-placing singers at Country Jam were Courtney Jourdain from Lac la Croix, an Ojibwe reserve in western Ontario, and Melissa Galvin of the Keeseekoowenin First Nation, an Ojibwe reserve in southwestern Manitoba. Both sang songs in a new-country style: Jourdain performed a country version of Prince's 1984 rock/pop hit "Purple Rain," drawing upon LeAnn Rimes's 1998 cover version;[2] Galvin performed "It's My Time," a song popularized by Martina McBride. Neither accompanied herself on guitar. The judges also acknowledged the do-it-yourself style, however. The third-place contestant, Bruce McIvor of the Cross Lake First Nation, a Cree reserve in northern Manitoba, sang a version of John Fogerty's country-rock tune "Southern Streamline," and the runner-up, Derek Gould of the Fairford First Nation, an Ojibwe reserve in the Manitoban Interlake, sang his own composition, "Wild and Free," which had lyrics in the style of a new-country song but a straightforward harmonic structure. Gould accompanied himself on guitar.

Thus, the female winners sang new-country songs, while the two top-placing men sang pieces in a more traditional style. The correspondence between gender and genre was evident throughout the competition: sixteen of the nineteen men sang songs that were in a traditional country style or that had easily predictable harmonic structures, while ten of the eleven women sang new-country songs. The discourse surrounding the stylistic distinction was perhaps similarly gendered: my male informants described classic country music as traditional and feelingful and considered new country to lack its rootedness and sincerity. Their differentiations were reminiscent of more widespread characterizations of new country as trivial, melismatically "frilly," and artificial, and of traditional country as direct, straightforward, and authentic.

Somewhat problematically, as it would turn out, "Purple Rain," the song performed by the overall winner, Jourdain, not only stood outside classic country but bordered on rock or pop.[3] Certainly there were elements of country music in the performance, most notably in the style of vocal production: Jourdain sang with a tensed throat, twanged her vowels, used vocal breaks, and scooped up to notes. But alongside this was melismatic passagework more characteristic of a pop showpiece. Still other elements of the performance evidenced the rock-and-roll provenance of the song, including Prince's ambiguous lyrics, describing a complex relationship, partly amicable, partly domineering, partly sexual. And while the accompaniment in classic country songs can often come across as a "lyric delivery mechanism," seemingly oblivious to the tragic narratives conveyed in the text, the chord changes in "Purple Rain" announced themselves with a kind of grand guitar-rock portentousness. They also lacked the straightforward tonic-dominant polarity of a typical classic country tune.[4]

Jourdain gave an electrifying performance, and by the end of the first line alone the audience in the hall was transfixed. In part it was the song, which I think was as surprising a choice for the rest of the audience as it was for me. "Purple Rain" was the last thing I expected to hear at Country Jam, and a *country* version of it was more startling still.[5] In part it was also the shock of Jourdain's vocal virtuosity. Many of the competitors at Country Jam sang in a relatively reserved style, but here was a fourteen-year-old belting out a version of Prince's hit (of all things), decorating the melody with dramatic breaks, scoops, and melismatic garlands. At the end of the performance the audience gave her a standing ovation. It was no great surprise when, later that night, she won first prize.[6]

Not everyone was happy, however: the rock-and-roll origins of "Purple Rain" led to complaints, and David McLeod told me that NCI received a number of phone calls and email messages asking why a non-country song had won at a competition that had the word "country" in its name. The issue was eventually taken up at a station board meeting, with the result that the event was renamed: in 2003 Country Jam became the NCI Jam.

The change of name can be narrated as the culmination of a series of socially consequential acts, each addressing and transforming a particular social context, each with broader implications than the last. First was Jourdain's performance, which engendered an outpouring of enthusiasm from the audience. Second was the decision of the panel of judges to award first place to the performance—even though it strained the bounds of the category of country music and even though they had been given a mandate to award special consideration to performers singing original songs. It seemed to me that above all the judges were responding to, and ratifying, the extraordinary support the audience had shown for Jourdain. Third was the decision by the NCI board to rename the contest. Their action responded to the controversy that had followed Jourdain's win, but also to ample evidence that "Manitoban aboriginal music" comprised a wide variety of styles, many of which were already heard more or less regularly on NCI, although not during prime broadcast hours.[7]

Consciously or not, these three acts—Jourdain's performance, the judges' determination, and the NCI board's decision—affirmed an aesthetic shift in aboriginal public culture, recognizing that styles other than classic country music were important to listeners and musicians. As this suggests, publicness is by no means static: it is rather a space in which tendencies toward repetition vie with readiness for transformation. In 2002 (as today) "Manitoban aboriginal music" was in flux: not only was classic country music, a dominant part of the live aboriginal music scene, losing some of its preeminence to new country, but other genres of music, including rock and pop, were taking up increasingly important roles. It made sense for Country Jam to become the NCI Jam.

The Cowboy Code

NATIONAL AND ABORIGINAL PUBLICS

Having arrived at a moment when a prominent aboriginal institution acknowledged popular styles *other* than country, it seems appropriate to ask why country music has been so important in the first place. Attempting to answer this
question (posed recently by David Samuels; see Samuels 2009) will entail, toward
the end of this chapter, a discussion of the lyrics of contemporary First Nations
and Métis song. But it will also involve exploring accounts of aboriginal performers and audiences at a number of significant historical junctures: at early
twentieth-century agricultural exhibitions, during the initial appropriation by
First Nations and Métis people of country music and western wear, and at the
moment when First Nations people could first legally enter drinking establishments. As will become evident, the history of aboriginal country music reflects
the complexities of the relationship between the settler public and its aboriginal
other, including their divergences, intersections, and inequities.

In a 2002 interview, Errol "C-Weed" Ranville explained to me how he had mar-
keted the single that would become his first Canada-wide number 1 hit, a cover
of The Band's "Evangeline." He told me he had sent out free copies of the song to
band offices on reserves across Canada:[8]

> [Our] community is syndicated already by the band offices across the
> country—another thing is the Friendship Centers across the coun-
> try.[9] So I kind of invented or pioneered...the aboriginal music indus-
> try...because I discovered that, "Oh, we already have...a system in
> place here for syndication.[10]...We can...contact each other." I can mail
> to all the reserves, all at one time, you know?
>
> Which is what I did with "Evangeline," the single....And lo and
> behold, consequently it became the number one across Canada. All these
> non-Native radio stations—'cause there was no Native radio stations
> in those days—were flooded with calls for this song that arrived at the
> band office last week.

Ranville's remarks point to a significant connection between the aboriginal
public on the one hand and the reserve system established by the Canadian federal
governments on the other. As chapter 1 explains, the numbered treaties and the
Indian Act created an indigenous subnation, confederating a diverse array of communities and peoples as a single "Indian" public and binding them by laws specific
to them alone among Canadians. These documents created a "striated" and homogeneous structure (see Day 2000: 42), constituting each band as a distinct reserve
but subjecting most of them to the same laws, the same kinds of oversight, and
similar forms of political organization, with little concern for preexisting cultural

particularities. Yet, in doing so, as Ranville's account suggests, they also established a formation that facilitated relationships between these far-flung communities. And this is what in fact happened: the reserve system was one of the networks through which indigenous forms of publicness could come into being.

All of this points to some important aspects of the relationship between the national and aboriginal publics in Canada. First, the Native public is a differentiated social formation—indeed, one that is legally distinguished from the national public. Second, as its origins in the treaty making and laws of the colonial era suggest, the indigenous public stands in an unequal relationship to the broader national public that gave it aspects of its basic form and political structure. Third, although these publics are differentiable, they are also permeable, and similar or similar-seeming discourses and performances circulate within them and move between them.[11] As much seems evident in Ranville's "Evangeline" strategy: the singer pursued an aboriginal audience as an initial step toward national attention.

SHARED PUBLIC SPACES UNDER COLONIALISM: ABORIGINAL PERFORMANCE AND THE EXHIBITION

These three characteristics of publicness—its differentiability, stratification, and permeability—have had consequences for indigenous publicness and for the relationships between indigenous and national publics. Because publicity is differentiable, indigenous Manitobans have been able to create distinct social imaginaries around preferred ways of making music, dancing, and socializing. Because it is hierarchical, indigenous publicness has been subjected to national derogation and asymmetrical regulation. And because of the availability of publicness (and of the circulating stuff that constitutes it), aboriginal Manitobans have been able to (a) accept invitations that may not originally have been extended with them in mind, (b) draw upon mass-mediated expressive forms to create aboriginal music and (c) appropriate the forms and technologies of publicness to create social imaginaries of their own. Such responses to the availability of performances, expressive forms, and publicness itself are evident well before Ranville's "Evangeline," in the case of early twentieth-century fairs and exhibitions, and in that of early indigenous country music. So too are the differentiability and divergent statuses of publics.

Public address is characteristically oriented (as though) to an unknown and unspecified audience, and during the colonial era aboriginal Manitobans took advantage of this, insistently understanding themselves to be members of the audiences hailed by, for example, popular songs and advertisements for events. In ways that were perhaps unexpected at the time, they claimed public venues and expressive forms as spaces in which they could contest their inequitable position. Significantly, they seem to have focused on those areas in which colonial ideologies were most directly expressed.

Manitoban communities began to host large agricultural fairs and exhibitions at the end of the nineteenth century. The most long-standing of these was launched in the western Manitoban city of Brandon in 1882 (Coates and McGuinness 1985: 6), but Portage la Prairie and Winnipeg also held exhibitions. Many such events featured performances of singing and dancing by First Nations people; Dakota communities in southwestern Manitoba seem to have played a particularly important role at these early powwows.[12] A 1910 *Manitoba Free Press* article suggests that aboriginal people began to come together, dance, and sing at the Brandon fair around 1896. One particular group was "admitted to the grounds each year as guests of the fair board" and held "an Indian dance in a canvas enclosure on the grounds" (*Manitoba Free Press*, July 27, 1910, 11).

Newspaper accounts of these exhibitions describe First Nations people, and especially their singing and dancing, in ways that ritually affirm colonial hierarchies (see chapter 1); the fairgrounds arguably did similar kinds of ceremonial work, juxtaposing science and superstition, advanced and primitive technologies, and civilization and savagery. Yet even as exhibitions and newspaper accounts affirmed the colonial discourses circulating within the national public sphere, indigenous people were making use of fairs to create alternative forms of publicness. First Nations people came to exhibitions in large numbers, and not only as performers but as attendees, as a description from 1913 indicates:

> As usual there is a mighty encampment of Indian braves and their squaws outside the grounds. It is stated that there are 1,000 under canvas. Scores of Indian ponies graze within the circle of the camp, and there is a miscellaneous collection of mongrel dogs and buggies, cooking utensils and swarthy papooses. The Indians are of the Sioux tribe, and they are permitted to hold a grand war dance inside a canvas enclosure within the grounds each day. The dancers, both men and women, are gaudily decked out in feathers, beads and red shawls. The monotonous beat of their tom-toms is one of the familiar sounds on the fair grounds. (*Manitoba Free Press*, July 17, 1913)

It could perhaps be asked whether aboriginal attendance at the Brandon event really evidenced publicness in the sense developed in this volume. Had the attendees come in response to a mass-mediated invitation, or did their yearly attendance represent a more local, face-to-face mode of sociability (after all, there are many aboriginal communities in the Brandon area)? There is some evidence that indigenous publics, organized around "imagining" forms of sociability, were indeed emerging. For instance, a 1910 *Free Press* article reported that a Dakota group had extended invitations to several aboriginal communities to join them in Portage la Prairie for that city's summer fair. The invitees included Dakota and

Ojibwe and Canadian and American communities, some more than one hundred miles distant.

> The largest gathering of Indians ever held in Manitoba will be held at Portage la Prairie on July 11 and will continue for three days, the same date as the annual fair. This is not done by invitation of the fair authorities, but a deputation of the Sioux [i.e., Dakota] tribe recently waited on them [sic] asked permission to have a place allotted for them inside the grounds and to be given police protection.[13] This request was granted and invitations have been sent to the tribes from the following points to attend: Swan Lake, Long Plains, Dog Creek, Duck Lake, Oak Point, Sandy Bay, Birtle, Griswold, Deloraine, Pipestone, [Turtle] Mountain, [Elphinstone], Minnedosa, Ruthland, Fort Totten and Tokio[,] North Dakota, and [Sisseton], [Sisseton] City and Havana, South Dakota.

The paper went on to report:

> All the tribes have accepted the invitations and it is estimated that at here [sic] will be 2,000 Indians in attendance. They have been given permission to put on pony races and other sports and have secured permission to hold a parade through the city daily. The fair management has offered prizes for the best costumes and it is expected that there will be keen competition in this line. ("Unique Pow-Wow to be Held at Portage," *Manitoba Free Press*, June 17, 1910, 1)

Again, it may be that the gathering proposed at Portage la Prairie grew out of modes of sociability (and indeed ways of imagining) distinct from the mass-mediated imagining that enables public culture (compare Anderson 1991: 67). Still, it seems reasonable to suggest that around this time traditional ways of relating to others increasingly existed alongside new modes of social imagining. Even as indigenous social life was being articulated to a national public through schooling and interactions with representatives of the federal government,[14] aboriginal people were beginning to make use of these modes of acquaintanceship themselves.

Thus, in the early twentieth century, aboriginal publicness seems to have emerged alongside dominant forms of it, and within some of the very same venues. The institutions and structures that articulated colonial ideologies were available for appropriation, and indigenous Manitobans attempted to make use of them toward their own social ends—including, as Pettipas (1994) suggests, to conduct sacred ceremonies and, as I propose (see chapter 1), to resist settler representations of indigeneity. All the same, this emerging Native publicness came into being in a context structured by colonial discourses, categories, and "race feeling" (again, see chapter 1).

SHARED PUBLIC SPACES DURING THE EMERGENT POSTCOLONIAL ERA: THE COUNTRY MUSIC SCENE

Another shared cultural forum emerged slightly later in the twentieth century: the country-music scene, in which First Nations and Métis musicians participated enthusiastically from the onset. Like early twentieth-century exhibitions, country music and related forms of cultural production were inflected by colonial power dynamics. "Cowboy" songs and films mythologized Euro-American encounters with aboriginal alterity and constructed heroic archetypes of white masculinity. Here too, however, aboriginal people found ways to make use of the technologies of publicness (and expressive forms) that addressed them, to participate in social imagining, and to contest colonial representations of indigenous difference. Native Manitobans taught themselves to sing and play the cowboy songs they heard on records and radio stations and began to avail themselves of broadcast technologies.

Two musicians of my acquaintance grew up during the decades when country music was beginning to make an impact in Manitoban aboriginal communities: Victor Courchene, who was born in 1927 on the Ojibwe reserve of Fort Alexander (Sagkeeng), and Nelson Menow, who was born in 1935 at Molson Lake in the bush country north of the Cree community of Norway House. Courchene told me that he had purchased a guitar when he was young and learned to play chords with the help of a friend. He later bought a record player and taught himself to sing songs by Ernest Tubb and Jimmie Rodgers. Menow told me that during the 1940s his father bought a battery-powered radio, and they would listen to Nashville programs on Saturdays: "I used to listen to the likes of Jimmie Rodgers and Hank Snow, Hank Williams, Roy Acuff, Kitty Wells and that old lady that used to always say, 'Howdy!': Minnie Pearl." He added, "The music that I was listening to was very fantastical to me. . . . I never played guitar before but I was listening to them and gradually I started earning for a guitar. I wanted to play it so badly like these country singers."

Both Courchene and Menow performed for friends and community members in socially intimate contexts—Courchene, for instance, used to sing in a band that performed at dances and fund-raisers—but they also performed for a broadcast public. As a young man Courchene sang with a friend on an Ontario radio station. Menow, during the years after World War II, participated in the *CJOB Western Hour*, a weekly singing competition sponsored and broadcast by a Winnipeg radio station. The contest took place before a live audience at the Starland Theatre in downtown Winnipeg. It was open to all comers, and both aboriginal and nonaboriginal performers took part. By Menow's estimation, as many as twenty-five singers performed during a program. The winner(s), who took home a prize of five dollars, were chosen by the audience: whoever received the loudest applause won. Menow often performed on the show as part of a duo with his friend Barney

Smith. According to Menow, both indigenous and nonindigenous performers participated and were judged fairly based on their merit as singers:

MENOW: People wouldn't favor anybody. We would just go out on the stage there. Like, I'm from up north, and Barney's from Peguis [a First Nation closer to Winnipeg]. Some people are from Winnipeg. You know, they wouldn't favor anybody.

DUECK: So, it was whites, it was Natives, it was everybody?

MENOW: Yeah, and whoever sang best got it. It's supposed to be that way. You don't favor anybody, you just pick out the best.

Thus, as far as Menow was concerned, racial prejudice was not a major problem at the *Western Hour*: Natives and non-Natives competed on equal terms.[15] Such parity stood in contrast to the state of affairs at early twentieth-century exhibitions, which tended to emphasize differences between indigenous people and Euro-Canadians. It was also at variance with other aboriginal experiences at the time: federal and provincial laws still discriminated explicitly against Status Indians. (The apparent absence of racial hierarchy in the country scene seems to have had implications for the subsequent development of popular music in Manitoba. Aboriginal performers have played particularly prominent roles in country music in the province, two of whose earliest national country stars, Ray St. Germain[16] and Errol Ranville, were Métis singers. To this day, the country scene remains a particularly integrated popular-music arena, so far as interaction between aboriginal and nonaboriginal musicians is concerned.[17])

In different ways, the agricultural exhibition and the country-music scene exemplify how Canadian public culture was simultaneously available to aboriginal people and unfriendly to them. Exhibitions, central venues of turn-of-the-century Prairie publicness (itself emerging), presented opportunities for aboriginal people to dance, socialize, and make money, and they seem to have made strategic use of these opportunities for public assembly. Nevertheless, such events were structured ideologically by colonialism, and indigenous participants clearly had second-class status, at least from the perspective of the settler press. The aboriginal experience of the country-music scene, at least as described by Nelson Menow, seems to have been more positive. Natives were free to participate in singing contests on the same terms as nonaboriginal musicians, and in forums that did not explicitly relegate them to a subsidiary role. Still, in its own way, early country music—alongside a larger body of popular culture idealizing the cowboy—configured indigenous people within an asymmetrical racial ideology.

THE "INDIAN COWBOY"

One of the guest performers at the NCI Jam in 2002 was Ken Boulette, the winner of the previous year's competition. He sang a version of "The Cowboy in Me," a song popularized by Tim McGraw, but substituted the word "Indian" for "cowboy" each time it occurred. The result was a performance that played upon the opposition between cowboys and Indians even as it appropriated the original song's rueful reflections on masculinity. "The Cowboy in Me" is a kind of ambivalent meditation on traits some might see as ideally masculine: rather than self-confidence, toughness, and motivation the song speaks of "foolish pride," stone-heartedness, restlessness, and dissatisfaction. Boulette went one inversion further, recasting the flawed manliness in the song as that of an Indian rather than a cowboy.

In sound and style, the cowboy has long played an important part in Manitoban aboriginal music making. Victor Courchene informed me that he and his First Nations friends began to play and sing songs they referred to as "cowboy songs" in the first half of the twentieth century. Country music continued to be popular with Native musicians in the decades that followed, as Nelson Menow's account suggests, and the cowboy theme remained important well into recent memory. In the 1980s Errol Ranville had a Top 10 Canadian hit with the song "Pickup Truck Cowboy," and in the 1990s he released an album called "The Cowboy Code."

Moreover, many working-class aboriginal men dress in western wear: cowboy hats, western shirts, jeans, and cowboy boots (although clothing influenced by urban music and hip-hop culture is increasingly popular, especially among young people). The stylistic choice seems significant, not least because aboriginal elders and political leaders often wear such garments—sometimes modified in ways that acknowledge an indigenous heritage—in public appearances and on special occasions. Indigenous adoptions of cowboy songs and western wear, like appropriations of fiddling and dancing traditions, do not appear to be parodic in character. They rather seem mimetic in the sense Michael Taussig identifies in *Mimesis and Alterity*. Taussig describes mimesis as a social response to the cultural differences encountered in contexts of colonial domination. He suggests that dominant and subordinate groups alike mimetically appropriate one another's differences, transform them, and in doing so attain symbolic power over one another. As he puts it, "The making and existence of the artifact that portrays something gives one power over that which is portrayed" (1993: 13). The bidirectional copying he alerts us to is evident in the various "cowboys" and "Indians" represented in both dominant and indigenous forms of public culture.

Mainstream representations of "Indians" and "cowboys" varied in the early twentieth century but overall tended to privilege whiteness and problematize indigeneity. The movie western played a particularly prominent role in the circulation of the ideologically charged opposition.[18] Yet while these films subtly construed their public as an audience of colonizers and civilizers, it was not only a settler audience that saw them. Thus Victor and Laureen Courchene, who grew up in Ojibwe communities in southern Manitoba, watched movie westerns in their youth, and by the mid-twentieth century they were being screened even in isolated northern communities such as Garden Hill and Ste. Theresa Point (*Winnipeg Tribune*, August 7, 1952).

In an interview I conducted with Nelson Menow in 2003, the singer and guitarist told me that soundless cowboy films and romances used to be shown for community entertainment in Norway House when he was young. When I asked him about the representations of Natives in cowboy films, he acknowledged that they were often negative, although, perhaps not wishing to offend me, he did not express anger:

DUECK: ... [Did] people sometimes get angry that Native people were shown in a bad light in these movies?

MENOW: At first we didn't realize that, eh, but later on we started thinking [laughs], "of course Indians are going to get beat."... But like I said, you know, Indian people, they're kindhearted, eh.... They don't keep things to themselves... for so long. They catch on and they just let it go.... But we finally caught on that we were the bad ones and we were always the dumb ones. [Laughs]

DUECK: Did that bug you, or...

MENOW: Well, for some people I guess it did.... But... they didn't really talk about it that much. They would just laugh and say, "Of course we Indians are going to get beat anyway." [Laughs] They knew the story well, how it was going to end.[19]

Given the movie western's opposition of cowboy and Indian and the negative stereotyping of the latter, some of the people I talked to (aboriginal and nonaboriginal) found it strange that Native people dressed in western wear and sang cowboy music. But to older Native people the cowboy code seemed unremarkable. During our interview I tried to ask Menow why it was that aboriginal people identified sartorially with people who, at least in films, were represented as the enemies of Natives. Menow did not make any reference to the cowboy-Indian dichotomy in his response:

DUECK: Well, I guess one of the questions I always had is, when you see... western wear, the cowboy hat and the cowboy buckles—lots of Indians wear those—and the cowboy shirts, and I always thought, well, doesn't that bug them?

MENOW: No, not really. You know, in our days, we didn't have nothing fancy, eh.... We didn't have no money, we couldn't make no money, but ever since people started making money they can afford to buy these things. So that's... why you see them wearing it now. They can afford it.... Some of them, mind you, not all of them.

Menow described western wear primarily as a desirable commodity: something initially out of reach that gradually became attainable. His explanation is a reminder of the economic inequities that have separated aboriginal and nonaboriginal Canadians historically and in the present day. It also points to the sweeping social and economic transformations of the second half of the twentieth century, a time when many Native men and women were moving to cities and being integrated as wage laborers in a market economy.[20] Western wear and country music are in this sense markers of an emerging postwar prosperity among working-class aboriginal men (see Fox 2004: 319–20).

A further layer of import might be proposed, however; namely, that aboriginal people were responding to dominant representations of whiteness and indigeneity through a kind of mimetic counterrepresentation. By taking the songs and style of the cowboy for themselves, they turned that representative of auspicious white masculinity into a figure who was both cowboy *and* Indian (see Figure 3.1).

Buying cowboy hats and singing country songs were mimetic acts (of not only consumption but also production) that gave indigenous people power over that which they reportrayed (see Taussig 1993: 188–92). The adoption of a "cowboy code" confused and disrupted the simplistic binaries pervasive in mainstream forms of publicness (see Hebdige 1979: 15–19). It denied the cowboy his exclusive whiteness and democratized his grandeur, making an audible and visible claim to parity. Again, First Nations people did not have the same rights as other Canadians until well after the Second World War, and even as consumers they faced restrictions, being unable to purchase beverage alcohol. Yet clothing, recordings, and musical instruments could be bought and deployed in ways that asserted equality.[21]

In some cases, musical and social precedents made mass-mediated cowboy songs and mass-marketed cowboy clothing culturally appropriate. Country music shares roots with the fiddle traditions that have long been popular in aboriginal

Figure 3.1 THE C-WEED BAND. An early promotional photo. From left to right: Don C. Ranville, Wally Ranville, Errol Ranville, Clint Dutiaume. Photo by Brian Ranville.

communities in northern North America. And Elaine Keillor (2002) notes that Plains and Plateau Amerindians frequently participated in ranching and rodeos and relates several genres of horse-related songs to indigenous people who held such occupations. Thus aboriginal people have held exactly the rural occupations celebrated in cowboy songs and country music, and a strict dichotomy between cowboys and "Indians" did not exist historically. It continues to be blurred in the present: when I interviewed Errol Ranville in 2002, it was on his rural ranch. Yet this does not explain why western wear was also adopted by First Nations people living in northern communities where hunting and trapping have been traditional occupations and ranching has never been viable. It seems reasonable to suggest that there, at the very least, sartorial choices had other reasons, including those suggested here.

Aboriginal musicians thus redeployed powerful mass-mediated images, rupturing the association between the cowboy and whiteness and presenting "Indian cowboys" (see Samuels 2009) to an indigenous audience and a broader public as well. It may appear that, toward the end of the era of Canadian high colonialism, aboriginal people were "taking their place" within a national public: purchasing commodities and appropriating popular music and thereby establishing themselves as normative Canadian citizens. But in the case of western wear and country music, participation in the market economy and popular culture does not seem to have been so straightforward. There was a differentiating and oppositional aspect to it. In appropriating the sartorial and musical markers of auspicious, white, rural masculinity, Native people disrupted the commonplace distinction between cowboy self and aboriginal other. This did not erase indigenous difference but rather produced it anew.

Indigenous Manitobans Move into the Public House

WRITING ABOUT DRINKING

As I explain in chapter 1, laws that explicitly discriminated against First Nations people were rescinded beginning in the middle of the twentieth century, but indigenous people have generally remained in inequitable positions relative to other Canadians, including in the areas of poverty, health, and life expectancy. Indeed, during the postcolonial period they have been increasingly subject to new forms of state intervention, including high rates of incarceration and child apprehension, that, although ostensibly colorblind, have had incommensurate implications for indigenous families and communities (it would seem that a tacitly biased postcolonial governmentality has replaced the old, openly prejudicial colonial one). Meanwhile, the state monitors all of these areas and others in ever greater detail, and the resulting data, and discourse concerning it, circulates in national and aboriginal public spheres alike.

Put another way, national and aboriginal publics are continually being constituted in relation to "Native problems." The national public comes into being in part through the circulation of discourses concerning its troubled and troubling indigenous population. Indigenous discourses, meanwhile, acknowledge not only the hardships many aboriginal people face, but also an awareness that these problems are being observed by a broader national public. Performances and publications addressing the aboriginal public sphere thus hail an audience familiar with poverty, poor health, incarceration, and child seizure; with child welfare organizations, the police, and the courts; and also with discourses that construe First Nations and Métis people variously as poor parents, delinquents, and criminals. Indigenous publicness, in short, comes into being around a sense of having been interpellated as a subject of national concern and intervention (see Althusser 1971: 170–83). It can accordingly evidence a form of what Michael Herzfeld calls "cultural intimacy"; that is, "the sharing of known and recognizable traits that not only define insiderhood but are also felt to be disapproved by powerful outsiders" (Herzfeld 1997: 3–4, 94).[22]

This dynamic is especially evident in the case of drinking. Aboriginal people are informed and concerned about the negative impact the misuse of intoxicants can have on families and communities, but they are also all too aware that indigenous drinking has been a long-standing concern of the national public, and that it remains a subject of analysis, intervention, and vicious stereotype. Indeed, related discourses, inflected by playful irony or apologetic recognition, circulate in aboriginal conversation and public culture. Thus the discussions of drinking in this book must weave their way through a number of potential pitfalls, including fastidious condemnation, rueful essentialization, and optimistic misrepresentation. If anything, the material that follows errs on the side of optimism, discussing aboriginal drinking in not-unfavorable terms. This is not a common choice, and it is rare to find similar positive characterizations in either national or aboriginal discourse. Yet my consultants occasionally framed drinking in a way that I hope to echo carefully here. Many of them were longtime teetotalers who spoke critically of their drinking years and of intoxicants in general. They nevertheless often seemed to suggest that something important went on—and perhaps continues to go one—amidst the drinking, and drinking songs, of Manitoba's postcolonial bar scene.

MAINSTREAM REACTION TO INDIGENOUS DRINKING

In 1956, the province of Manitoba passed legislation that allowed Status Indians to purchase and consume alcohol (Manitoba 1956), undoing one of the most significant discriminatory laws still on the books and allowing First Nations musicians and audiences to move into drinking establishments. A number of developments during the decades that followed merit attention in the coming sections: first, how the mainstream press portrayed newly legal aboriginal drinkers; second, the experiences of indigenous musicians who worked in drinking establishments; and, third, the emergence of a distinct aboriginal good-timing scene.

The extension of equal rights to aboriginal people did not mean an end to paternalistic discourses, and as First Nations people began to move into drinking establishments, the national public reacted with concern. Voices in the Manitoba mainstream, for instance, expressed disapproval regarding intoxicated behavior that transgressed expectations of what was normative (on drunken comportment as cultural behavior see MacAndrew and Edgerton 1969). Wrote James Gray in a 1966 newspaper article:

> And how are the Indians doing?
>
> All across the prairies, Indian hangovers get the cold-cure in city jails. The police pick up the drunken Indians wherever they fall, and they get the shortest shrift possible in the police courts as they take the normal 10-day penalty for drunkenness.
>
> It is true, of course, that only a minority of Indians are involved in the debauchery. None has the resources needed to continue drinking for very long. The trouble Indians have is that they are too gregarious. No Indian goes anywhere alone, if he can go with seven or eight others. So one thirsty Indian may trail a half a dozen friends along with him and all can wind up drunk. ("Drinking Habits Back 100 Years," *Winnipeg Tribune*, [July 15, 1966], clipping without page number consulted at University of Manitoba Archives and Special Collections)

Gray's article was published at a moment when colonial laws had been rescinded but colonial attitudes were still strong; it continues a long tradition of concerned North American writing about indigenous drinking.[23] Like other mainstream accounts of the 1960s and '70s, it characterizes aboriginal imbibing as worryingly extravagant: immoderate, unlawful, wasteful, overly "gregarious." Similarly, a 1966 *Winnipeg Tribune* article (reprinted from the *Ottawa Citizen*) described the good-timing of a northern Alberta band as follows:

> The Driftpile Indian Band near Faust, about 200 miles northwest of Edmonton, was granted full drinking privileges in January, but its members have been getting into difficulties at the Lakeside Hotel near their reserve.
>
> According to the assistant manager, Mr. Len Dircks, "our bar resembles a big party." The Indians tend to visit from table to table, and engage in noisy behavior and heated arguments. ("Lectures in Beer Parlor Etiquette Planned," *Winnipeg Tribune*, [February 26, 1966], clipping without page number consulted at University of Manitoba Archives and Special Collections)[24]

The article goes on to say that a series of lectures was being planned to teach "beer parlor etiquette" and thus help the Natives integrate into what it calls "the mainstream of Canadian society." Such lectures would presumably have made explicit just what was deemed normative.

So, at the beginning of the postcolonial era, white bourgeois discourses pathologized and minoritized indigenous barroom behavior. But they also did a kind of exclusive and expressive work, speaking as though to a national public that shared an idea of what constituted normal drinking comportment, on the one hand, and transgressions of it, on the other. These discourses addressed a "we" for whom certain drinking behaviors were familiar and others problematic, performatively constituting a national public around a vaguely moderate drinking style, feelings of concern for aboriginal people ("how are the Indians doing?") and, perhaps especially, distaste for certain ways of drinking (compare Povinelli 1998). These discourses may have expressed a kind of postcolonial melancholia, a disinclination to accept the ways that indigenous participation was transforming public spaces. But they also called for national action and response. Thus it was not simply aboriginal intoxicant use that constituted the indigenous public as a problematic counterpublic, but additionally and especially mainstream responses and interventions aimed at it.

ABORIGINAL MUSICIANS IN WINNIPEG DRINKING ESTABLISHMENTS

Given the negative perceptions of Native drinking, it was sometimes difficult for aboriginal people to find venues willing to welcome them. Blatant discrimination persisted in some quarters.[25] Nevertheless, aboriginal people began to make a place for themselves in Winnipeg's bars and hotels, and they appear to have done so in part through country music. Certainly this was the argument advanced by Stirling Ranville (Figure 3.2) when I interviewed him in 2003. Ranville is a Métis singer of country and gospel music who became an important figure on the Winnipeg country-music scene in the early 1970s. (Although he was for a number of years the leader of a well-established bar band, he no longer drinks, and for years he ran a gospel music ministry in Winnipeg's North End.)[26] According to Ranville, aboriginal country musicians began to bring live country music into Winnipeg beverage rooms around 1970, and in doing so opened up spaces for Native audiences. The group at the forefront of the movement was by his account his own. He and his brothers comprised the house band at the Brunswick Hotel, a large venue that once stood on Winnipeg's Main Street. Ranville told me:

> [Frank Sims, chairman of the Liquor Control Board of Manitoba] came up to me and he said, "Were you in the house band at the Brunswick Hotel?" I said, "Yeah, for three and a half years about." He said, "Well,

Figure 3.2 STIRLING AND YVETTE RANVILLE. Photo by the author.

in those three and a half years, that bar sold more than any other bar in Manitoba."

He went on:

[In] those days...there was a lot of bars that discriminated against aboriginal musicians....I mean, one manager of a bar actually came up to me and told me once—they'd hired us for two weeks, and I said, "Well, when do you want us back?" and he said—"You know, actually, we don't want you back. You have very good music, you have a very good band, but we don't like the people that you attract." They were trying to keep a nice little white bar....

So then we just stayed in the Brunswick Hotel as a house band. But then, all of a sudden, when I left the Brunswick, my brother C-Weed took over, Errol. And all of a sudden, they started breaking into other bars...they were playing in other bars. And other bars started opening up country music entertainment in their beverage room. They never had entertainment before. Then I started to put two and two together, then I realized what was happening.

Frank Sims, the chairman of the board at the Liquor Control, told me, "This guy, the owner of the Brunswick Hotel, proved to everyone else that if you hire a good country band, you're gonna sell." And now the rest of them, they looked at the situation: "OK, we can either keep a nice little white bar here, or we can make money. What are we in business to do?" And I think they thought about that. And then all of a sudden there was aboriginal people going into all the bars, and there was aboriginal musicians into all the bars, and I believe that we're the ones that broke through.

It was not only indigenous country music that moved into public spaces, but indigenous drinkers as well. In the same interview, Ranville said:

If you want to make money, this is how you got to go. I mean, aboriginal people like drinking. In those days, aboriginal people liked drinking. So... if you were in the business to sell alcohol, you had to go to the aboriginal people, and you had to give them what they like to get them to come to your bar. And they liked country music. And we proved it in the Brunswick Hotel.

The accuracy of Ranville's statements would have to be verified by others who were on the scene at the time. But it seems reasonable to accept the idea that aboriginal country musicians helped to make space for Native people and good-timing in Winnipeg venues in the 1970s, forcing nonaboriginal businessmen and politicians to take aboriginal musicians, music, and patrons seriously.

ABORIGINAL VENUES

All the same, a fully integrated bar scene did not emerge. Rather, eventually, distinct spaces of aboriginal sociability came to stand alongside others. For instance, a particularly important hub of urban aboriginal socializing during the late 1960s and the 1970s was the Main Street Strip, a stretch of bars and hotels along the main route connecting downtown Winnipeg and the North End. This is not to say that aboriginal public spaces were entirely separate from others: in those years, as today, aboriginal patrons probably visited bars with a majority nonaboriginal clientele and vice versa. Yet certain venues began to be identified as "Native bars" and others as "white bars" (see Sanderson 2006), some clearly courting particular clienteles. Nor was it simply race that distinguished the spaces, to return to an earlier argument: "Native" venues were constituted through distinctive styles of interacting and imbibing and, discursively, through commentary that pathologized them.

My older consultants had all been teetotalers for years by the time I met them, but many of them had lived through periods of riotous good-timing in Winnipeg during the 1950s, '60s, or '70s. Even though they had since come to frown upon drinking and regretted some of the things they had done while intoxicated, they had a less thoroughgoingly negative perspective of Native alcohol consumption than the nonindigenous writers quoted earlier. Their descriptions of the old drinking days included both positive and negative memories: drinking could lead to violence and family troubles, but it was also connected to song, dance, and memorable performances of charismatic personhood.

In these stories good-timing was often enabled by a gift-based economics of revelry in which those who had money ensured that poorer acquaintances also enjoyed themselves. One friend described coming into Winnipeg with a large pay-check, heading directly to the Balmoral Motor Hotel, and partying there with a group of friends for a week until he was completely broke. Drinking also occasioned remarkable feats. One friend described how his father, though a short man, had knocked an opponent clear across a pool table with a single punch; another described how he had once been able to jig while standing on his head. There were negative aspects to indigenous good-timing, and my friends were quick to remark on these; yet they also seemed reluctant to dismiss all of their experiences.

The idea that the good-timing scene was something more than the way it was portrayed in older media accounts, more than troubled drinking, comes across clearly in the third episode of the Canadian Broadcasting Corporation's 2002 radio documentary series *Original Citizens*, titled "Main Street." The program offers a nuanced description of the Main Street scene of the late 1960s and early 1970s, told from a variety of aboriginal perspectives. Interviewees comment on how Main Street offered a public space in which First Nations and Métis people felt welcome. Their words, too, are a fitting rejoinder to the journalists' remarks quoted above:

BRUNELDA WHEELER: I remember when I first went to Winnipeg I was going to University of Manitoba, and I was lonely. And at that point in history, you were very guarded about where you went, and what you did, but I knew that people conglomerated down on Main Street, and when I wanted to meet aboriginal people, if I was alone, I would go down to the Strip. I just wanted to have a feeling of belonging, and when I went down to the Strip, there were a whole bunch of aboriginal people down there like me.

MAN'S VOICE: People could frequent these stores and hotels and restaurants without feeling out of place, because there was always a lot of aboriginal people around. On Main Street, half the time I didn't know who the aboriginal people were, but I knew they were from a community around back home, and I knew that we could relate if we started talking. (CBC Manitoba 2002b)

GOOD-TIMING IN THE NEW CENTURY

Drinking establishments continue to play a significant role in the aboriginal country-music scene and in Native public culture more generally. The most prominent of these, Teddy Bob's Country Bar and the Westbrook Inn, both located some distance from the Main Street Strip, regularly book aboriginal bands for weekend stands. As in the early 1970s, drinking and good-timing at these venues still tend to differ from those at venues with a largely nonaboriginal or middle-class clientele—and from what is held to be normative in the mainstream public sphere. Partying is more likely to be an all-day affair, for instance. The headlining bands at one bar used to start playing at three in the afternoon on Saturdays, continuing until closing time at two in the morning, and many patrons pulled similarly long shifts (see chapter 1). Not coincidentally, I saw more intoxicated patrons at such venues than I did at other Winnipeg bars, and I was more likely to drink too much myself.

Drinking also tends to be more convivial: when I went out to the Westbrook or Teddy Bob's alone, I was almost always drawn into conversation or invited to sit down with a group of patrons, who introduced me all around. It was not unusual to find intergenerational family groups out for a good time, a rarity at other venues for live music in Winnipeg. Indeed, seating was typically arranged to accommodate large groups. Conviviality was especially evident in barroom economics: drinkers were much more likely to "borrow" and "lend" money and cigarettes and to buy drinks for one another ("borrowing" rarely involving any kind of straightforward repayment). Indeed, it is difficult for me to separate the sociability of the barroom from its economic aspects. This friendliness did have an opposite pole, however. "Aren't you frightened to be here?" I was often asked—in part a suggestion that I didn't belong, and in part a warning that things to be frightened about happened there.[27]

All of this should not be understood to indicate a homogeneous or stable culture of drinking. Good-timing is ratified, inflected, and challenged in countless individual performances (see Herzfeld 1997: 148–52), and it changes over time. Its negotiated character is particularly evident in two respects in Manitoba. First, a significant percentage of the indigenous population does not drink at all: Native people are twice as likely as other Canadians to be teetotalers, according to one source (Thatcher 2004: 23). Many aboriginal people condemn the use of alcohol and drugs, and I regularly heard my informants exhort their fellows to embrace a sober lifestyle. Such admonitions carried moral force in an environment where alcohol is closely associated with violence, child neglect, and abuse. Second, aboriginal political organizations and community leaders increasingly organize dry musical events: festivals, jamborees, coffeehouses, and dances where alcohol is not served (see chapter 5). These gatherings assert the possibility of good-timing without alcohol and sever seemingly natural connections between country music and the tavern. Through such interventions, indigenous teetotalers reconfigure the aboriginal country-music scene—and publicness more generally.

Again, the investigation of indigenous drinking is a thorny undertaking. Powerful negative stereotypes still circulate, influencing aboriginal and nonaboriginal discourses alike (see Thatcher 2004: 15; compare Herzfeld 1997). Even the framing of the question can help to reproduce potentially misleading assumptions—for instance, that race is the most appropriate optic through which to investigate alcohol consumption. (Why not "working-class drinking" or "drinking north of the 55th parallel"?)[28] Further, and as already noted, focusing on aboriginal drinking can obscure the significant population of indigenous non-drinkers and the dynamic and contested character of Native publicness. Still, it is important for a number of reasons to explore the connections between aboriginal drinking, country music, and the postcolonial period. Doing so recognizes an important area of negotiation in indigenous public culture, namely between wet and dry sociability. Additionally, it opens up space to explore how dominant publics at once differentiate themselves from, and stand in an inseparable relationship to, their counterpublics. It is not simply that drinking comportment in the national and aboriginal public spheres differs, but that the national public construes indigenous drinking as different and problematic, that it targets Native drinking through various interventions, and that aboriginal publicness comes into being in part in relationship to this surveillance and discipline.

The foregoing ethnographic and historical accounts reveal publics and the relationships that hold between them to be dynamic. In addressing imaginaries, performers and other social actors most typically perpetuate or extend them, but they also transform them, sometimes gradually and sometimes dramatically. Courtney Jourdain's performance at Country Jam 2002 helped to affirm the place of new country at the competition, but it also compelled the radio station's board to reconsider the centrality of country music at the contest. Aboriginal country performers such as Stirling and Errol Ranville brought Native music and audiences into drinking establishments that had formerly been perceived as "white bars." And today various agents contest the relationship between country music and drinking establishments by organizing alternative venues and contexts for country performance.

The preceding accounts have also explored connections and distinctions between publics. They have shown circulating genres, performances, and discourses to be available for redeployment by different groups of people, and likewise (to some extent) the means of producing publicness itself. Aboriginal musicians have availed themselves of country music, rock, and rap—and of the agricultural fair, the talent show, and radio broadcasting—creating venues and virtual spaces of their own. Notwithstanding the overlapping and "available" nature of publicness, imaginaries can be distinguished one from another. This is in part because (some of) the performances and publications that circulate within them differ—but it is also because of power. In the Canadian context, the national public has defined itself in part in relation to a problematic or worrisome indigenous one. This relationship has in some respects endured despite the collapse of an explicitly colonial ideology: whereas agricultural fairs of the colonial era constituted a settler nation in opposition to its uncivilized "Indians," during the postcolonial period the national public shared a sense of duty to intervene in troubling aboriginal behaviors, including intoxicant use. As this suggests, the distinctness of publics is in no way simple or discrete: they come into being in relation to one another. The discourses and acts of the national public define it, in part, in contrast to an aboriginal public, while the aboriginal public understands itself, in part, as the problematic object of the national public's concern and intervention.[29]

"#1 on NCI": What Aboriginal Country Musicians Sing About

The journey from Winnipeg north to Norway House First Nation is relatively easy when compared to travel to other, more isolated Manitoba communities, but it isn't one to make without first thinking about when and where to stop for gas. Once you get to Grahamdale, two and a half hours north of Winnipeg, there are no communities until Grand Rapids, another two hours north. From there it is another two hours until the service station at the Ponton junction, and then just short of two more, mostly on gravel, to Norway House. In the summer of 2005 I took this route to visit Edward and Audrey Guiboche during the community's annual Treaty and York Boat Days. I arrived on the night of the talent show, and so after some supper we went to watch it at the hockey arena. Singers from neighboring communities and across the reserve performed, accompanied by a pickup band of regulars from the aboriginal country-music circuit.

One stood out for me in particular: a young woman singing a version of Julie Roberts's country hit "Break Down Here." The song portrays a car and driver on the verge of breakdown, the driver close to tears and the car nearly out of gas, some fifty miles from the nearest town. Having spent the later hours of my own northward journey worrying about running dry between service stations, the lyrics were bound to make an impression. Yet they also seemed appropriate to the community the performer was addressing. Many Norway House residents have friends and relatives in Winnipeg, or work that they do in the south of the province, and they regularly make the same trip I had just completed. Even travel to closer cities such as Thompson or the Pas begins with something like a hundred-mile drive over gravel, sometimes in a car in much worse shape than the '94 Honda I had driven (compare Samuels 2004: 131–33). So, although the song might have described a scene in any one of a thousand places in North America, the performance rooted it in the time and place in which it was heard, made it speak about local roads, loves, and breakdowns. Like all performances, then, it was an act not simply of entextualization/enmusicalization, but of contextualization too (Silverstein and Urban 1996).

Why is country music popular with aboriginal Manitobans? And what makes country music aboriginal? I have suggested that country is important to Native people because it is connected to their twentieth-century history, including their experiences of participation in the virtual spaces (think of Courchene and Menow's radio broadcasts) and venues (consider the Ranvilles' performances at the Brunswick Hotel) of Manitoba's public sphere. I have also suggested musical reasons for its popularity. Country has much in common, melodically and structurally, with fiddle music and Christian hymnody, genres adopted decades or even centuries earlier in many communities. And its musical straightforwardness, especially in the case of classic country, facilitates amateur adoption.

But, as the account of the performance of "Break Down Here" suggests, country music is also popular because its lyrics and themes resonate with indigenous listeners. This final section of the chapter considers a few prominent themes in aboriginal country music, drawing largely upon songs performed at the 2002 NCI Jam and privileging compositions by Native songwriters. Three recurring themes are evident in these songs: rural homes, friends, and communities; drinking, partying, and alcohol-related problems; and, above all, love, longing, and heartbreak (see again Table 3.2).[30] While these themes are important in aboriginal country music, they are also common in mainstream country and indeed are explored by other scholars of the music. Aaron Fox discusses the musical and affective emplacement of rural, working-class sociability "out the country," as well as the character of the drunken and heartbroken "fool" in song and social life (2004). Cecilia Tichi explores the tensions between "home" and "road."[31] And Barbara Ching (2001) writes about the figure of the abject—and often drunk and heartbroken—loser.

Given that mainstream and aboriginal country music explore the same subjects it might be asked whether country is a particularly indigenous expression (see Samuels 2004, 2009). Does the ubiquity of these themes (and of country music more generally) reflect a broader working-class sensibility that crosses political boundaries and lines of race and class? This probably explains part of the appeal. Nevertheless, and as the following material hopes to show, the lyrics of country music also resonate with aboriginal people because they address concerns and experiences that are specific to that audience. Rural themes are significant not only because many listeners live on reserves far from Winnipeg, but also because many of their unique rights as aboriginal people are vested in these locations. Songs about drinking are appealing not simply because aboriginal listeners share with country's wider audience an appreciation for narratives about the ups and downs of good-timing, but also because indigenous drinkers have been subject to decades of targeted surveillance and discipline. Native songwriters furthermore approach the familiar themes of rural community, good-timing, and love in ways that subtly reflect indigenous histories, experiences, and sociability. For these reasons as well, country has been successful in addressing and constituting an indigenous Manitoban listenership.

"JAMMIN' IN THE JACKPINE": COUNTRY MUSIC AND THE COUNTRY

Aboriginal country music hymns the hinterland in the face of ideologies that celebrate the city.[32] Occasionally the affirmation of the rural is ambivalent, acknowledging widespread stereotypes of country life as backward and isolated. Many of the older country fans I knew loved Merle Haggard's "Okie from Muskogee," notwithstanding its specifically American references and apparent political conservatism. I suspect they appreciated the balance it struck between defiant pride and self-deprecation regarding being from an insular community with a funny name (compare Ching 2001: 41–44). There were similarly playful celebrations of rural "backwardness" at NCI Jam 2002, where Charlie Boulanger, a singer from the isolated Ojibwe community of Berens River, covered Tracy Byrd's "I'm From the Country,"[33] a song that acknowledges stereotypes about country folks while celebrating the closeness of relationships in rural communities.

Not all of the songs sung at the contest were so ambivalent about country life: a number affirmed it more forthrightly. "My Town," by Donald Bradburn of Norway House, described with affection the changes his community had gone through during the preceding decades: the roads paved, the bridges built to join its various islands, the hydroelectric power lines brought in to link it to the province's power grid. Some of these are mentioned in the second verse of the song, quoted here along with the chorus:

> I seen these forty years come and go;
> We have changed a lot of things in you:
> I seen you when they put those pavement roads;
> I seen them put up those hydro poles.[34]
>
> I've seen a lot of changes in my time;
> I've kept a lot of memories in my mind.
> Norway House, you've always been my town;
> Every time I leave, I come back home.

These improvements are more than "developments" or "modernizations." They are acts of care visited upon the community by its inhabitants: "We have changed a lot of things in you," Bradburn sings. "My Town" is a nostalgic song about the past, but only in part: it is also a statement of commitment to the ongoing vitality of the community.

Danny Bulycz drew together the past and a contemporary commitment to community in a different way. His "Jammin' in the Jackpine" invited listeners to come out to his hometown, Mafeking, to dance and sing under the northern lights. This would continue a long tradition: previous generations of aboriginal people had "jammed there in the jackpine," albeit without guitars or fiddles. Bulycz's take on history was more playful and less personal than Bradburn's, but similarly celebrated his community through reference to the past. The performance was in fact oriented in a very concrete way to community vitality: "Jammin' in the Jackpine" was the theme song for a series of music festivals of the same name that Bulycz organized on the outskirts of Mafeking in 2002, 2003, and 2004. Profits from the festivals would go toward the construction of a new recreation center for the community, he explained to me in a 2002 interview. His performance at the competition was thus more than a celebration of good-timing and rural community: it represented a commitment to the future of that community and to good times yet to come.

Bradburn and Bulycz's songs presented known, intimate spaces to unknown listeners, orienting the particularities of community experience outward to an aboriginal public. Complicating this trajectory from intimacy to publicness, Bulycz's public performance was undertaken in part to benefit his immediate community. This underscores a theme developed in the previous chapter: that performances are often multiply oriented, simultaneously addressing intimate social contexts as well as audiences of strangers.

To reinforce another point made in chapter 2, the rural communities represented in aboriginal song are often the places where Native languages and traditions are most actively preserved and where indigenous political and economic rights are strongest. Country music celebrates these communities in a context of considerable economic pressure to move off-reserve and pursue opportunities elsewhere (compare Tichi 1994). Many Manitoban First Nations were strategically located at the time the "numbered" treaties were signed: they were well situated with respect to hunting, trapping, and fishing territories and stood at key intersections in the riverine transportation and trade network. Nowadays many of them are considered isolated and deprived: difficult to get to and short of opportunities for employment and advancement. While these reserves often maintain continuities in terms of community, language, and traditional occupations, as well as some degree of political autonomy, they do not offer the same kinds of economic opportunities the urban centers of the south do. It is in this context that songs about rural homes and communities are sung and heard and, I suggest, offer a particularly appropriate affective language for expressing aboriginal experiences of, and ambivalences concerning, urbanization.

"I GOT A JOB PARTYING WITH ALL MY FRIENDS": GOOD-TIMING

Given the historical prohibition and contemporary surveillance of aboriginal alcohol consumption, as well as the fierce opposition to intoxicants in many indigenous communities, it is not surprising that songs about drinking play an important role in aboriginal country music. That the songs that mentioned drinking at NCI's 2002 singing competition (see again Table 3.2) tended to present it in negative terms was also perhaps to be expected. Some ("Killing Time Is Killing Me" and "Two More Bottles of Wine") portrayed drinking as the unhealthy retreat of those whose romantic relationships had failed, and there was a general connection between drinking and abjection.[35] Cal Richard's original composition "Family Tree" was unique in its defense of good-timing, although its justifications were perhaps hard to take seriously.[36] In the first verse the song's narrator describes how his mother encourages him to get a job, save money, and start a family. In the chorus, he replies that he already has already been doing just that:

> My mama warned me way back when I was young:
> She told me, "Son, I think you're having just too much fun.
> It's time you get a job and settle down, save some money, quit throwing it around,
> And maybe start another branch of the family tree."

> Well, Mama, I got a job partying with all my friends;
> As far as finances go, we all chip in;
> Every time I meet a newfound friend who likes to party just like me,
> Well, I take them home and add their names to the family tree.

His response comes across as a joke, of course: partying isn't a job, chipping in for the cost of a case of beer doesn't constitute financial planning, and drinking buddies aren't a family. All the same, it manages a clever rhetorical victory.

The exhortations in the song address behaviors stereotypically associated with Native people: drunkenness, laziness, irresponsibility, and prodigality. As "Mama's" concern perhaps suggests, some aboriginal people have come to consider these to be faults to which they as a group are prone (again, see Herzfeld 1997), and they acknowledge these negative self-conceptions with rue, shame, or defiance. One friend told me he had once told his boss, "I'm an Indian—we never work on payday!" He was angrily acknowledging the notion that aboriginal people were "irresponsible" or "lazy" and could not be counted upon to put in a full day's work once they had been remunerated.

Partly at issue—beyond racism, that is—is that certain differences are misapprehended across cultural lines. Manitoban indigenous people often do approach work, household economics, and good-timing differently from Euro-Canadians. The latter have often characterized such variation in terms of lack: an absence of ambition, a missing work ethic, an inability to plan for the future, intemperateness. Their reception identifies but misinterprets cultural particularities, slotting them into categories that, while straightforward to the majority, are inappropriate (see Bhabha 1994: 66–84).[37] Perhaps it is for this reason that, while Richard's narrator resists exhortations to toe the line in the areas of employment, family, financial prudence, and temperance, his defiance is comical. The playfulness of his rhetoric reflects the difficulty of confronting dominant discourses on their own terms.

Many country fans would hear the influence of Hank Williams Jr.'s well-known outlaw country song "Family Tradition" in Richard's "Family Tree." Both present dialogues between a defiant narrator and chiding interlocutors, both play on the meaning of the word "family," and both make sly arguments in defense of a dissolute lifestyle ("So if I get stoned," sings Williams, "I'm just carryin' on an old family tradition").[38] Clearly, then, mainstream country music also resists the disparagement of drinking and dissolution in dominant discourses.[39] It might therefore be asked whether "Family Tree" is any different, any more "aboriginal" than "Family Tradition." To what degree does the song simply adopt language, narratives, and postures from the country-music industry, which, with a number of notable exceptions, tends to be dominated by nonaboriginal performers, songwriters, and businesspeople? More broadly, to what degree does indigenous country music represent Manitoban indigeneity?

In the first place, certain broad preoccupations of country music simply resonate in deep ways with the experiences of aboriginal people. This certainly appears to be the case so far as the themes of drinking and rural life are concerned. (As I explain above, the prohibition of intoxicant consumption by indigenous people was a very significant element of Canadian colonialism, and concerns about drinking continue to shape cross-cultural relations, community life, and aboriginal self-conceptions.) But country music can also address the particularities of its audience in subtler ways. The lyrics of "Family Tree," for example, hint at aspects of sociability that are characteristic of Winnipeg's urban aboriginal public culture and, more specifically, the distinctive interactions that hold in drinking venues with a primarily indigenous clientele. When I went out to a "Native" bar or festival I regularly found myself added, in just the way Richard describes, to someone or other's "family tree." My newfound friends made sure I always had a beer or smoke in my hand, kept me company, and ensured that I was having a good time. Richard's song captures and celebrates elements of this conviviality while simultaneously acknowledging it as a social problematic. Even as it evidences the influence of Hank Williams Jr., then, it points to elements of a more immediate context.

"NEVER BE A CHEATIN' HEART"

It would be an error to underestimate the importance of love songs to the aboriginal public: they are a mainstay of live performances, recordings, and radio programming. They were certainly well represented at the 2002 NCI Jam, as Table 3.2 confirms, constituting twenty of the thirty songs performed. The majority of them expressed sadness or heartbreak, and even a number of the happier ones suggested that mutual love was rare and tenuous.[40] Les Shannacappo's "Never Be a Cheatin' Heart" occupied a middle ground between optimism and pessimism: in the chorus the narrator implores his beloved to tell him that she loves him, that they will never part, and that she will "never be a cheatin' heart."[41] The song holds forth a tentative hope for a love that will not fall prey to breakup or infidelity, even as it suggests such ends are very real possibilities.

Although the songs at the competition positioned committed, romantic, heterosexual love as an unmarked ideal, many of them focused on breakups, infidelity, and heartbreak—unfortunate but common transgressions of it. In short, many of the love songs expressed uncertainty about the possibility of attaining love-song love. It might be tempting to draw connections between the large number of songs about heartache and the high rate of so-called single parenthood amongst aboriginal Manitobans, or between unhappy love songs, family instability, and fiscal uncertainty.[42] I am not entirely comfortable with such arguments.[43] But it can certainly be argued, in a more general way, that the frequency of songs about unhappiness in love, and the guardedness of songs, such as Shannacappo's, that celebrated new relationships, suggested a context where dominant ideologies concerning love, sex, and family did not match up with lived experience (compare Berlant and Warner 1998: 552–57; Kipnis 2000; Berlant 2008; Stokes 2010). And it can furthermore be suggested that the singers who sang such songs at Country Jam 2002 construed their public as one with which this disconnect would resonate.

Breakups, heartaches, and infidelity are frequent subjects in mainstream country music (and other popular genres), but do songs by indigenous songwriters on these subjects acknowledge the particularities of their aboriginal audience? It seems to me that some lyrics do, in subtle ways. Chris Beach's (Figure 3.3) "#1 on NCI" is a case in point, hinting at aspects of sociability and self-presentation that I encountered in everyday interactions with Cree and Ojibwe people.[44] Beach had

Figure 3.3 MORRIS MONEAS, CHRIS BEACH, AND CAROLINE BEACH (*LEFT TO RIGHT*). Photo by the author.

his first NCI hit in the summer and autumn of 2002 with "My Soap Opera Woman," a humorous song about a relationship that falls apart when the narrator's wife can no longer distinguish between reality and the soap opera plots and characters that obsess her. The song maintained a position at the top of the NCI charts for several weeks, and the station awarded it the prize for "Single of the Year" at that year's NCI Jam. Two years later, in 2004, Beach released a sequel entitled "#1 on NCI," narrated by the same character, who explains how, once he stopped crying about the departure of his wife and started writing, he found fame:

> I used to sit and cry all night long,
> Then one day I decided to put it in a song.
> Then I took it to one-oh-five point five;
> Now I'm number one on NCI....
>
> Yes, I'm number one on NCI
> Since my soap opera woman said goodbye.
> She can keep the house and keep the car and that other guy,
> 'Cause I'm number one on NCI.

In the second verse he explains to his ex that if she wants him back, she'll have to line up behind the other women who have recently begun to express an interest in him, and he revels in the thought that she can't turn on the radio without hearing his voice: "I'm in your face every day on one-oh-one-point-five." But in the final verse he says:

> With you I was always number two.
> You wrecked our home and family and made me blue.
> And you can tell our three children not to cry
> 'Cause Daddy's number one on NCI.

There is a mixture of boastfulness, vengefulness, and sadness here—wrapped in that country-music jokiness that allows you to hear it all as a laugh, or maybe not (see Fox 2004: 129). The narrator is equally delighted by his success and by the fact it will make his ex-wife regret her decision to leave him. Yet one wonders just what consolation it will be for his children.

The combination of bitterness and pridefulness here can perhaps be found in examples of mainstream country music—in Toby Keith's "How Do You Like Me Now," for instance. Yet the mixture of remembered injury and self-regard also indexes distinctive ways of expressing antipathy and performing selfhood that I encountered during fieldwork. My Cree and Ojibwe consultants generally took great care not to criticize or censure their acquaintances and relatives; to do either could be a serious provocation. On occasion, nevertheless, people would make their resentment or enmity known.[45] Breakups and divorces were behind some of these; arguments over money and politics led to others.[46] Similarly, although social relations were generally egalitarian, individuals would occasionally reveal a surprisingly extravagant self-regard. Such behavior was irregular (although certainly not unknown) in a context where social parity was the norm and accordingly it was subject to various kinds of "leveling." People who were perceived to have too high an opinion of themselves were criticized, sometimes to their faces; alternatively, self-regard and success could provoke jealous responses in others. Complicating matters, these socially problematic behaviors were also enjoyed, particularly in arenas of expressive performance such as song. Audiences took pleasure in the spectacle of charismatic pride, and self-possessed performers were courted by social facilitators.

These ways of performing enmity and retribution, and pride and status, shape not only face-to-face relationships but publicness as well. This happens in a particularly dramatic fashion in Manitoban aboriginal politics, where bitter fallings-out and dramas of status and leveling are not uncommon. It also happens in the realm of popular music. Prominent singers often expect to be acknowledged at public events and invited to perform at important concerts and festivals, and they can respond with sincere indignation to perceived slights. Musicians occasionally reveal bitter rivalries with one another, and additional conflicts are often alleged by observers. I suggest that these aspects of sociability are also reflected in the mixture of hurt and boastfulness in "#1 on NCI." And perhaps in part for this reason, the song resonated with NCI listeners, who made it another number 1 hit.

Conclusion

As the account that opened this chapter suggests, country has a prominent place in the realm of Manitoban aboriginal popular music, but perhaps not the dominance it once had. All the same, it has played an important historical role in Manitoban aboriginal musical life and continues to do so. Why is country music number 1 on NCI? It is in part because it has been an arena in which to address the relationship between the national and aboriginal publics, both during the colonial era and afterward. Country music allowed aboriginal people to assert parity with the broader settler public, as "Indian cowboys" adopting western songs and clothing and joining nonaboriginal people in the nation's public houses. It has probably also been important because certain of its themes resonate strongly with indigenous experiences. Songs about rural communities and sociability celebrate the lands and homes where First Nations and Métis rights are often held to be rooted (and from which aboriginal people are often tempted by better economic opportunities). Songs about drinking express a range of stances toward substances and behaviors that have respectively been strictly controlled and closely surveyed by the nation—and that are subject to vigorous debate within Native communities. Further, country music has presented an avenue for reflecting upon characteristic elements of Manitoban Algonquian sociability: certain ways of good-timing, performing charismatic selfhood, and expressing one's relationships to others.

The preceding accounts have also exemplified in a number of ways the availability, distinguishability, and hierarchical character of publicness. Aboriginal country musicians have drawn upon circulating songs and genres—and the technologies of publicness more generally—and made them their own. In some cases, these have been incorporated with little transformation into contexts of aboriginal sociability: consider the performances of "Break Down Here" and "Purple Rain" described above. Indeed, aboriginal artists have become thoroughly fluent in the idioms of country music and attained national successes; C-Weed's career is a good example. As this suggests, "mainstream country music" is regularly and uncontroversially deployed in contexts of aboriginal sociability, while "aboriginal country music" occasionally moves beyond the indigenous public sphere to address a national or international audience. In this situation, trying to interpret the music Native people make as a combination of "Indian" and "non-Indian" elements seems to miss something fundamental, as David Samuels has argued (2004: see 257–62).

Yet despite the movements of songs and genres, it remains possible to distinguish indigenous and mainstream musical publics. The majority of mass-mediated aboriginal music circulates within, and helps to constitute, a sphere of broadcast, recording, and publication that stands largely apart from the national country-music scene. Winnipeg and other cities have social spaces, both wet and dry, that draw in predominantly aboriginal clienteles. Whatever the overlap with mainstream virtual and social spaces, there is separateness and distinctiveness, too. This is in part because the musical and social interactions that tend to be normative in spaces of aboriginal sociability differ from those in others. It is in part because, although a good deal of music is similar to what circulates in the broader public sphere, a substantial portion of it is different. It is further because aboriginal publicness has emerged in the shadow of a national publicness that has regarded aboriginal people and their behavior as troubled and troubling.

The foregoing account has explored aboriginal country music as a general response to broad social, political, and historical developments. The next two chapters tighten the focus. While they still consider genres and songs that circulate in mass-mediated form, they are concerned to a greater extent with how particular musicians deploy these in contexts of face-to-face music making, what they do with these songs and say about them, and how listeners and fellow musicians respond to them. In doing so, what follows explores further intersections between intimacy and imagining.

4

"Your Own Heart Will Make Its Own Music"

Gospel Singing, Individuation, and the Comforting Community

Part I: The Comforting Community

In early 2006 my friend and teacher Edward Guiboche, aged fifty-seven, died of cancer. I drove up to Winnipeg from Chicago to attend his wake and funeral. Edward was known in communities across Manitoba as a coach and choreographer of competition square-dancing teams and as a caller at social dances. I got to know him in 2002, when he led weekly gatherings at the Winnipeg Indian and Metis Friendship Centre (Figure 4.1). Fittingly, his wake was held in the same building where he had so often led friends and acquaintances through the choreographic patterns he loved. Edward never called the dancing from the stage; instead, he danced out on the floor with the rest of us, shouting out instructions and, when words failed him, pushing us in the right direction with urgent hands. His final request had been to see square dancing again; it was honored at a gathering a few days before he passed away.

During 2002 and 2003 Edward also organized a weekly gospel music coffeehouse at William Whyte School, where his wife Audrey was the principal. Aboriginal musicians from around the city and farther afield gathered in the echoing gymnasium on Wednesday nights to sing hymns and gospel songs and enjoy one another's company. The coffeehouses were low-key events, and, although attendees sang sacred songs, there was little in the way of proselytizing. As I did more fieldwork I gradually realized that the singing there was linked to a broader ritual practice common in many Cree and Ojibwe communities, namely the singing of sacred songs at funerary wakes. It was Edward who helped me understand this. Occasionally, after the coffeehouse had wrapped up at around ten at night, he would invite me to a neighborhood church or funeral chapel to attend a wake in progress. I typically hung out near the back of the sanctuary while Edward paid his respects and greeted friends. Sometimes he went up to the front of the room to sing with the musicians there—among them often singers I recognized from

Figure 4.1 EDWARD GUIBOCHE (1948–2006) AT THE WINNIPEG FRIENDSHIP CENTRE. Photo by the author.

the coffeehouse. There was music, some light talk, some quiet reflection, a little bit of food, some cigarettes outside, and coffee. Afterward I dropped Edward off at home. Thus he introduced me to aboriginal ways of holding wakes and impressed upon me what the living do for the departed.

I have often wondered why Edward put so much effort into the coffeehouse, and why he paid his respects at so many wakes. Did he already know that he was ill? Was he surrounding himself with the songs and musicians who would accompany him when he left?

Edward's own wake was well attended: there were family, friends, square dancers, gospel singers, politicians, clergy, and conductors of traditional ceremonies. I recognized many of them from the dances and coffeehouses he had organized when he had lived in Winnipeg. In fact, the wake was the third of three such events, each held in a different place. The previous night there had been one in Grand Rapids, the community in which he had grown up, and the night before that there had been one in Norway House, where he and Audrey had taken jobs in 2004. It is not uncommon for wakes to be held in two places so that more friends and relatives can see the deceased. Edward's tour of three communities attested to his renown in the square-dancing scene, to his and Audrey's travels over the years (both of them had worked at a variety of jobs across the province), and to his charisma and gregariousness.

Edward was a unique and memorable individual, and also a man of considerable artistic and social talents. At the time I came to know him, he was proud to point out that his square-dance routines were in use across the province. In some cases he had taught them to the dance troupes; in others the dancers had simply copied the steps. Sometimes new ideas for dances occurred to him in the middle of the night, he told me, and he would wake up Audrey (and, I learned, the children) to run through them together in the kitchen, with chairs as additional partners. It wasn't difficult to find real dancers to perform the routines he came up with: Edward made friends easily and had a knack for recruiting people to take part in the projects and events he organized. He occasionally revealed a grudge against someone, but the majority of his energy was devoted to building alliances, connections, and friendships. When he was younger, he had been a drinker and a fighter, he told me, and he sometimes related stories of his wild days to me as we traveled together to dances and competitions. By the time I knew him he had been sober for years, but he continued to maintain the consequential social profile he had as a young man. On evenings out he never stayed still for long, making his way around the room, greeting acquaintances, teasing friends, telling outrageous jokes, and making conversation. Once met, he was never forgotten.

When I arrived at the wake I shook hands with Edward's family, then stood for a moment beside the casket with my hand on Edward's hands, as I had often seen him do. He was wrapped in a star blanket and wearing his traditional ribbon shirt, and he looked much older and thinner than when I had last seen him. A short time after I arrived, Nelson Menow and Josephine Flett began to set up on the Friendship Centre stage; they would guide the musical proceedings for the first part of the evening. They opened with an instrumental arrangement of "Where the Roses Never Fade," with Menow playing the melody on his electric guitar and Flett chording along on acoustic. Later they sang some Cree and English songs. Over the course of the evening a number of Winnipeg singers came up to perform with them, including Jerald Funk, known around the city as "the Cree Singer," and Kendra and Mary Sinclair, close friends of Edward and cofounders of the William Whyte coffeehouse. Later several speakers said a few words, including an Anglican clergyman, a born-again Christian, and one or two traditional ceremonialists.

After they had finished, a group of around eleven singers from northern Manitoba, including a number from Sapotaweyak Cree Nation, gathered around a table on the Friendship Centre stage. Two of them had guitars and led the singing. They gradually made their way through the hymnal, calling out the number of the appropriate song at the beginning of each new piece.[1] They sang in unison in strained voices, and although the drumlike strumming of the guitars remained steady, the music had the metrical unpredictability of much of the singing I had heard at Edward's coffeehouse. More singers came up to join them as they continued. When they had finished, a second group came up to sit around the table. They had also traveled a long way, I believe from the western Manitoba community of Moose Lake and farther away in Saskatchewan.[2] They too sang in a metrically irregular style to guitar accompaniment, performing Cree hymns, gospel favorites, and a Cree song entitled "Kē Kē Pā Sakihitin."

The latter was particularly dear to a number of my Winnipeg friends. In its lyrics the deceased, speaking in the first person, comforts the bereaved who have gathered at the wake, telling them he or she loves them and will not abandon them. The third verse and chorus follow below, in Cree and in the English translation included alongside it on a song sheet I copied from some friends.[3]

Unōch katipiskak
Ke pas wetupimina waw
A mino sipwātāyan
Kawinu ma matook
Kawina ketimik
Tu miyo pukitiniyāk

Kawinu Mawikasin
Misuwash Mo Wēkatch
Ni ku kitimakisin
Kawina Mētasin
Misuwash Mo Wēkatch
Ku nukutitinawaw

Tonight
You came down to sit down with me
So I can go in peace to my Lord
Do not weep for me
Do not be lazy too
For you must let me go today.
Do not weep for me
For I'll never be poor

Do not weep for me at all
Do not weep for me
For I'll never leave you
All alone in this wicked world.[4]

As the early hours of the morning passed, attendees went home to sleep. Late at night it seemed that only Edward's immediate family was left. Some of them played cards; others sat, or thought, or talked. The singers from western Manitoba left at about three-thirty in the morning, explaining that they had been traveling around the province all week and needed to get some sleep. Audrey found a portable stereo to play some recordings of fiddle tunes, Edward's favorite music. I told her I was leaving to get some sleep as well, and she asked me to pick up some colored ribbons the next morning at the store for the pallbearers' armbands.

* * * * *

The hymns and gospel songs performed at Manitoban aboriginal wakes and coffeehouses are vehicles for the performance of both personhood and collectivity. At wakes, their communal role is particularly in evidence: they convey to the bereaved the collective solace of the community. At the same time, they are often performed in ways that highlight the uniqueness of performers, distinctions that are experienced in particularly immediate ways by fellow musicians. Sacred song is thus socially efficacious: through it, groups of people constitute themselves as communities, soloists and groups extend comfort to those who are bereaved, and individual performers instantiate their particular personhood in the course of social and musical interactions. Northern Algonquian individualism has been of great interest to anthropologists and ethnohistorians, sometimes to the detriment of discussions about community. Examining how Christian song repertoires are employed in Manitoba Algonquian contexts offers opportunities to think about both, considering the connections between personhood and collectivity, including how individuation emerges in the course of corporate musical activity, and how the gifts and actions of particular musicians are oriented to larger social groups.

Like all of the genres of music considered in this book, hymns and gospel songs move between networks of mass-mediated circulation and socially intimate contexts: many aboriginal musicians get to know such songs through published sources such as hymnals and recordings, and many orient their performances to a public through recordings and radio broadcasts. But given the important role that these genres play in the collective observance of mortuary rituals, and the dramatic way in which northern Algonquian individuality emerges in the course of face-to-face performance, the focus here will be largely upon musical intimacies.[5]

THE WAKE

Manitoban Cree and Ojibwe peoples are connected by linguistic and cultural commonalities, a longtime alliance, and the historical experience of colonialism. They also share certain rituals and observances, including one that seems to have taken on real significance following the spread of Christianity: the wake. In my experience a wake is usually held for one or more nights before a funeral. It typically gets under way in the evening, at which time members of the deceased's family and community begin to arrive at the church, family home, community hall, or funeral chapel where the body is resting. The date of the wake often depends on the logistics of travel for out-of-town attendees. Many Manitoban aboriginal communities are located some distance from one another and from the cities in the south of the province, and it can be difficult to get back and forth, particularly between communities that are not connected to the transportation grid by regular roads. Nelson Menow (Figure 4.2) remarked in a 2003 interview:[6] "You know, this Indian nation is a very big nation. There's a lot of people that...have relations from all over. So sometimes they have to wait for the relations to come." At the wake, attendees sit together, listen to hymns and gospel songs, and comfort the bereaved. They talk in subdued voices, although there are occasional jokes.

Figure 4.2 NELSON MENOW. Photo by the author.

Typically there is food and coffee for those who want them. Toward the beginning of the gathering, there are often words or a short meditation from a clergyman (Edward and I usually arrived well after this point). When Menow described a typical wake to me, he emphasized this part, remarking that a wake was "run by the minister. Whatever these people want, they tell the minister, 'This has to be done.'" Although Menow's remarks suggest that the minister plays an important role, they give special priority to the mourners, who give the minister instructions. And indeed in my experience a wake was a paraliturgical space in which lay, rather than clerical, activity was important.

Wakes continue until late at night and apparently in some cases until morning. Menow told me that communities "used to have them right through the night. They cut down to two o'clock, three o'clock, 'cause a lot of people are working."[7] On occasions when I stayed late, there typically came a point when only family members and very close friends remained. Until then there was usually singing, typically with guitar accompaniment. On some occasions singers came up one by one to perform songs and were accompanied by a sort of house band. At other times, larger groups took turns singing. Often, according to Menow, singing groups from different churches show up to pay their respects and comfort the family:

DUECK: Who sings at the wake?
MENOW: Well, it's mostly people that are singing in the churches and people
    that are singing the gospel songs that go there. It's a mixture. You see...the
    Catholic group would be singing; next will be the Anglican group—they give
    themselves time. And next it would be the other group. And they just work it
    out nicely.

In response to further questions, Menow told me that there is no favoritism so far as the singing is concerned: even family members do not necessarily sing any longer than other singers.

Wake singers often come from outside the community, sometimes traveling long distances to do so. The community and family of the deceased look after visiting singers, another consultant told me, making sure that they have food, shelter, gas money, and comforts like cigarettes. At Winnipeg wakes, musical contributions were often diverse, since in that cosmopolitan city it was not uncommon for aboriginal people of different backgrounds to become friends (or indeed marry). I attended one wake where singers from the northwestern community of Moose Lake sang in Cree and English, followed by singers from the southeastern community of Little Black River, who sang in Ojibwe.

Lest the wake be understood to be a thoroughly homogeneous practice across and within Manitoban indigenous communities, Menow did mention other kinds of wakes at which singing did not occur. When I inquired further, he hesitated, and then talked about a way of doing things that he found troubling.

MENOW: The Indian culture, they have a different way of doing it too, eh. This
    I don't really go for, but, it's not that I want to call them down, but it's a
    simple fact for me that I don't really go for...the way they handle things.
DUECK: What is it that you don't agree with?
MENOW: Well, some people...don't sing....They do it the opposite way.
    Some of them drink right there and they play cards, according to what
    I heard....I don't really know too much about it. I don't want to talk too
    much about it, but according to what I hear, I don't like it.

In characterizing this second way of having a wake as "the opposite way," Menow acknowledged the frequently strict distinction between wet and dry spaces of aboriginal sociability (see chapter 1). His description accords with what I observed about such spaces more generally: the presence of alcohol tends to rule out sacred song, while the presence of sacred song tends to rule out drinking.[8]

It should be remarked that Menow did not presume to speak for all aboriginal people in the interviews he granted me, and that, amongst the scores of aboriginal communities in Manitoba, funerary practices vary in ways beyond those he described. So, for instance, Audrey Guiboche, upon reading the opening of this chapter, explained that in Duck Bay, where she had grown up, there had not been much singing at wakes, and that it had been common to play cards. All the same, she told me, people did not drink, and at moments throughout the night they said the rosary. Her intervention was a reminder that, even after much fieldwork, my understanding of Manitoban aboriginal traditions was only partial.

All the same, it seems that certain practices are very widespread in funerary observance. Most of my older consultants associated wakes with Christian song, for instance. As I remark in chapter 1, hymns have been part of indigenous musical life in Manitoba for well over one hundred years in many communities, having been translated into Ojibwe and Cree in the 1800s. As I mention in chapter 1, the first book published in what is now the province of Manitoba was James Evans's *Cree Syllabic Hymn Book*, and it seems likely that Ojibwe-language hymnals were in wide circulation by the end of the nineteenth century.[9] This is not to suggest that hymn singing has remained the same since that time: my older consultants had witnessed changes. Nelson Menow and Stirling Ranville had grown up (in Norway House and Eddystone, respectively) singing hymns in church, accompanied by the organ; they characterized guitar accompaniment as a relatively recent development. Ranville remembered that his Métis parents had considered the use of guitar in sacred repertoires controversial. In a 2003 interview Ranville seemed to indicate that the adoption of "country gospel"—sacred songs sung to guitar accompaniment in a style influenced by country music—had occurred around the 1970s, initially in evangelical tent meetings and later in sacred services. Nowadays even older hymns are typically sung to guitar accompaniment. The change in instrumentation may have had other musical entailments: Nelson Menow told me that contemporary hymn singing was "a little faster" than the singing he remembered hearing when he was young (see Dueck 2005: 285–86; on the change in style compare McNally 2000: 167–71). Contemporary mourning practices, thus, however particular and emplaced, sediment a history of engagement with various mass-mediated forms: printed hymnals initially, and later mass-mediated popular and devotional styles.

Funerary practices may also stand in dialogue with ideas that precede the introduction of Christianity. Many of the songs sung at wakes—but also in less formal contexts of musical socializing—concern heaven and the life that awaits the deceased there. That these should be the preferred subjects of sacred song seems to resonate with aspects of traditional eschatology. For instance, A. I. Hallowell writes that the Ojibwe of Berens River traditionally understood people to undergo a journey to *djibaiaking*, the Land of Ghosts, upon death (1992: 77–78). The deceased maintained consciousness, memories, and some form of corporeality (1992: 74–75), and the living kept up relationships with them, giving them gifts of food and tea and sometimes communicating with them or witnessing their appearance at special ceremonies (Hallowell 1992: 77–78). Contemporary mortuary ritual—even practices that appear Christianized—may continue, in new ways, older ideas of the afterworld and traditions of respectful engagement with the departed. The comforting words in "Kē Kē Pā Sakihitin," coming as though from the deceased, merit consideration in this regard.

MORTUARY OBSERVANCE, SONG, AND COMMUNITY

During a fifteen-month period in 2002 and 2003 I attended more wakes and funerals than ever before in a similar span. There were a number of reasons for this. First, deaths were sadly frequent: there are inordinately high rates of homicide and suicide among young aboriginal people in Manitoba, particularly young men.[10] Three of the ceremonies I attended were for men or boys under the age of twenty: one had committed suicide, one had been killed by an acquaintance in a violent accident, and a third had been sexually assaulted and then killed in a tragic and widely publicized incident. A second factor had to do with my consultants, many of whom were older than fifty and lost friends, parents, and siblings while I was doing fieldwork. Because I had a vehicle and many of them did not, I often drove them to ceremonies and sat with them. Third, and most important, I attended wakes and funerals because they were a significant part of social life for my friends and acquaintances, who attended them frequently, even when they did not know the deceased particularly well. Funerary ceremonies were moments of general congregation, when communities came together in acts of collective support, the latter often expressed through musical performance.

One of the funerals I attended, held on an Ojibwe reserve in eastern Manitoba, exemplified the corporate character of mortuary observance. I arrived with two friends on the day of the ceremony after a lengthy drive from Winnipeg. Community members and visitors had begun to fill the lawn and the road in front of the family's house, where the wake had been held in a front room. All other activity on the reserve seemed to have come to a halt, and when we stopped by the community store we found it closed, even though it was a weekday. At the funeral, every seat in the church was full, and many attendees stood against the walls of the sanctuary or in the foyer. A large group of people waited outside the church, some standing, others sitting in cars. The service was long, and one impatient man began to honk the horn of his truck.[11] When it had ended the more fully participatory events of the ceremony took place: the burial and the feast. At the burial, following a drum song and words from the officiating clergyman, community members dropped a little bit of earth into the grave with the body. Then everyone went to the community hall for the feast. So many people showed up that the food had to be carefully apportioned.

A similar communality was evident at funerary events I attended in Winnipeg. Such ceremonies, whether rural or urban, were welcoming and well attended. I was never made to feel awkward for showing up, even if I had only a distant relationship to the deceased (as a friend of a friend), and my colleagues never hesitated to invite me along. While my attendance might have seemed peculiar to some, it was no stranger than my showing up at a reserve powwow or square dance, and nobody ever intimated that it was inappropriate. As all of this suggests, the wakes and funerals I attended were broadly inclusive. They were also integrative, presenting opportunities to acknowledge, affirm, or realize roles as family, friends, members of the community, and contributing musicians. The ceremonies brought together kin and acquaintances, united communities across religious and political divisions, and effected rapprochements between estranged individuals and families. They also provided opportunities to establish or strengthen musical relationships and reputations.

The crisis of death calls kin and friends to affirm in the course of ritual their social relationships to the deceased and to one another (positions they sometimes occupy at some physical remove).[12] As the preceding accounts suggest, however, it is not only close family members and friends who come but often a much larger group. Mortuary observance can thus be one of the more significant occasions at which broad aboriginal communities experience themselves as such. Put another way, important modes of Cree and Ojibwe collectivity come into being through corporate mourning, comfort, support, and the singing that conveys them.

Because funerary ceremonies are often widely attended, they can provide opportunities to transcend social divisions, albeit temporarily. Aboriginal communities are frequently segmented by religious and denominational differences—and, often, attendant differences in sacred repertoires. The wake can be a space in which people from a range of denominations participate, especially through song, as Menow's comments above suggest ("the Catholic group would be singing; next will be the Anglican group ... next it would be the other group."). Similarly, there are linguistic divisions within some aboriginal communities and within the social groups that form in urban centers, but the wake can provide a space for performers to sing in a variety of languages.

Some differences seem sharper than others, however, and the musical inclusiveness of the wake does not always extend to traditional and neotraditional song. I did not often hear drum songs and Christian songs performed together at mortuary ceremonies. Indeed, at one funeral I attended, the body of the deceased was moved through a series of distinct spaces delineated by contrasting musical and spiritual practices. At the beginning of the day of the funeral the body lay at the house of the family, attended by gospel song; as the body was being taken from the house, drum songs were performed; at the church during the funeral service there was gospel song and Anglican liturgical music; afterward, at the grave site, another drum song was sung. The distinctness of these musical spaces suggested a strict differentiation between Christianity and traditional observance; nevertheless, the inclusiveness of the day's activities suggested that representation from both constituencies was valued and important, and that all kinds of songs contributed to the collective articulation of the ritual.

My experiences indicated that mortuary rites were integrative in more particular ways, too, presenting opportunities to move past old arguments and differences. My friends and consultants generally cultivated warm and generous interpersonal relationships, but these were counterbalanced by certain personal grievances and jealousies of passionate intensity. Following a death such antagonisms might be put aside. I knew one family that bore considerable ill will toward a former in-law and his relatives; the man in question had left a member of their family for another woman. Yet when the former in-law's mother died, the members of the offended family showed up to honor her at wake, funeral, and feast. Even the matriarch of the family, a woman who responded fiercely to perceived slights to her children, showed up. Thus funerary rites are moments when the collective expression of comfort can supersede personal animosities, creating opportunities for the amelioration of strained relationships.

My interpretation here is in some ways in line with foundational social-scientific understandings of religion and ritual. Emile Durkheim suggested a century ago that funerary rites acknowledge and strengthen social bonds: on the one hand by regulating social behavior, demanding of members of the community certain ritual obligations, and on the other by integrating communities, reinforcing the relationships between their members (1995 [1912]).[13] According to Durkheim, the process of integration is closely bound up with collective religious representations—that is, with shared sacred concepts—and with the heightened emotion that often accompanies ritual gatherings and is often mediated through music, dance, or both. Much of this seems evident in the accounts presented above. The death of a member of an aboriginal community obliges that community to come together to comfort the bereaved, often through the singing of sacred songs. Ritual is associated with emotion, expressed and cued by songs that are serious and sad, although often understated in character. In many cases, moreover, ritual and ritual music reflect widely shared beliefs that the soul of the deceased will go on to a better place—a shared representation that even traditionalists and Christians who disagree on other points may hold in common.[14]

MUSIC AND COMFORT

Thus, funerary observances are integrative and participatory events that allow communities to come together, at times despite personal antagonisms and differences of denomination, faith, and language. (This is not to suggest that integration always occurs or that, when it does, it is necessarily complete. There are exceptions, as my accounts and Menow's comments both suggest.) These ceremonies—and the singing that occurs at them—are also socially efficacious in other ways, and consultants employed an abundance of terms to describe what they do: comfort, uplift, ease, help, support, lighten the hearts of mourners, demonstrate love, and counter mournfulness, heavy-heartedness, and discouragement. Nelson Menow said:

> For us Indian people, we try and help one another. And we know this person is hurting. So the best way we can do is...have a wake [when] they lose a loved one. I don't know why they have two, three nights' wake sometimes; it's hard for them to part with somebody they love, I guess. So the best way we can do is by helping them...go and sing gospel songs for them. And somebody might preach to them [too]. And it takes that burden, that heavy burden away from them.
>
> ...Suppose I had a cousin of mine passing away. I would go there and these people...would ask, "Can you come and sing over there?" I would

ask somebody, "Can you come and help me?" 'Cause I'd feel discouraged just sitting there, just looking at the body like that, without hearing everybody singing or preaching to me. See, the Word of God reaches out to people.

It is not only music that comforts mourners: Menow mentioned the role of preaching and of the Word of God, and another consultant explained that simply having the community around soothes the bereaved. Yet music has a privileged place in mortuary ritual. Indeed, Emery Marsden (Figure 4.3), an Ojibwe singer originally from Lake St. Martin, described a wake without singing as heartbreaking when I interviewed him in 2003:

> When I started going to wakes . . . the first thing that I heard was "Amazing Grace" and "In the Sweet By and By" and all these songs. . . . I used to see people get uplifted by these songs, and they'd sit there all night and sing these psalms and comfort the family that would be mourning. But I'd sit there at times myself . . . there's times when my loved ones passed away . . . I used to sit there and I'd listen to the people that would sing . . . It would be like having a cup of coffee. I'd sit there and I'd listen, and the mourning part of me would be at *ease* because of the music. And so I started asking myself, I'd see other people when their loved one would pass away; I'd attend some wakes where . . . there'd be no one to sing, and they'd just sit there, and that would just break my heart. . . . And I would say to myself, "I wish I could sing. I'd sing for them. I'd sing."

Marsden returned later in the interview to the comparison between the comforting effect of song and that of a cup of coffee. When I asked him what he liked about the sound of gospel music, he replied:

> It's like having coffee. Every thing of it: the rhythm, the timing of the music, . . . the comforting words of a song. . . . I can feel it, I can feel those songs. . . . It was in my heart, boiling, and here it is.

Singing boils out of the singer, but it also warms and comforts the bereaved. On the day I interviewed him at his home, Marsden made sure that I had coffee to drink, and even gestured at our cups as he made some of the remarks above. Just as a host puts guests at ease by giving them coffee, he was suggesting, so do singers comfort mourners by giving them songs.[15]

Marsden's metaphor establishes iconic connections between the sonic experience of hearing music, the embodied experience of drinking coffee, and the social and affective experience of being comforted. Iconicity, in the linguistics of Charles Sanders Peirce, is a semiotic relationship in which a sign shares some similarity of form with the object it represents (see Peirce 1960: 143, Parmentier 1994: 6–7, or Turino 1999: 226–27 and 242–44). In music scholarship, the term has often been used to describe connections between musical sounds and various visual and aural objects, or between musical experiences and various social and affective experiences (see Turino 1999: 234; Turino 2008: 42–44; Feld 1990; Samuels 2004: 138). The approach taken here is similar, understanding musical experience to have potential iconic relationships to social and affective states, and for the "similarity of form" to exist along many potential lines (including not just the visual but also the aural and tactile).

Marsden's metaphor is productive in two ways. First, it renders both music and comfort "substantial," rhetorically lending them a heft that suggests their social consequentiality and effectiveness. Song is not ephemeral in his characterization but rather socially, emotionally, and physically present, something that, like coffee, can be given and received, something whose warming effects can be felt. In imbuing song with corporeality, Marsden helps to explain its agency at the wake: how it comforts, uplifts, eases, helps, supports, and lightens the hearts of mourners. Singing is not simply an icon of the community's comfort, then, but also the means by which consolation is effected.[16] Put another way, singing both represents and accomplishes the community's intervention. (And, in fact, song is much more palpable, more present, than the solace of which it is a sign: it is only through acts such as singing that comforting is effected.)

Second, and more broadly, in drawing connections between musical experience, the experience of a physically palpable substance, and the affective and social experience of receiving comfort, Marsden's metaphor suggests how embodiment informs musical, affective, and social experience (see Clayton and Leante 2013). The idea of music as coffee, and coffee as comfort, captures something of the surroundingness and ongoingness of both song and solace. Moreover, these similarities of form may help to explain the apparent cueing relationship between them in the context of ritual: musical experiences prompt, with palpable impact, social and emotional ones to which they have an iconic connection (and vice versa).[17] When silence envelops mourners, they feel heartbroken; when song surrounds them, they feel comforted.

Marsden and Menow thus emphasize the socially consequential aspects of singing at the wake—its "indexically entailing" character, to use Silverstein's terminology[18]—rendering it an instantiation of the community's comfort and help. Indeed, Marsden's description invests music with a particular substantiality and corporeality, portraying singing as a palpable work of comforting and soothing.

This discussion of grieving and consolation brings to mind other foundational social-scientific writing on funerary practices: namely, Robert Hertz's idea of death as a "transitory state" (1960: 81); Arnold van Gennep's concept of mortuary observances as "rites of passage" between "one cosmic or social world [and] another" (1960: 10); and the elaboration of both of these by Peter Metcalf and Richard Huntington (1991). The latter authors suggest that funerary rites can be explored from three perspectives: by examining how mourners ceremonially dispose of the body of the deceased; by looking at the eschatological explanations concerning the dead body, the departed soul, and the relationship between them; and by considering how the community of the living gradually reintegrates itself in the absence of the departed.

Though all three routes of investigation might productively be pursued with respect to the wakes considered here, it is the last of them that seems most closely bound up with what musicians at the wake understand themselves to be doing: extending comfort. Singing at wakes acknowledges and seeks to ameliorate the early stages of the transitional period during which those who mourn reintegrate themselves as a social group without the deceased—and during which, from an eschatological point of view, the departed soul passes "from the visible society of the living into the invisible society of the dead" (Hertz 1960: 86). As Hertz remarks, "The brute fact of physical death is not enough to consummate death in people's minds: the image of the recently deceased is still part of the system of things of this world, and looses itself from them only gradually by a series of internal partings" (1960: 81). The comforting and soothing that Menow and Marsden describe might be understood as attempts to address the initial jarring moments of what will be a long and difficult passage. They are additionally, however, acts that acknowledge and affirm particular social and musical ways of approaching such transitions.

Part II: Christian Song and Social Particularity

Although the wake is the most auspicious site for the performance of Christian song, hymns and gospel music are heard in many other contexts, including church services and revival meetings, as well as at more secular events such as coffeehouses and jam sessions. And although Christian song is often a medium through which the community expresses its support, it also lends itself to performances of personhood and small-group allegiance. In the ritual context of the wake, the emphasis is on community and solidarity; but in other contexts, individualism and struggles over leadership are more evident. This is not to say that idiosyncratic behavior or conflict are never in evidence at wakes, but rather that their more dramatic manifestations tend to be muted inside ritual spaces and more evident in secular ones. Sacred singing, then, does not only express community solidarity and comfort, although this is its most important role; it also provides opportunities for expressions of social particularity, assertions of leadership, and negotiations between persons and groups. As the discussion moves, in this second half of the chapter, toward the spikier and more contentious aspects of the musical sociability I observed, it is important to remember that they constitute only part of the story. Manitoban aboriginal musical life is neither an unrelenting struggle nor a series of alienated performances; the solidarity manifest in funerary observances is just as important or more so. But the communal interactions at the wake, and the individuality and contentiousness that come into focus outside it, are better understood in relation to one another. Considering them side by side presents a more complete picture of the social and musical lives of working-class northern Algonquians.

EARLY ANTHROPOLOGICAL ACCOUNTS OF NORTHERN ALGONQUIAN SOCIABILITY

R. W. Dunning, A. I. Hallowell, Ruth Landes, and Leonard Mason, who conducted ethnographic research in northern Algonquian communities in Ontario and Manitoba from the 1930s to the 1950s, describe a sociability characterized by small-group solidarity and individualism and in which leadership and power were regarded with ambivalence (see Dunning 1959, Hallowell 1955 and 1992, Landes 1968, Mason 1967). Their characterizations of mid-twentieth-century social interactions, outlined in brief here, resonate in certain respects with my own observations of musical mutuality, even as they seem problematic in other ways.

At the time these authors did their research, small, relatively independent kin-based groups had an important role in northern Algonquian social life and economic activity. Bands whose economies centered on hunting and trapping typically lived together in villages during the summer months, their subsistence needs met by fishing. During the winter, however, the summer village split up into smaller groups. Each of these was typically led by two male trappers and worked a clearly delineated territory (Hallowell 1955: 119; Mason 1967: 30, 39; see also Dunning 1959: 54–64; Landes 1968: 5–7). These territories were large, and accordingly groups tended to live some distance from one another. The early ethnographers perceived an analogue between these atomistic living arrangements and broader social structures, suggesting that, although social bonds could be close within small groups, there was relatively little integration at the level of the larger community (see Mason 1967: 39). And while community leaders existed—typically male elders gifted with knowledge and special spiritual powers—there were no strong or permanent governing or judicial structures (Mason 1967: 39; Hallowell 1955: 361–62, 1992: 35–36). Indeed, there seemed to be resistance to certain forms of social hierarchy: Mason reported (based on fieldwork conducted largely in 1940) that the Oxford House Cree had "no need for a supervisor or chief to direct their activities" (1967: 46).

These anthropologists also identified individualism and autonomy as significant aspects of northern Algonquian personality.[19] Hallowell, for instance, emphasizes the importance of personal experience in northern Ojibwe spiritual life and in the dream fast, one of its central rituals. He explains that before reaching puberty, Ojibwe boys would fast in the forest alone for several days, awaiting a dream in which a guardian or tutelary would appear (Hallowell 1992: 87–88). This other-than-human person would help the young man throughout the rest of his life, determining to some degree his destiny, giving him blessings that assisted him in hunting or healing the sick, and in some cases imparting magical abilities (Hallowell 1992: 88). The relationship with this guardian was a source of personal assurance. As Hallowell writes, "[During the dream fast, every] boy met the 'persons' on whom he could most firmly depend in time of need, and a few acquired exceptional skills and powers that carried the greatest prestige in Ojibwa society. To a man, relations with other than human persons were an enduring source of his inner security" (1992: 88). Such relationships were further personalized in that there were prohibitions against talking about one's guardian or one's dreams of them (1992: 88–89). Thus in Hallowell's telling the encounter at the core of an Ojibwe man's spiritual development was highly individualized: not only did it occur in the course of a dream and during a solitary fast; it was also meant to be kept secret from others.[20]

Although the foregoing account emphasizes the role of spiritual experiences in the lives of men, both men and women could meet dream visitors, receive blessings from them, and become renowned spiritual leaders. Those so blessed were frequently able to promote health and long life, but they also, in some cases, had the power to make enemies sick or even kill them (Angel 2002: 161–62; Hallowell 1992: 36; see also Landes 1968: 9–20, 57–67). Thus their leadership was a mature manifestation of the individuated and individuating powers and abilities bequeathed by a personal guardian spirit. But while this spiritual power was greatly valued, it could have a negative valence, being associated also with the ability to harm others.

These early ethnographic accounts suggest that charismatic leaders and their "dream power" (McNally 2009) were regarded with ambivalence: with fear and suspicion as well as respect. Some powerful figures, for instance, were suspected of attacking persons in secret in response to social slights (Hallowell 1992: 36; Landes 1968: 9–20, 57–67). Dream power thus seems to have been both valued and problematic: even as it aided in hunting and healing, it could lead to jealous competition and generate fear, suspicion, and resistance.[21] If dream power was two-sided, it was also dynamic and contested. Powerful individuals engaged in struggles and even duels with one another, conducted through spiritual rather than physical means.[22] Further, spiritual power was subject to spectacular falls and reversals. Powerful persons were often expected to transgress against others and consequently "to be felled eventually by supernatural retribution" or by more conventional and secular means (Landes 1968: 14–15, 44).[23]

Michael McNally (2009) argues that there has been an excessive preoccupation with individualism in the early anthropological literature on the Ojibwe. As a corrective, he points to historical evidence of social structures extending well beyond the family hunting group and the band, and to the collective character of a great deal of traditional sacred practice. He observes that traditional Ojibwe speech practices, including the use of kinship terms for non-relatives (or rather those who "might be relatives"), locate speakers in "a web of relations and obligations" and shape a "disposition that looks expectantly for relationship," even among those who are not kin (2009: 85–86), remarks that have rich implications for my arguments concerning the privileging of intimacy in chapters 6 and 7. He goes on to point out that this network of kinship and obligation includes spiritual beings and other-than-human persons within the natural environment (2009: 86–88).

During fieldwork I too was struck by the importance of community, and of larger networks of obligation and interrelation, and for this reason spend much of this chapter, and this volume more generally, reflecting on musical manifestations of collectivity (both intimate and imagining). All the same, certain observations made by earlier ethnographers also resonated with my experiences. Individualism, small-group allegiance, charismatic leadership, and a complex set of negotiations and ambivalences regarding authority were significant aspects of my social and musical encounters, and I accordingly turn my attention to them here. Throughout, it should be borne in mind that these ostensibly atomistic aspects of sociability inevitably stood in productive dialogue with commitments to community, a seeming contradiction I attempt to resolve below and in chapter 5.

In turning to the pricklier aspects of sociability I observed, it seems appropriate to remark on some aspects of the work of the anthropologists cited above—and my own writing. The quoted authors wrote from a disciplinary stance of methodological relativism (see M. Brown 2008) and out of a concern for the preservation of cultural differences threatened by colonialism. They did not seek to extend criticism or condemnation from some supposedly higher ground—although Harold Hickerson has interpreted anthropological writing on northern Algonquians in this way (see 1967: 321; for a more nuanced yet nevertheless critical account of this literature, see Angel 2002). Rather, they attempted to convey indigenous differences using language that was sometimes uncongenial to neutral representation. This book in some respects follows in that tradition, examining some of the productive tensions in northern Algonquian public culture while highlighting the stakes of difference in a national context where what is perceived to be troubled and troubling alterity easily becomes an excuse for further attempts to assimilate.[24]

For some readers, the arguments about northern Algonquian sociability set forth here may seem to be in danger of reiterating the essentialism of earlier authors, adding to them a kind of insistent autochthonism. It is accordingly important to advance these arguments in careful and nuanced fashion, but also to explain why they are being made. This has to do with the larger national context in which indigenous alterity exists. It is not simply that this volume seeks to convey, to those who may be unfamiliar with them, something about Manitoban aboriginal approaches to rhythm and ensemble; drinking and abstinence; individuality, collectivity, and leadership; and so on. It also hopes to show how these can differ from those that are dominant and unmarked within Manitoban or Canadian public culture. In that context, indigenous cultural differences can seem aesthetically, socially, and politically disreputable—a manifestation of counterpublicity. The aim is in part, then, to render northern Algonquian cultural practices more intelligible to cultural outsiders, and to render the often unquestioned practices and judgments of these outsiders less transparent and more visible, less universal and more provincial. But it is especially to draw attention to how the relationship between Canadian and aboriginal publics is shaped by what the former holds to be socially and aesthetically normative, and by its impulse to intervene and assimilate.

Drawing attention to the implications of these socially problematized differences is complicated—but not precluded—by the fact that northern Algonquian cultural practice is neither homogeneous nor unchanging. "Aboriginal Winnipeggers" are diverse with respect to history, language, belief, experience, cultural practice, and class. Moreover, their cultural practices change over time, subject to contestation and historical transformation[25] (the latter occurring not only internally or through contact with other indigenous groups, but over centuries of contact—precolonial, colonial, and postcolonial—with nonindigenous people and institutions). Yet, at the same time, the differences between indigenous and unmarked mainstream habitus are solid enough that they impact the way nonindigenous Manitobans react to the music, social comportment, and political activities of northern Algonquians. Such reactions have implications for arts funding, for mainstream public discourse, and for Canadian law. It accordingly seems to me less irresponsible to attempt to discuss such differences than to hesitate to address them at all.

"YOU BECOME YOURSELF": MUSIC AND INDIVIDUALITY

Returning to the main thread: although sacred song has a particularly close connection to the collective observance of rites of passage, it also affords opportunities for the performance of individuality and charismatic leadership—as well as the negotiation of the latter. The musical events I observed and took part in during my fieldwork were moments when performers revealed—and performed into being—deeply distinctive musical personalities. Singers often approached hymns and gospel songs in idiosyncratic ways, especially when it came to rhythmic elements (compare Whidden 2007: 84–89), and accordingly coffeehouses, jam sessions, and even wakes brought together singers and instrumentalists who had distinctly different conceptions of the same songs. In such situations, accompanists had to set aside their own musical ideas and respond on the spur of the moment to soloists' unexpected musical trajectories. Participatory discrepancies (Keil 1987) abounded in these unscripted collaborations, as musicians imposed their individuality upon one another's minds and music-making bodies.[26]

Musicians affirmed that singing was a manifestation of personhood. When I interviewed Emery Marsden, I asked him what he liked about the gospel music that he sang. His response, quoted earlier in more abbreviated form, led into a discussion of musical individuality.

DUECK: What do you like about the sound of country gospel music?

MARSDEN: It's like having coffee. Every thing of it: the rhythm, the timing of
the music,...the words, the comforting words of a song....I can feel it, I can
feel those songs....It was in my heart, boiling, and here it is—when I sing
it, when I play it—here it is, here's what's in my heart! Here's what was in
my heart that wanted to come out—here it is! Just like that. And I believe
that every, each individual has that...I believe you got, you got music in you,
too....You hear music and then you say to yourself, "Oh, I, I hope I can sing
like that if I tried singing." And then all of a sudden you're fighting in yourself
up there, saying, "I can't do it." Well, and then you're not going to do it! Why
don't you just reverse that thought and say, "I can do it!" And then you'll do
it! Maybe even if it takes for you to imitate somebody, imitate that person!
But...somewhere down the road after you imitate that person, the *real you*
is going to come out. And all of a sudden *you're* going to be the singer, all of a
sudden *you're* the man with the wheel. And that's how it goes.

At this point in the interview I told Marsden that since beginning my fieldwork in
Winnipeg I had heard many singers, each with his or her own different approach
to rhythm and melody. I asked whether it was important to him to be unique.

MARSDEN: Yes. Just what I just told you. All of a sudden, you become yourself.
All of a sudden you have your own timing. All of a sudden you have your
own melody. All of a sudden your heart is singing different from—from
someone else's heart. And that's what I mean about, "first imitate someone."
And then later on what happens is that music boils inside you, and all of
a sudden it comes out in a different form. Just like you say, a different
melody,...different timing, different—same words—but different sound.
That's why I say, "Your own heart will make its own music."

Two important ideas emerge in Marsden's response. The first is a concept of musical individuality. At the beginning, he explains, you may need to imitate someone,
but eventually "you become yourself," coming into your own melody and your own
timing. Musical performance is the outward-oriented communication of an inner
uniqueness (a distinctness differentiable, it seems to me, from that celebrated in
familiar Western concepts of the artist).[27] Second, Marsden returns to the coffee metaphor he introduced when describing music at the wake. Earlier in the
interview, this metaphor rhetorically rendered music substantive, vesting it with
a physicality and warmth that (I suggest) helped to account for its social effectiveness as a comfort to the bereaved. Here, something similar occurs. Music, boiling
out of a musician's heart, is the tangible manifestation of uniqueness (compare
Lassiter, Ellis, and Kotay 2002: 112). Indeed, even in the telling of it, Marsden's
words boil out of him: "Here it is—when I sing it, when I play it—here it is, here's
what's in my heart!"

The metaphor suggests a way of reconciling community and individuality, the two concepts structuring this chapter. At the wake, song is a gift: it comforts the bereaved and honors the deceased (or indeed helps the deceased to depart): "Here it is!" Song may boil out of an individual, but it contributes to the communal task of extending comfort: for all its personal specificity, it is incorporated in the fundamentally communal work of the wake. Hallowell suggests a similar reconciliation, writing of the special relationship initiated through the dream fast: he argues that the individuated powers and gifts acquired through relationships to guardians allowed adults to make their most significant contributions to community life: as hunters, leaders of ceremonies, and healers (Hallowell 1992: 88).

SMALL GROUPS

Small-group solidarity also remains a significant element in contemporary musical and social life. My Winnipeg consultants did not divide their year, as did rural Cree and Ojibwe in the mid-twentieth century, into a winter spent trapping with a small, kin-based residential group and a summer spent in a larger communal village, although some of the older ones trapped in their younger years. Nevertheless, small groups, particularly family groups, were significant. Socially, family allegiance was strong and often primary: an offense to a relative meant that the family had been aggrieved—whether or not the relative was in the wrong, it often seemed to me. I quickly learned to speak more carefully about people's relatives than I had been accustomed to, lest I jeopardize friendships.

Family also played an important role in aboriginal music and dance scenes, including in square dancing, where members of dance groups were often related, and country and country gospel music, where family-based ensembles were also common. In such groups, as well as in small sacred choirs such as those that sang at Edward Guiboche's wake, performers often settled into relatively agreed-upon yet metrically or otherwise irregular interpretations of songs and tunes. In short, highly individualized takes on songs became the basis for collective music making. As with the fiddle tunes discussed in chapter 2, the ability of such groups to navigate the twists and turns of a metrically irregular song was a manifestation of the social and musical intimacy of the collaborators—a sounding together that bore witness to lives lived together.

Collaborations were frequently necessary, both within and beyond the family unit, because money was tight (compare Samuels 2004). Partnerships allowed musicians to share vehicles and transportation costs and to travel long distances to events that mattered to them but that they might not otherwise have been able to attend: wakes, funerals, coffeehouses, and jam sessions. Material considerations determined collaboration to only a certain extent, however, in a context where performers were often resolutely independent. Within groups, arguments and fissures were common. Family allegiances were generally sturdier than others, but even there tensions could erupt. There was a kind of atomism (as Hallowell puts it) in musical life: performers got into disagreements, fell out, and allied themselves with new partners, occasionally getting past old differences to collaborate with former colleagues. Yet this centrifugal tendency was part of a larger pattern: these groupings and regroupings, however fractious, made possible larger, collective musical gatherings, wakes in particular.

A tendency toward fission was also evident in the great range of religious, denominational, and repertorial affiliations among the musicians I knew. Many people maintained connections with Anglican and Catholic churches, which have had long-standing, although often problematic, connections to First Nations and Métis communities. However, Evangelical and Charismatic churches had made significant inroads in Native communities and in the city of Winnipeg. Meanwhile, traditional sacred practices were undergoing a revival and reimagining. The upshot was that aboriginal people could associate themselves with a wide variety of spiritual paths and song repertoires. Singers' religious affiliations determined to some degree the songs and collaborators with which they were most comfortable as well as the extent to which they could participate with other musicians at wakes, coffeehouses, and traditional events.[28]

These differing musical repertoires helped to produce and distinguish social spaces, something particularly evident in the case of drum songs. Although these were sometimes performed at wakes and burials, they stood apart from other mortuary music in significant ways: they were musically distinct from hymns and gospel songs, and they were frequently performed separately, on different instruments (conceptualized in very different ways), by different musicians. Feelings ran high about drum songs. Some embraced them, along with traditional ceremonies, as a part of a heritage that had been suppressed by colonialism and Christianization, and they regarded Christianity and its associated musical repertoires negatively. Others, in sharp contrast, shunned drum song, considering it "the devil's music." Still others appreciated both drum song and gospel music and practiced Christianity alongside traditional spiritual observances.

Songs associated with the Charismatic movements of the 1990s (see Poloma 1997: 258) also created musical divisions. These often strayed from the harmonic structures characteristic of older hymns and gospel songs, and, accordingly, from the musical lingua franca that tended to facilitate collaborations between gospel and country musicians at jam sessions and coffeehouses (see chapters 3 and 5). This could make interactions difficult; nevertheless, such songs were regularly performed in the same places as other kinds of Christian music. When songs left dominant conventions too far behind, other musicians would simply sit out, letting those who knew them best accompany themselves.

This repertorial factionalism notwithstanding, there were a number of socially and musically aggregating elements to these interactions, as already suggested. Many performers were familiar with certain harmonic and formal conventions that structured a range of genres, including country music, fiddle music, hymnody, and gospel song. This knowledge allowed them to move confidently between styles, and consequently between social spaces, and to make musical contributions even in contexts where they were not entirely familiar with certain songs or tunes. A second factor involved a group of widely known hymns and gospel songs, most of which were structured according to the aforementioned conventions. This loose repertoire, typically sung in English and in a popular country style to guitar accompaniment, went by the name "country gospel music." Singers and listeners from many different denominations performed it, and clergy accommodated it at a number of the Anglican and Catholic services I attended. The shared repertoire likewise eased first-time collaborations, including at wakes and coffeehouses (see chapter 5). The wake, as mentioned, was a third socially centripetal practice. At such gatherings, repertorial and denominational differences were typically of secondary importance to the broader tasks of honoring the deceased and comforting the bereaved. A range of sacred traditions was often welcome at such events, albeit sometimes in clearly delineated spaces.

GOSPEL MUSIC, LEADERSHIP AND RESISTANCE

During fieldwork there were many occasions when consultants revealed an ambivalence regarding authority, sometimes in ways that were reminiscent of the accounts of mid-twentieth-century ethnographers. Certainly they honored elders and deferred to them (see McNally 2009), but they regularly expressed misgivings about, and demonstrated resistance to, other kinds of leaders. This was frequently the case, for instance, with community and political leaders, whom I often heard accused of misdeeds, embezzlement, and the inequitable distribution of collective resources. Many such allegations seemed speculative, but occasionally egregious behavior on the part of some leader or other came to light, resulting in a dramatic reversal of fortune.

Leadership was also a problematic when it came to musical events. This was in part because musical and political spheres overlapped: indigenous governments and institutions regularly sponsored festivals, concerts, and jamborees, and musicians performed to support politicians during election campaigns. Whether or not musicians were invited to perform at particular events was regularly and disapprovingly characterized as "politics"; that is, as a reward for political allegiance or support. But leadership was also subject to contestation and controversy at more local, interpersonal levels. At one coffeehouse I visited regularly, attendees complained or joked loudly when the master of ceremonies preached too long or made what they considered to be inappropriate requests for money. And rumors circulated regarding the organizers of musical events and (especially) what they did with any monies raised at them.

A specifically musical negotiation of leadership often took place in the course of musical interaction. This was especially true at participatory events such as coffeehouses and jamborees, where a steady stream of singers would perform over the span of an evening, accompanied by a house band. Here musical collaboration was often inexact, and accompanists had to stay attentive to soloists, readjusting their musical responses from moment to moment. Sometimes this was because they did not know the song being performed. Yet even when the song was familiar, it was often difficult to predict the direction in which a singer would take it. This was not helped by the way some singers paid almost no attention to their accompanists. Conversely, singers sometimes had to accommodate instrumentalists who had their own ideas about how the rhythm should go. Frequently there resulted a kind of heterophonic homophony, in which musicians fell in and out of step with one another (see chapter 5).

Tensions could arise between leaders and supporting players. Some of these were verbalized, with those who preferred a metrically regular style criticizing others who performed more freely. Emery Marsden performed in a freer style, so when I interviewed him I asked about the difficulties of making music when musicians had different ideas about how a song went:

DUECK: If everyone sings the same song different, then when you have a bunch of musicians on the same stage trying to do the song, does it sometimes get tough?

MARSDEN: All the time, all the time. One thing is, people...just like you say, it is always tough—for the perfectionist. But if you're not a perfectionist, and if you're liberated, you'll let it go. But if you're a perfectionist, get your own band. Stick with your own band. Stick with your own group. Don't go and get angry at somebody that's making music to God. Because you're actually getting mad at God when you get mad at someone that's singing—I just told you. Because it's coming out of your heart—that's music! [Laughs] That's how it goes.

Marsden acknowledged that musical differences could generate tension between musicians who played in a rhythmically free style and "perfectionists"—a category that, I presume, included those who insisted on playing with the "correct" timing. He also suggested a solution: perfectionists could quit playing with strangers and work with musicians they knew—and with whom they could always get what they wanted. But his response was also a defense of the unpredictable style: music came from the heart and accordingly varied from performer to performer.

Musicians who performed in a metrically regular style typically took a different view. Stirling Ranville, founder of Winnipeg's oldest and longest-running weekly gospel coffeehouse at the time I interviewed him, was committed to metrical regularity and critical of musicians who performed "out of time":

The *worst* thing, the *worst* thing that can happen to you as a singer on that stage is when someone is out of time. Even the most *seasoned* singer

Figure 4.3 EMERY MARSDEN. Photo by the author.

and musician cannot perform if someone's out of time. If you're on the wrong chord, you can wing it. Someone hits a wrong chord, you can ignore that. But if someone's out of time, it's just—it's no longer music.

He went on to say that out-of-time performances used to bother him so much that he would get angry and walk off the stage. When I interviewed him, however, he had reconciled himself to playing with musicians who played out of time, although he did consider it his duty to try to help them to change their ways.

Thus Marsden and Ranville both acknowledged the potential for musical differences to generate interpersonal tensions. Moreover, they deployed two distinct definitions of music, appealing to two different guiding principles. On one side: music comes from the singer's heart and will accordingly have its own unique timing: "That's music!" On the other: performances should follow established rhythmic codes: "If someone's out of time...it's no longer music." One appealed to the heart, the other to convention. The disagreement suggests the dynamic negotiations of authority that went on in musical interactions. Attempts by some to get music to sound "correct"—by according with metrical principles, for instance—were continually frustrated by resistance from singers who were confident that their way of doing things was just fine.

An analogous struggle was often embodied in musical interactions themselves—and, more specifically, in the moment-to-moment negotiations that occurred when one or more musicians performed in different metrical styles. Ranville described such encounters:

> If you miss a beat in a song once, the *whole band* has to *shift* somewhere along the line...and...unless you have a *good* band, it might take them a whole verse before they click back into where they should be. It's like a train going off the rail. Or the beat goes upside down. Like if you're going "one-two, one-two, one-two" and then all of a sudden it's going "two-one, two-one," you know? And then everybody looking at each other on the stage and wondering what's going wrong.

In ensemble situations among nonintimates, singers often performed individualized versions of gospel songs that confounded accompanists' expectations and contradicted their ideas about how the music should go. Inevitably, there were moments when "the beat went upside down" and accompanists had to scramble to get back on track. In the course of such encounters, singing soloists impressed their musical individuality and authority upon collaborators in a physically palpable way.[29]

This is not to suggest that the musical leadership of singing soloists was uncontested. I sometimes observed a kind of nonchalance or imperturbability among accompanying musicians, a disinclination to attend too closely to the way the parts were wandering in and out of sync with one another. Indeed, on some occasions singers who performed in a metrically regular style led ensembles made up of accompanists who were accustomed to playing nonmetrically. In these situations it was the singers who experienced in an especially embodied form the negotiation of authority. This sense of contestation is evident in Stirling Ranville's description of how he sometimes had to pull musicians into step with him, lest he lose his place himself: "[In] most cases, a musician behind me can't pull me off the track, because I've learned how to *wrestle* them back."[30] Later in the same interview Ranville described how a respected Manitoban fiddler had dramatically brought a musically disorganized house band into line:

> [There] are some musicians who can really *pull* a band together no matter who they are. A good example that I heard one time was Cliff Maytwayashing. Fiddle player. There was a really confused-sounding band on the stage, and it was a jamboree, too, 'cause it was different people coming up, I think. Nothing they did was good, and I was wondering: what an awful band. Cliff Maytwayashing was called up. He took up his fiddle, went up, and started to play, and he *pulled* every one of those musicians together. Just like a—reminds me of a really good dog team. When the lead dog just yanks, he puts them all in line.

In a variety of social situations, it was problematic to interfere with the autonomy of others, and consequently the leadership of those other than elders was often subject to resistance (in various forms, including wariness, criticism, jealousy, and acts of leveling). In musical contexts, too, people valued autonomy. It is perhaps for this reason that musical leadership could seem to involve *pulling* people together and *wrestling* them into position, to use Ranville's words. Being imposed upon was often met by embodied resistance.

Yet, to return to a point raised earlier, musical individuation is a fundamentally social relation to others. In aboriginal gospel singing it emerges in especially dramatic ways during moments of musical performance, when charismatic singers impress their idiosyncrasies upon the minds and bodies of accompanists and collaborators. Complicating matters, musical individuation can become the basis for certain forms of musical collectivity. As is argued in chapter 2 with respect to fiddling, members of small performing groups sometimes come to share a unique approach to certain vocal and instrumental pieces, which thus become musical manifestations of solidarity and intimacy. And when solo singers share their musical particularities at a wake, they take their place amongst a community of iconoclasts similarly extending comfort to the bereaved.

The ritual and expressive practices explored in this chapter and chapter 5 should be understood to be guided by aesthetic priorities somewhat different from those that structure prominent concert practices: these are "participatory" rather than "presentational" performances, to use Turino's (2008) useful categories.[31] They nevertheless differ in significant ways from those Turino looks at: there is little of the "security in [rhythmic] constancy" or "cloaking of individual contributions" Turino describes as characteristic of participatory practices.[32] I would suggest that this is in part because musical sociability in northern Algonquian communities is often individuating as well as collective. This should hardly be surprising given the traditional importance of highly personal experiences and knowledge (sacred, musical, and occupational) in Cree and Ojibwe life.

Conclusion

Manitoban Algonquian people deploy Euro-American genres of music and assembly (the latter including the wake and the coffeehouse), but in ways that seem distinctively aboriginal. The wake, in indigenous practice, has become an arena in which the blessings and songs of gifted individuals contribute to communal gestures of comfort and assistance. Less formal performance venues such as the coffeehouse, meanwhile, provide arenas for the performance and collective musical negotiation of personal distinctiveness and authority. In these respects and others, Christian singing traditions resonate with aspects of social and religious practice described in the works of anthropologists writing in the middle of the twentieth century.[33]

Paradoxically, performances of Christian song can be manifestations of both comforting collectivity and social particularity.[34] This is aptly reflected in Emery Marsden's coffee metaphor, which represents singing as both a vehicle through which a person's heart makes its unique contribution and the means by which the community extends its comfort to the bereaved. More broadly, practices of Christian song appear effective on more than one level. They extend collective comfort, establish the musical and social distinctiveness of individuals, and create arenas in which charismatic leadership is asserted and challenged. In doing so, however, they also affirm and extend certain long-standing modalities of northern Algonquian sociability.

* * * * *

Christian song is not only heard in socially intimate contexts such as the wake; it also fills coffeehouses and concert halls, plays over the radio and on YouTube, and circulates on compact discs and MP3s. In short, it addresses and constitutes a public. The publicness that emerges is nevertheless deeply grounded in indigenous intimacies: the music of comfort, the sounds of family collaboration, and the sometimes spiky interactions of musical iconoclasts. This publicness, and these intimacies, are the subject of chapter 5, which focuses on music making in a public venue in Winnipeg's North End.

Preface to Chapter 5

Musical Materials, Performance, and Efficacy

The following short study looks at a recorded performance that exemplifies the metrical irregularity characteristic of much contemporary aboriginal Christian song. This in turn allows a detailed discussion of the metapragmatic theory that informs the understandings of intimacies, publics, and musical and cultural practice laid out in this volume. A few key points can be introduced here at the outset. First, musical and social action establishes coherence as it both responds to and is consequential within its context of occurrence. Second, it establishes coherence in part through the regimentation of other responding-and-consequential actions (hence the "meta" in "metapragmatics"). Third, these features of responsiveness, consequentiality, and regimentation are evident in micro and macro contexts alike: a musical performance comes into being through the same kinds of processes as do genres—and, similarly, publics and cultural practices. Understood in this way, musical and cultural activity is never static or solid (although genres, musics, and cultures often give the impression of "complex wholes"), but rather always being performatively extended. Finally, agents from different cultural backgrounds often respond to and regiment the music and social activity they encounter in different ways; in doing so, they not only extend their own cultural practices but also undertake the transformation and translation of others.

During fieldwork I came to know of Hubert Thomas as a respected singer of Cree hymns who regularly performed at wakes and other gatherings.[1] His eminence stemmed in part from his public profile: around the time I began my research, he had released a five-volume CD set entitled *Cree Hymns* on Cherish, the gospel music imprint of Sunshine Records. He was also, clearly, a proficient singer in the tradition in which he performed: Sunshine's owner, Ness Michaels, told me that Thomas had recorded several compact discs' worth of songs—scores of hymns—in a single long session.

Transcribed in Figure P5.1 below is the first verse of "Keya Oopimachihiwāo," as recorded on *Cree Hymns Vol. 1*. The hymn is a version of "Sun of My Soul, Thou Saviour Dear," written by John Keble in 1820 and published in 1827 (Taylor 1989: 174).[2] Thomas probably sang it from a reprint of the 1927 edition of

Tactus (notated as quarter note) proceeds at 108 bpm. Eighths are swung.
Small noteheads indicate melodic embellishments.

Figure P5.1 "Keya Oopimachihiwāo" (traditional). Shown here is verse 1 as performed by Hubert Thomas on *Cree Hymns, Vol. 1.*

Reverend J. A. Mackay's *Psalms and Hymns in the Language of the Cree Indians of the Diocese of Saskatchewan, North-West America*.[3] The melody is a version of the well-known tune "Hursley," used to set English-language versions of the hymn. The tune is not notated in the Mackay hymnbook, however. Indeed, most aboriginal-language songbooks in Manitoba contain only words, and it seems probable that the melodies of hymns have been transmitted primarily by ear since they were introduced in the nineteenth century.[4] Thomas is likely to have learned the tune aurally; I did not know any gospel singers who read music.

Nelson Menow translated the lyrics of the first verse from the Cree as follows: "You are the Lord, Sun of my soul. [Not a shadow in this world] will fall on me."

Thomas's version of the hymn is metrically irregular: although the tactus (again, the main beat, notated here as a quarter note) is steady, the grouping is

Table P5.1 **Structure of "Keya Oopimachihiwão"**

Section	Subsection	Length (pulses)	Harmonic content	Cadence strength and type	Ant. or cons. phrase group
Intro		7	I	—	—
Verses	Phrase 1	13	I–V–I	Weak (perfect auth. cadence)	Antecedent
	Phrase 2	13	I–V	Strong (half cadence)	
	Phrase 3	12	V–I	Weak (imperfect auth. cadence)	Consequent
	Phrase 4	13	IV–I–V–I	Strong (perfect auth. cadence)	
Coda		2	I	—	--

not. It seems to be in twos at some points but indeterminate or in threes at others. As the beaming of notes and patterning of accents indicate, the guitar accompaniment establishes a duple pattern at the beginning of the performance and at the ends of the first, second, and fourth lines of each verse. At the beginning of the first sung phrase, there is no clear sense of grouping, but a little later a faint sense of tripleness emerges, largely imparted by the placement of the harmonic changes, but perhaps also subtly evident in the strumming of the guitar. These rhythmic irregularities do not betray an overall lack of organization: the performance is in other respects rigorously structured. Thomas repeats the rhythmic idiosyncrasies of the first verse in each subsequent one, for instance: throughout, the first, second, and fourth phrases are thirteen pulses long, and the third phrase, twelve pulses (see Table P5.1).

Pragmatics and Metapragmatics in Musical Performance

Silverstein's metapragmatic theory of language and culture (see Silverstein 1993, 1997; Silverstein and Urban 1996) understands socially significant action to have a dual relationship to its context of occurrence: it is both *appropriate to* and *effective in* it.[5] Human sign activity—which is to say, socially significant acts, whether the wave of a hand, the strumming of a guitar, or the utterance of words or sentences—both acknowledges its environment and accomplishes something within it.[6] On the one hand, then, it is contingent, addressing or presuming other elements of its context; on the other, it is consequential, extending or transforming this context (see Figure P5.2).

Moreover, successful and coherent social activity is appropriate and effective at both micro and macro levels of interaction. On the micro level, it addresses its immediate "co-text." It acknowledges the interactive goings-on that surround

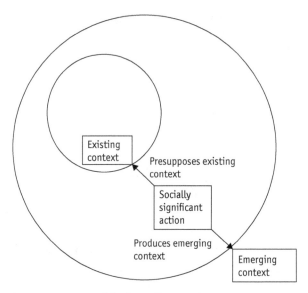

Figure P5.2 Metapragmatic model of socially significant action.

it—perhaps the preceding gesture in a musical performance or the last thing said in a rehearsal—and contributes something new. At the macro level, it takes into account the broader cultural context in which the interaction takes place—the likely presumptions of fellow musicians, for instance, or the broader expectations that surround a genre, such as when it should be performed and what it typically accomplishes. It also helps to extend them—typically affirming, but occasionally resisting or reshaping. In this way effective action also takes ideologies into account.[7]

As a consideration of musical elements in Hubert Thomas's performance of "Keya Oopimachihiwāo" suggests, musically significant activity is rooted to its context of occurrence by relations of contingency and consequentiality at even very basic levels. For instance, guitar downstroke <q> in Figure P5.3 follows downstroke <p> at roughly the same temporal interval that separated the preceding adjacent pairs <mn>, <no>, <op>, and so on. These spans are related by a similarity of length: they are temporal icons of one another.[8] But just as important,

Figure P5.3 Verse 1, line 3 of "Keya Oopimachihiwāo" as performed by Hubert Thomas.

they are connected by relationships of contingency and consequentiality. The temporal interval <pq> is contextually contingent upon the rhythm that has been set up by preceding downstrokes. At the same time, it is contextually consequential because it effects the incremental continuation of this rhythm and of the musical context more broadly. Such sign activity is efficacious in other ways, too, as is evident when we take into account listeners who engage with it. A regular pulse such as the one shown in Figure P5.3 engenders in listeners a corresponding, synchronized, and anticipatory response. Listeners entrain to the pulse, mentally anticipating the next beat (see Clayton, Sager, and Will 2004: 14–15; my account will focus on the sign activity that enables entrainment, rather than entrainment itself).

The appropriateness and effectiveness of basic melodic events might similarly be remarked upon. Each stable pitch that Thomas sings sustains a rate of vibration that distinguishes it from six other melodic pitch classes (or seven other pitches, since D appears in two octaves) that are salient within the context of the performance. On the one hand, this rate of vibration is contextually contingent, since it establishes the distinct identity of one pitch class only with respect to others. On the other hand, it is consequential, since it helps to establish an overall melodic context in which seven pitch classes stand in contradistinction to the others. Of course, this diatonic collection clearly preexisted Hubert Thomas's performance. And thus, again, deployments of musical signs engage, in addition to an immediate musical co-text, a broader music-cultural context: in this case, a tradition of melodic diatonicism. Yet such performances are not simply dependent upon music-cultural givens: in a small way they also affirm them, bring them into existence, qualify them, or contest them. (Similarly, listeners, hearing Thomas's performance and reacting to it, draw upon, and affirm, extend, or qualify, aspects of their own cultural provision: a Cree speaker might attempt to place Thomas's accent, while a classically trained singer might evaluate Thomas's singing with reference to Western ideologies of proper intonation.)

Thomas's performance in the recording studio was thus an "entextualization" or "enmusicalization" that brought a potential song into actual, coherent being in real time and in a particular social context.[9] It was additionally a realization and confirmation of a number of more abstract music-cultural structures. Complicating matters, the performance confirmed some such principles but not others. This is in part why it may sound distinctive—or wrong—to listeners who enmusicalize it themselves (that is, to those who listen to it). I will discuss this in more detail later.

I have suggested that coherent musical activity both acknowledges and extends its context, and on both micro and macro levels. But this coherence is possible because, or only insofar as, some musical activities regiment others. Such organization allows strumming on a guitar to be understood as a pattern, and this pattern to be understood as part of a song. This is in part why Figure P5.2 depicts a circle within a circle: to suggest a metapragmatic relationship in which signs

Figure P5.4 Verse 1, line 1 of "Keya Oopimachihiwāo" as performed by Hubert Thomas.

not only acknowledge but also structure other sign activity. Such regimentation occurs at many different levels but is perhaps easiest to see at the micro level, in the way certain musical signs organize others within their immediate musical co-text (see Silverstein 1993: 36–37).[10]

Metapragmatic regimentation is evident, for instance, in the organization of rhythmic elements in Thomas's performance of "Keya Oopimachihiwāo." The singer's guitar strumming consists of a series of downstrokes and upstrokes. He plays with a light swing, which makes the downstrokes slightly longer, and he also plays them slightly louder. These regimenting features help to designate the downstrokes (to enculturated listeners) as the set of musical onsets that carries the tactus.[11]

Occasionally a slightly longer rhythmic figure appears in the strumming: during the introduction and at cadence points (see Figure P5.4), Thomas introduces a pattern made up of two downstrokes and two upstrokes, <down–up–down–up>, that articulates the accent pattern <strongest–weak–strong–weak>. In this pattern the first downstroke (indicated by an accent in the transcription) sets all six strings vibrating, while the second (indicated by a tenuto mark) hits only the highest strings; upstrokes (unmarked) are comparatively quiet. This structure has coherence by dint of both internal and external regimentation: internally through the pattern of differentiated accents and externally through repetition: the accent pattern begins again after two beats, indicating the ending of one unit and the beginning of another (compare Lerdahl and Jackendoff 1983: 74–75).

For many listeners, the repeated strumming pattern will suggest duple meter. Other moments in the performance can suggest different kinds of metrical organization, however. Consider for instance the harmonic shift to D major that occurs near the end of the first line of the song, supporting the sung syllables "-chi-hi-" and the neighbor-note melodic figure <A–B–A>. These three beats are followed by a harmonic shift to G major, supporting the sung syllable "-wāo" and a melodic arrival on a prolonged G. All of this creates a brief sense of triple meter.[12] And yet there is little sense of any global metrical organization, either duple or triple.

Thoroughgoing triple meter is in fact in play throughout another enmusicalization of the same melody: the four-part arrangement of "Hursley" published

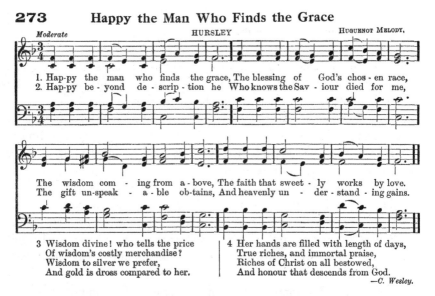

273   **Happy the Man Who Finds the Grace**

3 Wisdom divine! who tells the price
Of wisdom's costly merchandise?
Wisdom to silver we prefer,
And gold is dross compared to her.

4 Her hands are filled with length of days,
True riches, and immortal praise,
Riches of Christ on all bestowed,
And honour that descends from God.

—*C. Wesley.*

Figure P5.5 "Hursley" as it appears in *The New Canadian Hymnal*. ([Methodist Church (Canada)] 1917).

in the Canadian Methodist Church's *New Canadian Hymnal* of 1917 and shown in Figure P5.5. (The term "enmusicalization" is here extended to include acts of arranging and publication.) In the arrangement, harmonic shifts entail a clear sense of meter: when there is only a single harmonic change in a measure, for instance, it always arrives on the first beat (see mm. 1, 3, 4, 8, 12, 13, and 16). This metrical sense is reinforced by musical notation that specifies the durations of notes relative to one another, by barlines that appear after every three beats in the score, and by the time signature.

In fact, on the page the hymn evidences what might be called "maximal metricality" (see Dueck 2013b). The tactus (notated as a quarter note) falls into regular triple groupings that are nested within larger, quadruple, "hypermetrical" groupings, which are in turn nested within a still larger quadruple grouping.[13]

So, although the printed version of the hymn is thoroughly metricalized, Thomas's performance of it does not fall into any such steadily recurring pattern. The main beat stays steady, and duple and triple groupings occasionally emerge. Again, this is not to suggest large-scale musical structures are not present: both Thomas's version of "Hursley" and the one in the *New Canadian Hymnal* nest motives within phrases, phrases within antecedent-consequent groupings, antecedent-consequent groupings within verses, and verses within the song as a whole.[14] Nevertheless, Thomas does not appear to pursue this kind of structural thoroughness in the realm of rhythmic organization.

What Thomas's performance makes evident is that, in enmusicalizing songs and musical formulas, musicians realize some musical potentialities but not others, and that their realizations are informed by cultural practice. For instance, the <strongest–weak–strong–weak> strumming pattern often signals that what follows will be in duple meter, but this does not come to pass in Thomas's version, an outcome that is in keeping with the fluid approach to meter evident in many other Manitoban aboriginal performances. At the same time, he does realize some of that pattern's latent music-cultural associations, using it to establish an idiomatic sense of placeholding, expectation, and transition between phrases and verses. Similarly, the harmonic rhythm evident at a number of points in Thomas's performance would suggest triple meter to many listeners, yet the singer does not maintain that metrical structure. In this way his performance uncouples both the strumming pattern and the harmonic structure of the hymn from the maximally metrical matrices that often surround them, deploying them in a way apparently guided by a more minimal metricality. That he leaves some musical potentialities unrealized should not be understood as a fault in the performance; it rather indicates a kind of aesthetic "translation" of the elements in play (see Chakrabarty 2000: 88–96, 62–71).

It is not clear that Thomas's performance evidences a completely minimal metricality, in which the tactus constitutes the only stable metrical layer.[15] It seems evident, however, that the presence of certain metricalized elements (i.e., the strumming pattern and the harmonic rhythm of the song) does not necessitate the consistent continuation of the metrical structures that inform those elements. There are, of course, listeners and performers for whom the presence of such elements would create the expectation of consistent continuation, and for whom the combination of a triple-meter song with a duple-meter strumming pattern would seem infelicitous.

It is here that the broader contingent-and-consequential dynamics of musical practice come into better view—not between co-textual musical elements, but rather between musical performances and the social worlds in which they circulate. Publishing a recording or a hymnal is an act that (1) presumes and addresses a particular social context, "regimenting" it and (2) produces consequences within it. To begin with the first point, Hubert Thomas's recordings address an audience of listeners who find Cree hymns edifying,[16] who like them performed in a country gospel vocal style to guitar accompaniment, and who prefer, enjoy, or are simply not bothered by performances that take a flexible rhythmic approach. The *New Canadian Hymnal* hails an audience of Methodist singers and instrumentalists who find English-language hymns edifying and who prefer, enjoy, or are not bothered by music that is carefully regulated with respect to meter. Moving to the second point, when these mass-mediated forms are enmusicalized—listened to in the case of the CDs; sung, perhaps in congregational worship, in the case of the hymnal—they produce a wide variety of consequences, including in the realm of rhythmic response. The apparently metricalized elements in Thomas's performance engender metrical reactions in some listeners, the strumming pattern perhaps producing the expectation that subsequent musical events will continue to be organized by duple meter. Yet these elements do not cue the same metrical expectations in others, who simply expect the music to continue to maintain a steady tactus. Enmusicalized, the recording subverts the rhythmic expectations of some while unsettling those of others not at all.

This has implications for the ability of metrically irregular music to successfully constitute a listening public. Such music alienates some listeners, leaves others ambivalent, and captivates still others, all of this occurring in a social context in which the idea that music should have "good rhythm" continues to carry considerable ideological weight. In this context, acts of publication such as Thomas's *Cree Hymns* discs or the *New Canadian Hymnal* are both contingent upon and consequential within social imaginaries. They address publics whose members have in common certain kinds of sounds and practices, but they also actively extend and differentiate these publics, recruiting audiences to distinct rhythmic subject positions.

This is not to argue that there is some preexisting aboriginal public that only listens to metrically irregular music, or a nonaboriginal public that only listens to metrically regular music; as has been noted at several points already, such clear-cut distinctions do not exist. It is to argue, however, that *Cree Hymns*, and other such publications, are acts of world imagining that configure indigenous publicness in relation to particular rhythmic practices. It is furthermore to argue that performers, arrangers, and composers structure their music making with reference to culturally acquired patterns, and in a manner they understand to be appropriate to culturally attuned, listening subjects. Finally, it is to say that, as members of their publics perceive patterns of musical regimentation in the course of real-time engagement with this music—as they listen, analyze, or contribute to the accruing of music—they do so in accordance with cultural structures. And, crucially, they do not always perceive the same kinds of regimentation to be at work; indeed, they often have very different perspectives about what is "really" going on (see Silverstein 1993: 37; Goffman 1974). Broadcasts, recordings, and publications may address audiences of ideal listeners, but not all of these listeners are those idealized—and that is precisely where things get interesting.

* * * * *

This brief study has attempted to bring together metapragmatic theory and music analysis. It should be remarked that while metapragmatics offers a productive way to approach analysis, it does not supplant existing approaches. The point is not to advance audacious analytical interpretations that would be impossible to achieve using extant methods; indeed, the analytical interpretations presented in this preface are very straightforward. The point is rather that metapragmatics can be reconciled with music analysis and, more important, that the former complements the latter by emphasizing the social performativity of musical materials.

Metapragmatic analysis is here concerned, on the one hand, with how musical performances come to take coherent shape, and, on the other, with the relationships between these performances and their broader social and cultural environments. In this respect it is well suited to ethnomusicological research that moves between close examinations of musical performances and wider discussions of their social import (as shown in Monson 1996). But it is also valuable because it facilitates discussions of musical *interactions*, in terms that often get left out of studies of "the music itself": namely, agency, efficacy, and role. These are explored in chapter 5.

5

"We Don't Want to Say No to Anybody Who Wants to Sing"

Gospel Music in Coffeehouse Performance

The William Whyte School Coffeehouse

The North End, located above the railway yards that cut from east to west across much of central Winnipeg, has been a culturally diverse working-class neighborhood for at least a century. In the early 1900s, it had a largely eastern European population consisting of Jewish, Ukrainian, Russian, and Polish immigrants.[1] By the beginning of the 2000s the demographics had changed considerably: years of aboriginal urbanization had created one of the largest metropolitan concentrations of indigenous people in North America (for figures on early twenty-first-century residential patterns see Silver, Keeper, and MacKenzie 2005: 2–6). If the demographics had changed, the neighborhood's reputation had stayed much the same, for, as in the early twentieth century, the North End was widely held to be a troubled area. News reports and conversations with consultants who lived (or had lived) there identified poverty, violent crime, intoxicant abuse, and street gangs as particularly worrisome problems.[2]

On Wednesday nights during the 2002–3 school year, I regularly attended a coffeehouse at William Whyte School in the heart of the neighborhood. The school had introduced a number of social events on weeknights that year: in addition to the coffeehouse, there were social dances and square-dancing classes. Audrey Guiboche, the principal, and her husband, Edward (see chapter 4), understood these gatherings in part as safe spaces where people could enjoy themselves in an environment free from drugs, alcohol, and gang activity. The school supported the events by making the gymnasium available on weeknights, purchasing a public-address system and instruments, and arranging for the canteen to provide snacks and an inexpensive hot meal for attendees. Edward Guiboche organized the evenings and promoted them energetically in the community, frequently playing the role of master of ceremonies at them. As one of the most outgoing of my contacts in Winnipeg, he was eminently equipped for these tasks.

The events were open to all, but in various ways were particularly oriented to working-class indigenous people—from the North End and farther afield.[3] The school canteen typically sold aboriginal comfort food such as bannock and hamburger soup, and the gatherings prioritized genres of music and dance that were popular with Native people: gospel song, square dancing, and fiddle music. Thus the activities at William Whyte hailed a particular kind of public: a predominantly aboriginal audience whose members shared a similar habitus (on habitus see Bourdieu 1977).

On a typical Wednesday night, a steady stream of singers went up to the stage end of the gymnasium to perform with the house band, a loose group of regulars who accompanied on lead, rhythm, and bass guitar. The central figure in the ensemble, and its most regular member, was the lead guitarist, Nelson Menow, of Norway House (see chapter 3). Other frequent participants included Jack Meade and Edward Guiboche, who accompanied on rhythm guitar, and Emery Marsden, Albert Audy, and Eugene Moar, who played bass and rhythm guitars, depending on what was needed. I often played bass myself, typically early in the evening, before better bassists arrived, or later, when they got tired. Occasionally, fiddler Tommy Knott and keyboardist Fern Wood stopped by. The school provided a bass guitar and amplifier and an acoustic guitar in addition to the PA system; a number of musicians, including Menow, Knott, and Wood, regularly brought their own gear. As for the singers, many were amateurs who simply appreciated an opportunity to perform for an audience, but a number of more experienced musicians also attended. Some of the latter were involved in music ministries and were regular performers at events such as revival meetings, church services, and wakes. Others were active on the aboriginal country-music scene and sang at festivals, jamborees, and nightclubs. Many of these semiprofessionals, sacred and secular alike, disseminated their performances through recordings.[4]

Musical interactions at the coffeehouse enacted and extended a particular understanding of indigenous music culture in the public space of the William Whyte gymnasium. In order to take part effectively, musicians in the house band had to be familiar with certain repertoires and the musical grammars that organized them—as well as with certain aboriginal inflections of these. The physical space, instruments, and sound equipment at William Whyte might have facilitated musical performances in a number of genres, but the coffeehouse focused on Christian song—"country gospel," as organizers and participants referred to it. Country gospel was in many respects the same music heard at aboriginal wakes. It included hymns, gospel songs, and country songs on sacred themes, sung in English, Cree, and Ojibwe.

While country gospel might appear to have been constituted around a diverse set of musical genres, it was in fact unified by a set of stylistic norms it shared with classic country music (see chapter 3). The songs tended to be strophic; employ a basic I–IV–V harmonic palette in the keys of G, D, C, A, or E; make use of antecedent-consequent phrasing; and have a hierarchized cadential grammar (in which, for instance, weaker cadences on the dominant were paired with stronger ones on the tonic). Singers employed a somewhat pinched and nasal vocal sound, decorated melodies with expressive vocal breaks and bends (see Fox 2004: 279–83), and were supported by lightly swinging rhythmic accompaniments and rocking bass lines. There were occasional instrumental solos and interludes. The near-ubiquity of this style facilitated competent interactions between coffeehouse participants who had not played together before, as well as in situations where accompanists were unfamiliar with the songs soloists had chosen.

The elements of this style were almost never discussed at the coffeehouse. Edward remarked to me that he did not even know the names of the chords he strummed. Musical notation was almost entirely absent: the songbooks and hymnbooks I saw contained lyrics, but not melodies, and only very rarely were chord symbols present. As might be expected, some songs fell outside of country-gospel norms, drawing upon the harmonic vocabulary of rock or making use of the more complex harmonic palette employed in contemporary Christian music.[5] These exceptions often proved difficult for musicians in the house band to follow, a fact that further evidenced the centrality of the classic country style.

Although the repertoire at the coffeehouse was very close to that sung at the wake, it nevertheless tended to be more "secular": participants sang fewer hymns and more songs popularized by famous country singers, albeit typically on sacred themes. Occasionally they performed nondevotional music: when Tommy Knott stopped in he typically played some dance tunes, and singers sang secular songs from time to time. Still, the coffeehouse had a distinctly sacred character; someone usually said a prayer at the opening of the event, for instance.

This overt spirituality was in my experience deeply characteristic of indigenous public culture, and one of the features that distinguished it from mainstream publicness.[6] Some sort of sacred observance—Christian or traditional—was common at most of the dry events I attended, even those whose purpose seemed nonreligious. The lack of a strict dividing line between sacred and secular brings to mind an observation made by A. I. Hallowell about the Ojibwe of Berens River:

> I soon discovered that any facile distinction between the secular and the sacred from the Ojibwa point of view was not so easy to draw. If I missed the first few minutes of what I thought might be a purely secular "dance," I also missed a smoke offering to "our grandfathers." (Hallowell 1992: 81–82)

The disinclination to separate sacred and secular worked in the opposite direction as well: singing gospel songs was not understood to be a particularly sacred activity. In organizing these events Edward Guiboche was committed to creating a space for community members to enjoy gospel music, but he was no holy roller, and he told me he considered himself more of a traditional person than a Christian. In fact, several men who regularly sang gospel songs at the coffeehouse declined to be identified in any straightforward way as Christians (it tended to be male, rather than female, singers who explicitly took up such a stance).

On a related note, indigenous sacred expression was, in my experience, less theological and more practical than was common in other Manitoban forms of Christianity. The participants at William Whyte came together around singing and fellowship rather than religious doctrine: they were more concerned about moral conduct and Christian observance than theology. This was made particularly evident to me one Christmas Eve when I accompanied two friends to mass. When it came time to take communion, my friends insisted that I go up to partake, although they knew I was not a Catholic. This would have been problematic for many of that faith, the sacrament not being meant for people who do not belong to the church or believe in transubstantiation. For my friends, however, proper action was the concern.[7] Similarly, and more broadly, my consultants preferred singing to sermonizing, and they were much more likely to spend Wednesday nights at William Whyte than Sunday mornings in a pew: few of them attended church with any regularity.

The coffeehouse—and similar events centered on Christian song—thus called an aboriginal public to certain kinds of *practice*. Sacred singing was one of these, but another important one was abstention from intoxicants and the immoral behavior associated with them. Such gatherings were explicitly conceptualized as spaces where people could meet away from the presence of drugs and alcohol. As argued in previous chapters, Manitoban aboriginal public culture draws sharp distinctions between drinkers and nondrinkers, wet and dry spaces, and good-timing and sober living. But even as coffeehouses and similar events rejected the bar scene, they were simultaneously reflections or inversions of it: "the opposite way."[8] Like Winnipeg bars that catered to a largely aboriginal clientele, they offered music in a country style, a space in which to enjoy the company and make the acquaintance of other Native people, and a place where aboriginal musical aesthetics and modes of sociability prevailed.

While gospel music and sober sociability were central concerns for the William Whyte coffeehouse, there were two other, more immediate conditions of possibility for its founding. One was that a number of musicians had become dissatisfied with another coffeehouse, also organized by and for aboriginal people (of this, more later). The second reason involved a recently bereaved mother and daughter, Mary and Kendra Sinclair. Shortly before the coffeehouse was founded, Mary had lost her partner, Phillip Sinclair, a songwriter and gospel musician. Phillip, Mary explained to me, had been like a father to Kendra, and the two of them had begun to perform gospel music regularly together in the time leading up to his death. I heard the story of Sinclair's passing many times and from many different people. One night in 2002, as he and Kendra were singing "I Would Not Be Denied" at a Winnipeg coffeehouse—

> When pangs of death seized on my soul
> Unto the Lord I cried.

Till Jesus came and made me whole,
I would not be denied. ([Sinclair binder] 2003: 23)

—he collapsed. He was taken to hospital but never recovered.

The coffeehouse was thus established in part to support the Sinclairs, a purpose it accomplished in a number of ways. Kendra and Mary were regularly given opportunities to sing, and proceeds from the end-of-evening draw went to a fund designated to help Kendra pay for the making of a gospel CD. Additionally, on the first anniversary of Sinclair's death, we held a feast in honor of him. That this memorial event seemed appropriate to hold at the coffeehouse points to the close connections between the gatherings there and the funerary observances discussed in chapter 4. As I have already remarked, the music performed at the coffeehouse was a repertoire closely associated with mortuary practice (indeed, one consultant told me that it was difficult for him to associate "Amazing Grace" with any context other than a funeral). Beyond this, both coffeehouse and wake were spaces for vernacular, laical devotional practice, both had an inclusive and egalitarian ethos, and both commemorated the passing of a community member while offering support to the bereaved. Yet while the coffeehouse had much in common with the wake, it was a public event and not a rite of passage (the night of the feast being an exception); it was bound up in the "imagining" sociability discussed in earlier chapters.

The coffeehouse sought to constitute its public around and through ethical and devotional practice, and to this end extended an invitation to enjoy fellowship in an intoxicant-free environment and to hear and sing sacred songs, many of them on themes of death and the afterlife. It is perhaps not surprising, then, that few attendees were schoolchildren or younger adults: they tended rather to be middle-aged or older. Many of them had given up the drinking and partying that they enjoyed (and that had at times hurt them and others) in their youth and had moved into stable, sober roles as parents and grandparents. Most had seen the passing of parents and of relatives and friends of their own generation, and the funerary repertoire was one that they understood to be a significant part of their social worlds and roles.

Individuation and Collectivity, Performed

In chapter 4 I suggested that singing accomplishes two contrasting but complementary social entailments: individuating musicians and effecting collective expressions of comfort and support. Here my goal is to explore how musicians accomplish similar, seemingly contradictory ends in the course of performance. As I will argue, musical interaction is an arena in which participants enact and affirm egalitarian collectivity, individuation, charismatic leadership, and the inevitable tensions between them—often implicitly, even wordlessly, through music, but at times explicitly too, in voiced reflections and exhortations concerning that music.

Agents articulate these modes of sociability as they collectively create coherent interactional structures—musical and otherwise—in real time. I will examine two of these: a coffeehouse held in June of 2003 and a performance of the hymn "Oh 'Twas Love" at that gathering.[9] Understanding these structures, and how they enable the expression of modes of northern Algonquian sociability, will require attention to three aspects of the interactions. The first of these is their *structuredness*, the way their constituent elements relate to one another. As will become evident, certain elements of the coffeehouse and of "Oh 'Twas Love" were relatively stable: they had been deployed many times in the past and would be deployed many times more in the future in much the same form. Others were more contextually contingent, and integrating them in the emerging interactional structures involved more improvisation. Thus the examination of structuredness will take into account both fixed and contingent elements, and both established and more improvisatory ways of accommodating them. Second, in establishing interactional structures, musicians inhabited and recruited other agents to *roles*. How effectively participants occupied these roles, and what they did in them, helped to shape the emerging structures and their coherence. Third, the interactions at the coffee house both relied upon and performatively instantiated *cultural practice*. Cultural practice is of course the source of the structures and roles just mentioned (see Silverstein 1997, 2004), but it is also the point of origin for the models of behavior and sociability that the various agents drew upon, reproduced, and transformed in their interactions.

In sum, then, the analyses that follow examine how participants at the coffeehouse deployed culturally available structures and roles in the course of microsocial (Born 2005) musical interactions, and how, in mobilizing them, these agents also enacted aspects of northern Algonquian sociability. Indeed, in the course of interaction they brought some of these modalities of sociability into productive juxtaposition: egalitarianism with charismatic leadership, and individuation with collective endeavor.

The analyses have two broader implications. The first is that studying "the music itself"—musical materials and the moment-to-moment interactions of the people who set them in motion—means exploring sites of negotiation, in which cultural practices are dynamically produced and reproduced. From this perspective the study of the minutiae of musical performance is in fact the study of social agency. The second is that the microdynamics of musical interaction stand in a dynamic relationship with much larger social formations (see Born 2005), helping to shape forms of publicness and give them their specificity. In short, the subtle intimacies of performance are the very stuff of larger social and political projects of world making.

Structure and Improvisation

The next-to-last coffeehouse of the 2002–3 school year was held at William Whyte on the night of Wednesday, June 11. Attendees gathered in the echoing gymnasium, where musical equipment, PA system, and tables and chairs had been set up. By this point the coffeehouse had been running for some time and regular attendees knew one another well, socially and musically. I often sat in with the house band and frequently socialized with friends from William Whyte at other events and in other places. On the night in question, I documented the evening's goings-on with a video camera and minidisc recorder. Twelve singers got up to perform over the course of the evening, six of them in duos. Of the twelve, the majority were involved in some form of music ministry, in the country-music scene, or both: a number frequently sang at wakes, church services, or gospel jamborees, and two were country singers whose recordings received regular airplay on NCI. All told, the twelve singers performed a little over thirty songs, accompanied by Nelson Menow and the rest of the house band.

The first singer began with "Dear Brother," a country gospel song by Hank Williams in which a sibling informs a brother that their mother has gone to a place "where there is no pain." She went on to sing "Mansion over the Hilltop," which pictures an extravagant home in heaven.[10] (The themes of death and heaven returned throughout the evening, in pieces including "I'll Fly Away," "Traveling On," "When God Comes and Gathers His Jewels," and "Suppertime." Songs about death and the afterlife were generally well represented at the coffeehouse. Still, a number of other themes were explored on the night in question, including the conversion experience, in "I Saw the Light," and salvation, in "He Came a Long Way from Heaven.") Following the opening songs, the first singer led the other attendees in a short prayer.

The casual interplay between sacred and secular that typified activities at the coffeehouse was evident during much of the evening. Although most singers performed country gospel music, several sang country songs, one choosing Waylon Jennings's "Amanda" and "Good Hearted Woman." Another joked from the stage that a woman other than his wife had accompanied him to the venue—albeit in code, referring to his "little spare." Nevertheless, performers treated the coffeehouse as a venue where sacred song and temperate comportment was expected. The same singer who had joked about infidelity seemed to acknowledge that some attendees might disapprove of him playing secular music, telling the audience that he would sing a country song "if you don't mind" before performing Ernest Tubb's "Walking the Floor over You." All the same, later in the evening, when one musician presented his spiritual testimony and another responded tearfully, it marked a shift in tone at an event where the religious had not been particularly prominent.

Table 5.1 **Organizational structure of the coffeehouse**

Basic Frame	Section	Subsection
Preparation: setup of sound equipment, tables, seats		
Opening activities	Introductory music making	
	Prayer	
Performances	Turn 1	Song 1
		Song 2
	Turn 2	Song 1
		Song 2
		Song 3
	Turns 3, 4, etc.	Songs 1, 2, 3, etc.
Closing activity: drawing and awarding of prizes		
Clean-up: teardown of sound equipment, tables, seats		

The coffeehouse tended to have the same simple structure from night to night (see Table 5.1). There was sometimes a short warm-up featuring songs, instrumental tunes, or simply some noodling on guitar. This lasted until enough attendees had arrived to get the event proper under way. Things really began with an opening prayer, typically delivered by a regular attendee, an elder, or a visiting clergyperson. After this the emcee (usually Edward) called singers or small groups up to the front to sing with the house band; each typically performed two or three songs. Attendees who wanted to sing added their names to a list, and organizers seemed to try to give everyone an opportunity. After the final song, a draw was held and prizes were awarded. At this point most attendees left; a few stayed around to help Edward put away the sound equipment, tables, and seats.

Thus the coffeehouse's typical structure: introductory and concluding events bookending a series of structurally equivalent turns at center stage, each turn containing one or more songs. Co-articulated with this event framework were other, more improvisatory structures, contingent upon who was in attendance and the sequence of events on any given night. One of these was the body of songs performed. Participants typically chose pieces that had sacred themes and fell within the stylistic boundaries of country gospel music, but two more criteria also shaped their decisions. First, they generally avoided performing a song if it had already been performed that night, and, second, they typically avoided performing pieces they knew to be the "property" of other singers present. In short, normative song selection was retrospectively nonrepeating and predictively nonpreempting.

There were exceptions, however. The rule of nonrepetition was violated when singers were unaware that an earlier performer had already sung the song in question, when they had a limited repertoire, or when they chose to flout convention. Similarly, singers sometimes performed other singers' favorites: when Jack Meade performed "Cup of Loneliness" on the night of June 11, he joked that he "stole that one from Stan Cook," another regular who happened not to be present. Thus, while normative song selection did exist, there were transgressions of it: performers could test the patience of the audience by singing a song that had already been heard that night, or they could challenge other performers by stealing "their" songs. Of course, participants had varying perspectives on the appropriateness of their contributions, as one might imagine in the case of a singer who arrived two hours late or a newcomer who unknowingly picked "someone else's" song.

In short, the aggregate of songs performed over the course of an evening was a structure that emerged and cohered in real time, that extended across turn boundaries, and that was contingent upon the assembled participants, their familiarity with one another (and one another's preferred repertoires), and the degree to which they were willing to defer to their audience and their peers. More broadly, event structure at the coffeehouse emerged simultaneously with other, more improvised and contextually dependent structures. And how these emerged on the night of June 11 suggests something about the nature of relationships between participants, and northern Algonquian sociability more generally.

Egalitarianism, Authority, and Role

The steady progression of structurally equivalent performance turns evident in Table 5.1 was well suited to the kinds of interactions I regularly observed at Manitoban aboriginal social gatherings. It gave each soloist or group a turn at center stage, allowing individuals to evidence their unique musical gifts and small groups and families to demonstrate their solidarity. Additionally, the structure was egalitarian: each performance slot was on par with the others (although, as will be seen, not all slots were equal in value). This formal parity accorded with an emphasis on inclusiveness and participation in talk about the coffeehouse. Edward Guiboche often remarked that anyone who wanted to sing could do so at William Whyte, and attendees occasionally contrasted his venue with another coffeehouse, where the emcee did a good part of the singing himself, and there were fewer opportunities for other musicians to perform. At the latter venue the emcee chose who would be invited up on the stage on any given night, and some complained that from time to time he ignored singers who had come hoping to perform. Thus some stakeholders framed the William Whyte coffeehouse as a musical space based upon principles of inclusiveness and egalitarianism that they perceived to be compromised at another venue, and as a gathering that offered an alternative to the model of authority in operation there.[11] Certainly not everyone saw it this way: so far as Audrey Guiboche was concerned, the William Whyte coffeehouse had been established for the benefit of schoolchildren and the broader community, and not to antagonize or oppose another hardworking community leader (indeed, it seemed to me that she made a point of maintaining cordial ties with the organizer of the other coffeehouse). All the same, most of those who were committed to the William Whyte coffeehouse would have agreed that it was set up to be a gathering where everyone was welcome to contribute.[12]

Although egalitarianism was built into the structure of interactions at the William Whyte coffeehouse and inclusiveness was a central principle, privilege nevertheless had a part to play. Every singer called to the stage assumed temporary authority over the house band, for instance: he or she chose the song or songs to be performed, and the band usually followed the singer's performance decisions (paradoxically, this practice effected parity by making it possible for any participant to take up a leadership role). Other, potentially more socially problematic disparities were also evident, for instance in subtle instances of preferential treatment. Popular and talented singers were typically given performance slots near the end of the evening, and on some occasions they were permitted to sing more songs than other participants. On the evening described in this chapter, for instance, the prestigious final spot was given to a singer who at the time enjoyed considerable popularity and regular airplay on NCI. In such instances, the organizers of the coffeehouse seemed tacitly to acknowledge the status or ability of certain performers.

Thus privilege and authority became manifest as the coffeehouse unfolded in real time in much the same way as the aggregate of songs discussed above. Certainly performers had accrued varying degrees of renown outside the venue, but the coffeehouse affirmed and performatively extended this standing. Just how this happened was extemporaneous and contextually contingent: who received the final singing slot varied from night to night, depending on who showed up and what time he or she arrived, for example. It depended on the ability of singers and instrumentalists to fulfill roles competently. And it was furthermore negotiated, dependent not only on whom event organizers preferred and how well musicians performed in their roles, but also on the support and affirmation of fellow performers and attendees. All of this is made clearer in the following account of an instance in which authority was, to all appearances legitimately, usurped at the coffeehouse. The example shows more than this, however, demonstrating how these social and musical interactions involved the simultaneous articulation of sturdier event structures and more contingent, extemporized ones; the occupation and negotiation of roles; and affirmations of certain kinds of cultural practice, including distinctive modes of sociability.

About halfway through the evening, the emcee called a relatively inexperienced singer to the stage for an unprecedented second appearance. The reason for this was somewhat unclear, but it was probably that not enough people had signed up on the singing roster, and the only way around the problem was to call somebody up again. Once on stage, the singer paged through a binder of songs, apparently trying to find something she knew but had not already performed.[13] As they waited, the members of the house band seemed to get impatient, and eventually the rhythm guitarist—a well-known singer who possessed an extensive repertoire of songs—stepped up to the microphone to announce that he would sing something while they waited for her:

> OK, we're going to do one more while she's getting her song ready. Nelson just told me, too, that this is all set up for practices for people . . . like me, and that little spare over there, and Nelson, and all of you. It's for practice and [we're not] too serious on all of this.

Acknowledging the situation, but somewhat obliquely, he was in part encouraging potential performers to come up to sing, even if they were unsure how well they would do. He was also, it seems to me, gently admonishing the hesitant singer for spending too much time picking a song that would work for her. His interruption contravened some norms of conduct at the coffeehouse. By preempting the singer, he broke with the convention that whoever was in front of the house band was its temporary leader. He also came close to openly criticizing her, which would have been truly surprising. Disagreements did occur at the coffeehouse—there were arguments over the volume of the bass amplifier, for instance—but a participant never, in my memory, pointed out another's faults in front of the audience.

The indecisive singer had been honored by being called to the stage twice in one evening, but by taking too long to start singing she demonstrated less than complete competence in fulfilling her role. Whatever the more experienced singer thought of the matter, he took action to get the music started again, and in doing so usurped her role as bandleader. She did not protest but rather continued to search through the songbook as he performed, singing a gospel chorus of her own when he had finished.

As this account suggests, a series of negotiations over role was coarticulated with the event structure of the coffeehouse. When the more experienced singer interrupted his fellow performer, he was calling into question her ability to fulfill her role. He was additionally asserting not only his own competence in that area, but also the right to intervene in matters where even the emcee rarely stepped in. This appropriation of power was successful, moreover: the audience and singer assented to it, affirming his status—he was already a well-known and respected performer—and in a small way, perhaps, extending it. (He interrupted not only the indecisive performer, of course, but also the turn structure of the coffeehouse. Interestingly, that structure demonstrated some resilience: when the confident singer finished, the interrupted singer performed, taking up her turn where it had left off, so to speak. In retrospect, the interrupting singer had simply interpolated a turn within a turn.)

There is more going on here than the not-quite-smooth articulation of event structures and negotiations over role: these are additionally an instantiation of cultural practice. Evident in the tension between the inclusiveness of the coffee-house and instances in which primacy was asserted is a confrontation between egalitarianism and authority. Such tensions were recurring elements of the social interactions I observed and took part in. Charismatic, even rule-transgressing authority was valued, but so was parity.[14] People valued persons, their distinctiveness, and their unique gifts, but they valued such things in themselves, too. In this context authority and privilege were both appreciated and socially problematic. Authority quickly met with resistance when it impinged upon personal autonomy or bruised someone's sense of self-regard. So, while leaders often projected a confident sense of self, they took care not to offend those who were socially weaker (see chapter 6) or to interfere in the lives and decisions of others. And while there was respect for elders, leveling strategies were nevertheless deployed against certain authorities: rumors circulated regarding the wealthy and successful, who were often accused of conducting shady deals to attain their successes, and perceived slights easily became excuses for grudges or open criticism. A moment such as the one recounted could be a tense one because of the potentially deep offense that might be taken.

A Visit from Joe and Juliet Little

Toward the end of the evening two strangers made their way to the front of the auditorium: Joe and Juliet Little (Figure 5.1), singers from Garden Hill, one of a group of isolated Oji-Cree communities in northeastern Manitoba. Their performance would change the emotional and spiritual tone of the entire evening. Most of the preceding singers had sung Christian songs, but their comportment had been understated. Joe Little, in contrast, carried himself with great self-possession, addressing attendees in the manner of someone speaking at a revival meeting. During the first song he removed the microphone from its stand and strolled around the stage area as he sang, occasionally raising his other hand in gestures of praise. At the beginning of the second song, he commandeered a guitar from a member of the backing band, leaving him without an instrument and with no dignified option but to quit the stage. Finally, following the end of the second song—it had initially been agreed that the Littles would only perform two—he gestured to the emcee to inquire if they could perform another. Members of the audience greeted this proposal with enthusiasm, and he received the go-ahead, although it was getting late and one big-name performer had yet to sing.

Figure 5.1 JOE AND JULIET LITTLE. Photo provided by Juliet Little. Photographer unknown.

Joe Little prefaced each song with some personal testimony. Before the first, he explained that his ability to communicate in English had been a gift from God:

> Before I accept the Lord I don't know how to speak English. But I'm gonna stay in the bush all the time. When I grow up, my Daddy's trapper and then fisherman. I never got a chance for school. . . . When I accept the Lord, and I asked the Lord if He want to use me, give me a little bit different language, and He gave me, and then I'll go places, places. I travel places, places. . . . My English I call broken English. [Applause.] Amen.

Before the second song, he explained that God had given him the ability to preach and to play the guitar (it was at this point that he took the backing musician's guitar to demonstrate his gift). And before the final number, he explained that God had blessed him with songs:

> He give me a song, the Lord, He give me. . . . He gave me eleven songs. . . . Remember . . . what the Bible says? Jesus said, "Earth . . . pass away. But my Word never pass away." That's what He said. The call of God: what a thing.

He subsequently performed one of those songs, a meditation on Matthew 24:35 and I Corinthians 13:11.

Joe Little's statements suffused his contributions with sacred significance, revealing even the simplest elements of his performance to be manifestations of

God's generosity. His "broken English" demonstrated God's gift of language; his presence before the southern audience was a fulfillment of the promise that he would go "places, places"; his guitar playing and songs embodied the musical gifts that the Lord had given to him. This was metapraxis at work: "regimenting" that revealed song, and other speech, to be something more than it might otherwise appear. It is in part through such practice that coherence and meaning emerge in the course of social interaction. Here it transformed what many other performers at the coffeehouse could do—sing, speak English, and play guitar—into something miraculous.

Little was not the only participant to imbue his performance with significance. When the Littles had left the stage, Edward Guiboche called up Chris Beach, who was to be the final singer of the evening. Before Beach could begin, however, Nelson Menow, who had gotten up from his chair to join him at the front of the stage, started to speak from the heart. Menow related a parable of a woman who had been told to expect a visit from God. As she waited, he told us, she turned away two children dressed in rags, as well as a soldier suffering from the cold. He went on to explain that it was exactly in the form of those needy people that the Lord had come to visit her, and that, because she failed to help them, she missed her chance to meet Him. "God is with us tonight," he continued, establishing a tacit parallel between the visitors in the parable and the Littles. "That's why He tells us every day, 'Be prepared.' We have to prepare ourselves. Jesus is coming soon. And I thank God that these people came here tonight. I really felt something in my life." He added, a little later:

> You know, the Lord is talking to us in mysterious ways. He appears to us in mysterious ways....That is why we let all sorts of people come down here. We don't want to hate anybody. We don't want to say no to anybody who wants to sing, regardless of what, because that's the way Jesus wants us to be: to love one another, not to hate one another....You know, there is a song that goes like this: "What would you do if Jesus came to spend some time with you?" Think about it. And I'm very thankful, I'm very glad tonight, that these people came down here. You know, when I first started playing I couldn't even play. I didn't even feel right, when I started playing. But when these people came, it made a very big difference in my life.

Menow talked for a while longer, exhorting attendees to get right with the Lord, and then returned to his seat and guitar at the rear of the stage. Beach, who had been waiting for Menow to finish, took his turn at the microphone, concluding the musical portion of the evening with the hymn "How Great Thou Art" and his popular country song "My Soap Opera Woman."

Menow's response instilled the Littles' visit with sacred import and located in it a spiritual justification for the way the coffeehouse was run. Their coming, he seemed to suggest, was like that of the people in the parable: an unexpected manifestation of the presence of God. Indeed, their visit had changed his playing and transformed how he felt, he told us, and his tears a little later on attested to its impact.[15] Menow further rendered the Littles' performance a vindication of one of the founding ideas of the coffeehouse. "We don't want to say no to anybody who wants to sing," he told us, asserting that the coffeehouse was an inclusive venue where all were welcome. As the parable he had related suggested, it was exactly because of such openness that the coffeehouse could be blessed by the presence of God, who appeared "in mysterious ways which we don't even know." Menow was referring to events that we had just witnessed, but his words had a forward-oriented, stipulating character, too. They characterized what the coffeehouse aspired to be and pointed to the Littles' performance as an example of the kind of blessings that could come when we realized this aspiration.

Menow's speech exemplifies how event structure intersects with improvised elements, but also how coherence and significance build during the course of collaborative undertakings. His short sermon was the second time during the evening that someone had delayed another's turn. While these interpositions might appear, on the face of it, to have disrupted the smooth unfolding of the event structure, they in fact established coherence. In both cases they advanced characterizations of proper coffeehouse protocol that extended across not only turns, but gatherings, and that sought to define the culture of the coffeehouse. In the first interruption the impatient band member was not only responding to the vacillations of an indecisive singer, but also describing the coffeehouse as an informal event: "[we're not] too serious on all of this." This statement was not simply descriptive but prescriptive: even as it characterized the coffeehouse as a space of informal "practice," it exhorted participants to get into the proper spirit. Menow's extemporized homily likewise extended a characterization of coffeehouse ideals across turns and weeks, but at a higher emotional pitch. It was a response to the Littles' performance and a meditation on the spiritual significance of their unexpected visit, but it also predicated something of the coffeehouse more generally. It reflected upon one of its founding principles—its inclusiveness—and upon the unexpected blessings that resulted from it. Like the previous interruption, Menow's response regimented its context in two ways: while extending a characterization of the openness of the coffeehouse, it also admonished attendees to behave in a manner that was in keeping with this ideal.

"Oh 'Twas Love of God to Me"

To sum up one strand of the foregoing argument, at each instantiation of the coffeehouse, participants collectively elaborated relatively fixed event structures alongside other, more improvised and contextually contingent formations.[16] They imbued these interactions with additional layers of coherence through explicit verbal pronouncements about, for instance, the ideals to which (they believed) the event aspired. They nominated one another to, occupied, and negotiated various roles. And, in the course of interactions, they also acknowledged and affirmed certain modes of sociability.

Musical performances at the coffeehouse unfolded in a similar way. As songs were enmusicalized, participants deployed relatively stable formations (including strophic structures and metrical patterns), but they simultaneously brought into being configurations of a more contingent nature—for instance, the sequence of singers and soloing instrumentalists who took the lead during any given tune. During performances, participants occupied a range of roles—lead singer, accompanist, instrumental soloist, and so on—and in the negotiations over these and the musical structures they laid down, they articulated musical modalities of some of the kinds of sociability discussed in this chapter and the preceding one.

Complicating matters, participants often came into these interactions with distinct or even conflicting ideas about the musical structures in play. Performance was a dynamic site in which musicians negotiated how "the song" or "the timing" went. (More broadly, of course, they were negotiating what kinds of songs and rhythmic approaches were legitimate within aboriginal musical practice.) In this context, the members of the house band at William Whyte continually encountered challenging new performance situations: unfamiliar singers and songs, and familiar songs performed in unfamiliar ways. In the latter cases, the newness often involved what musicians referred to as the "timing" of the song: the durations accorded to the notes and silences in the main vocal or instrumental melody, and especially whether these were calibrated to some sort of metrical structure. Interestingly, despite rhythmic twists that might have challenged some professional players, musicians at the coffeehouse usually found some way to compensate, and rhythmic anomalies almost never brought performances to a halt.

The musicians in the house band could confidently navigate these challenging musical encounters because they shared with most soloists an acquaintance with a core repertoire of hymns and gospel songs, a familiarity with the musical grammar of country gospel music, an understanding of certain music-cultural roles, and an awareness of the kinds of behavior appropriate to these roles. There was also a shared set of expectations concerning how singers and soloists approached "timing." All of this helped to enable the performances on the evening of June 11, especially in those moments when the members of the house band accompanied the Littles.

The second song the Littles performed that evening, "Oh 'Twas Love of God to Me," is a Cree version of "God Loved the World of Sinners Lost," an English-language hymn with lyrics by Martha Stockton.[17] I found Cree versions of the hymn in several hymnals (see [Northern Canada Evangelical Mission] 1977, 1979, 1980), although not in exactly the same version the Littles performed.

Omitting the verses of the hymn, the Littles sang the chorus four times, twice in Cree and twice in English:

> Maamaskaateyihtaakwan
> Jesus e saakihit
> Ispimihk e gii otohtet
> E wii pimaacihit[18]

> Amazing, so wonderful,
> That Jesus loves me so,
> He came down from heaven above
> To save me by His grace.

Nelson Menow translated the Cree text as follows (acknowledging that the Littles' Cree was different from his own):

> It's a wonder
> That Jesus loves me.
> [He came from above
> To save me.][19]

Table 5.2 **Formal structure of "Oh 'Twas Love of God to Me"**

Bracketing sections	Choruses	Phrase breakdown	Chord progression	Cadence at end of section	Meas. no.
Instrumental introduction		I. Short progression (not a phrase)	I–V–I	–	1–3
		B. Consequent-like phrase	I–IV–I–V–I	–	4–9
	Chorus 1: Cree	A. Antecedent	I–IV–I–V	Half	10–15
		B. Consequent	I–IV–I–V–I	Authentic	16–21
	Chorus 2: English	A. Antecedent	I–IV–I–V	Half	22–27
		B. Consequent	I–IV–I–V–I	Authentic	28–33
	Guitar solo	A. Antecedent	I–IV–I–V	Half	~33–37
		B. Consequent	I–IV–I–V–I	Authentic	38–41
	Chorus 1¹: Cree	A. Antecedent	I–IV–I–V	Half	42–47
		B. Consequent	I–IV–I–V–I	Authentic	48–53
	Chorus 2¹: English	A. Antecedent	I–IV–I–V	Half	54–59
		B. Consequent	I–IV–I–V–I	Authentic	60–65
Concluding tag/coda		B¹. Repetition of last half of previous phrase	I–V–I	Authentic	66–67

"Oh 'Twas Love" had a straightforward strophic structure in performance, as Table 5.2 shows. A short instrumental introduction and an even shorter sung coda bracketed five iterations of the chorus, four sung and one instrumental. The choruses were of antecedent-consequent construction, with the first half of each one cadencing on the dominant and the second half on the tonic.

The melody of the hymn was supported by a familiar harmonic pattern that appears in at least three other well-known songs: "Amazing Grace," "Where Could I Go but to the Lord," and the verse of "When the Roll Is Called up Yonder." (The first two were known and performed widely in Manitoban aboriginal contexts.) But while the Littles made use of the sequence of harmonies that occurs in this pattern, they did not maintain the durational ratio that holds between these harmonies in dominant performance traditions. In short, their version was not guided by a metrical structure (on the relationship that typically holds between harmonic rhythm and meter in Western music see Lerdahl and Jackendoff 1983: 80–84, 87–89). Table 5.3 compares the harmonic rhythm in canonical versions of "Amazing Grace" (row a), "Where Could I Go" (b) and the verse of "When the Roll Is Called" (c) with the harmonic rhythm in the Littles' performance of "Oh 'Twas Love" (rows d and e). The arabic numerals in the table denote harmonic durations in beats of the main tactus. Notice how all harmonic durations in "Amazing Grace" are divisible by three, all in "Where Could I Go" by four, and all in "When the Roll is Called" by two. This strongly suggests that harmonic rhythm in these songs is structured with reference to meter. In contrast, the harmonic durations in the phrases chosen from "Oh 'Twas Love" have no common denominator larger than one—a fairly good indication that in the Littles' performance meter was not a priority.

Table 5.3 **Comparison of harmonic rhythm**

Antecedent Phrase	I	IV	I	I		V
(a) "Amazing Grace"	6	3	3	6		6
(b) "Where Could I Go but to the Lord"	8	4	4	8		8
(c) "When the Roll" (verse)	4	2	2	4		4
(d) "Oh 'Twas Love," chorus 1	16	8	12	11		12
(e) "Oh 'Twas Love," chorus 3	18	8	12	11		12
Consequent Phrase	I	IV	I	I	V	I
(a) "Amazing Grace"	6	3	3	3	3	6
(b) "Where Could I Go but to the Lord"	8	4	4	4	4	8
(c) "When the Roll" (verse)	4	2	2	2	2	4
(d) "Oh 'Twas Love," chorus 1	18	8	12	7	5	16
(e) "Oh 'Twas Love," chorus 3	18	8	13	7	5	16

Note: In this comparison of harmonic rhythm in canonical versions of songs employing the "Amazing Grace" changes (a, b, and c) and Joe and Juliet Little's version of "Oh 'Twas Love" (d and e), rhythm is measured in pulses of the main tactus. Subphrasing creates a sense of a "restated" I chord halfway through both the antecedent and consequent phrases.

The Littles performed "Oh 'Twas Love" accompanied by Nelson Menow on lead guitar and Albert Audy on bass (Audy is a Cree singer and musician who was raised in Pelican Rapids). I interviewed the two backing musicians in the summer of 2008, at which time they confirmed that neither of them had met the Littles before the night in question. Both of them knew "Oh 'Twas Love" before meeting the Littles, but Menow was inclined to sing the song in a more metrically regular version, while Audy at first barely recognized the version the Littles performed.[20] At any rate, the Littles did not speak to Menow or Audy before starting into the song, and thus the two accompanists were in the dark as to what was being performed until the singing began. As Figure 5.2 shows, they nevertheless jumped in to accompany almost immediately. Their confidence was entirely characteristic of interactions at the coffeehouse, where musicians made their way as best they could through challenging situations, rarely worrying about getting things exactly right.

Joe Little opened the performance by strumming a G major chord on the guitar, shifting to D major for eight beats (the tactus is notated as an eighth note in the transcription) and then returning to G major. His introduction sent a number of signals, perhaps unintentionally, to Menow and Audy, who joined in eight beats after the return to G major (not counting Menow's pickup notes; see mm. 3–4). Their simultaneous entry was a response to the rhythmic structure of Little's opening chord changes, which had seemed to indicate the presence of quadruple meter. Indeed, their entry helped to sustain the sense of quadruple meter for the next little while (for metrically attuned listeners, at least). Evident already in the interaction was the contingent-and-consequential dynamic discussed in the preface to this chapter, now distributed amongst a number of participants. Little's playing engendered in Menow and Audy an expectation of metrical organization, and they responded by "regimenting" his guitar strumming through metricalized and metricalizing contributions of their own.

Other elements of Joe Little's introduction signaled a particular stylistic vocabulary, especially his use of open-position chords and a lightly swinging rhythm. Menow and Audy interpreted these as markers of the country gospel style and responded accordingly: Menow entered with a standard country guitar lick, a chromatically decorated melodic sixth, while Audy struck up a rocking bass line, a figure that simultaneously suggested a country feel and quadruple meter.[21] Again, their contributions were performative, not only acknowledging but also extending the style "proposed" by Little's strumming. (Their responses additionally affirmed broader realms of musical practice: the style common at the coffeehouse and in Manitoban aboriginal music making more generally.)

Menow and Audy's entry momentarily established a sense of meter, but this was soon undone, since Joe Little did not stay with any consistent metrical pattern. As a result, Menow and especially Audy were frequently caught "wrong-footed" and forced to make adjustments.[22] At the end of the second vocal line in the first chorus (mm. 14–15), for instance, the Littles sang "Jesus e saaki-"

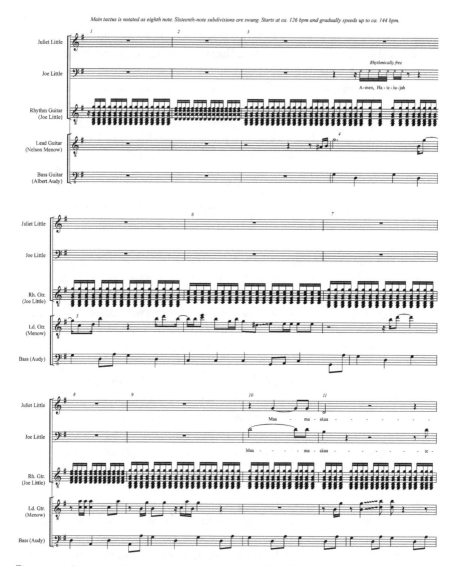

Figure 5.2 INTRODUCTION AND FIRST CHORUS OF "OH 'TWAS LOVE" (TRADITIONAL). Barlines only occasionally indicate meter in Figures 5.2 and 5.3; they tend rather to indicate important structural moments, including harmonic changes, cadences, and the arrival of final syllables in poetic lines. Their inclusion also facilitates specificity of reference in the text (i.e., reference to particular measures). There are some exceptions to the general rule: in mm. 4–5 (Figure 5.2) and mm. 35–40 (Figure 5.3), Menow and Audy seem to be calibrating their contributions to a metrical pattern. At these moments the measure numbers move down to a position above Menow's guitar part, indicating his temporary success in establishing a sense of meter. Transcription, by the author, appears with the kind permission of Juliet Little, Nelson Menow, and Albert Audy.

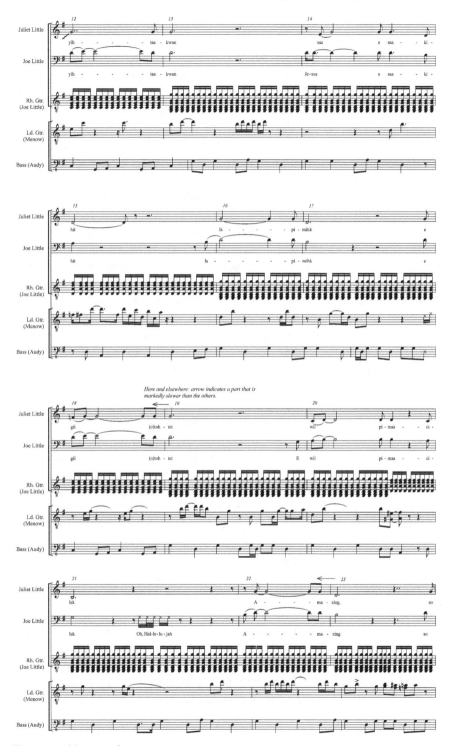

Figure 5.2 (Continued)

as an eleven-pulse group, cadencing on the dominant on the subsequent syllable, "-hit." This arrival occurred exactly halfway between points in the pulse pattern of Audy's rocking bass line, forcing him to recalibrate rhythmically.

These early moments of interaction had a number of significant outcomes for the performance. First, they designated Joe Little's guitar downstrokes (rather than Audy's rocking bass line) as the tactus-bearing strand in the musical texture. Second, they set up a fluid, even minimally metrical, rhythmic context in which the tactus fell into no consistent pattern of metrical grouping. This created some problems of ensemble, particularly for Audy, whose bass line moved at half the rate of the tactus and did not easily accommodate odd groupings. Third, in accomplishing the foregoing, they also affirmed Joe Little's role as the leader of the proceedings.[23]

All of these outcomes were engendered collectively rather than by the Littles alone. Albert Audy's frequent rhythmic recalibrations accommodated various points of arrival in Joe Little's guitar playing and vocal melody, thus giving precedence to those musical signals. Juliet Little, Menow, and Audy all deferred to Joe Little's musical decisions, in doing so ratifying his role as leader and accepting theirs as accompanists. Their rhythmic "corrections" exhibited, again, an acknowledging-and-accomplishing dynamic: they were simultaneously a response to Little and a performative mobilization of musical roles. (Nor were these one-time-only roles, of course, but rather well-established positionalities in the realm of country gospel performance.)

Joe Little was an unpredictable leader whose rhythmic approach varied even from chorus to chorus. His musical idiosyncrasies continually presented his fellow musicians with unexpected developments, and in this way his charismatic musical leadership impressed itself upon them mentally and physically throughout the performance. This appeared true even in the case of his most privileged collaborator, Juliet Little, who clearly knew the song and her harmony part, yet had to pay close attention in order to stay with him. Her vocal entries invariably followed his, sometimes by a full beat. The "participatory discrepancies" (Keil 1987) here were of a particular kind, then: co-performers were continually accommodating the musical personality of the leader.

Nelson Menow's guitar solo, midway through the performance (see Figure 5.3, mm. 33–41), further illustrates the negotiation of leadership in the course of musical interaction. After the second chorus, Joe Little stopped singing and began to speak. Menow and Audy, following him, began to cycle through the harmonic progression of the chorus a third time. After a few beats of this, Menow moved out of his accompanimental role and into the lead, laying down a clearly phrased melody with a regular metrical profile (mm. 36–40). As the transcription illustrates, Audy soon fell into rhythmic step with him.

Menow established his leadership with the help of elements of the "Amazing Grace" changes that had until then not been in play. The Littles had employed the basic sequence of harmonies, but Menow set them in a metrically regularized durational relationship. Table 5.4 presents one canonical version of this relationship, borrowed from "Where Could I Go."

As the roman and arabic numerals in bold in Table 5.5 indicate, Menow managed to track this version for just over half of the length of his solo. While much of his solo was metrical, his role as leader only came into effect around m. 37, when Audy began to follow him. (There were subsequent differences between the harmonies implied by Audy's bass line and by Menow's guitar solo, but from this moment onward Audy was more rhythmically attuned to Menow than to Little.) Audy thus occupied a position as a kind of kingmaker, his allegiance determining who was the leader. Indeed, it was particularly significant in doing so, since Joe Little did not easily relinquish primacy; at a number of moments during the instrumental break he held on to harmonies significantly longer than the others did (see mm. 38–40).

At the end of the instrumental break, as Menow neared the conclusion of the chorus (see Figure 5.3, mm. 40–41), he began to signal cadential closure by means of a descending melodic formula.[24] Little, however, denied Menow the harmonic

Figure 5.3 Nelson Menow's guitar solo in "Oh 'Twas Love."

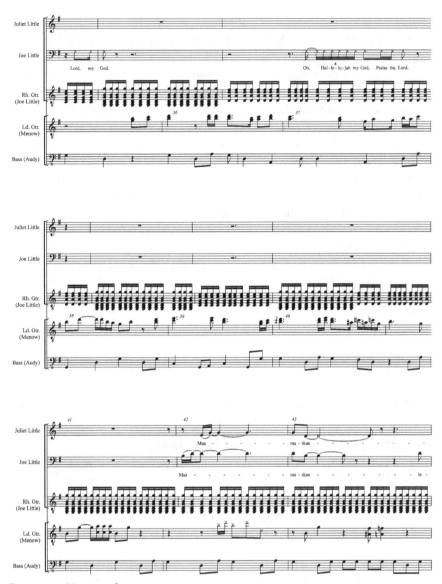

Figure 5.3 (*Continued*)

support that would have effected a collectively articulated cadence: instead of moving to the tonic G chord on the point of arrival that Menow's melodic material seemed clearly to be setting up, he held on to the penultimate D chord for four additional beats (see m. 40). Here Audy, too, sustained D major, putting his musical support behind Little and leaving Menow the odd one out. When, five years later, I played the recording for Menow, he laughed out loud when he heard his bid for closure so denied.

Table 5.4 **Harmony, duration, and meter of the chord changes in "Where Could I Go but to the Lord" (a version of the "Amazing Grace" changes)**

	Property	Harmonies/units					
	Harmony	I	IV	I	I		V
Antecedent phrase	Duration in pulses	8	4	4	8		8
	Metrical cycles	2	1	1	2		2
Consequent phrase	Duration in pulses	8	4	4	4	4	8
	Metrical cycles	2	1	1	1	1	2

In sum, then, the Littles and their accompanists collectively articulated a number of musical structures in their performance of "Oh 'Twas Love." These included relatively stable formations: lyrical, melodic, harmonic, and formal structures. They also included two distinct metricalizations: Joe Little's relatively minimal metricality, in which a steady, subdivided tactus represented the deepest consistent level of rhythmic regulation, and the more maximally metrical framework put forward by Nelson Menow (see Figure 5.4).

They also established a number of more contingent or extemporized structures, including a sequence of shifting role occupancies that we might call a "structure of

Table 5.5 **Meter and harmony in Nelson Menow's guitar solo, "Oh 'Twas Love"***

	Property						
	Implied harmony	I	IV	I	**I**		**V(7)**
Antecedent phrase	Duration in pulses	*16*	8	8	**8**		**8**
	Metrical cycles	–	–	–	**2**		**2**
	Measure number	33	34	35	36		37
	Implied harmony	**I**	**IV**	**I**	**I**	**V**	I
Consequent Phrase	Duration in pulses	**8**	**4**	**4**	**4**	**4**	12
	Metrical cycles	**2**	**2**	**1**	**1**	–	
	Measure number	38	39		40		41

Note: Durations are given in pulses of the tactus. Boldface type indicates those parts of the solo that were clearly synchronized both metrically and harmonically with the "Where Could I Go"/"Amazing Grace" changes. Regular type represents parts that accorded harmonically but not metrically. When a harmonic duration cannot be inferred clearly from the musical context, it is presented in italics.

* This analysis grants the penultimate harmony, V, four beats. Some readers may feel that Menow's solo in m. 40 implies six beats of I and two of V. Indeed, Audy plays on the notes of the tonic chord during much of the measure. The melodic B ("covered" by D) that arrives in the middle of m. 40 in the guitar part can nevertheless be heard to signal the arrival of the (dominant-functioning) cadential 6/4. I have gone with this interpretation.

leadership." These various structures had implications for one another: it was the alternation of roles, for instance, that allowed performers to present two distinct forms of metrical regimentation.

Thus, "Oh 'Twas Love of God to Me" came together as agents collectively realized musical structures and occupiable roles in real-time interaction. Significantly, participants at the coffee house were not only enmusicalizing songs, structures, and roles, but also affirming these formations as possibilities within the realm of music-cultural practice they shared. Indeed, the performance of "Oh 'Twas Love" was in some ways a negotiation of very different conceptions of "how music goes." From one perspective, the result of this negotiation was the ratification of a minimally metrical approach: although Menow and Audy preferred to play in a more rhythmically regular style (as they indicated to me in separate interviews), they mostly deferred to the Littles. From another point of view, the negotiations affirmed an *inclusive* approach to performance in which disparate, even apparently irreconcilable rhythmic styles could stand side by side.

Scholars of music have tended to locate agency and contestation in lyrical content, metamusical discourse, and paramusical goings-on, but they also exist in

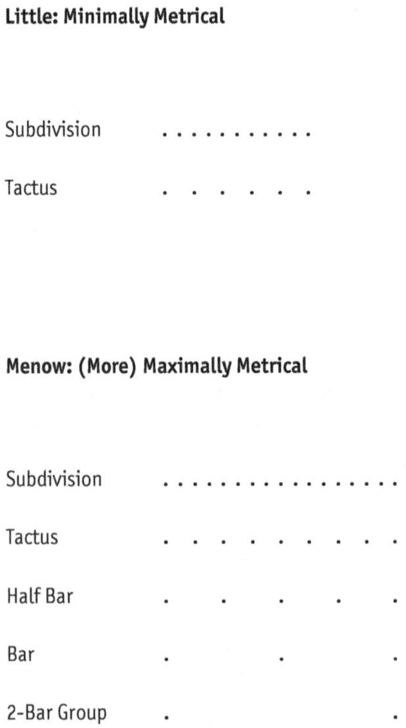

Little: Minimally Metrical

Subdivision	. . . .
Tactus	. . . . . .

Menow: (More) Maximally Metrical

Subdivision	. . . .
Tactus	. . . .
Half Bar	. . . . .
Bar	. . .
2-Bar Group	. .

Figure 5.4 BEAT STRUCTURE FOR MENOW AND LITTLE. (After Lerdahl and Jackendoff, 1983)

the most basic of musical interactions. The preceding analysis seeks a rapproche-
ment between close analyses of musical interaction and broader explorations of
music's social import (see Monson 1996: 190–91). The idea is to deploy musical
analysis as an analysis of cultural practice. Understood in this way, it need not
be (dismissed as) an undertaking that eschews questions of power and agency.
Nor need the exploration of the minute particularities of musical interaction be
(understood as) a retreat from larger social issues. As has been argued throughout
this volume, it is exactly such intimacies that stand in complex relationships with
larger, imagining social formations.

Northern Algonquian Sociability in Musical Performance

The preceding discussions of musical intimacies have been concerned in part with
exploring how music mediates the modes of sociability described in chapter 4.
Performances of music at the coffeehouse were also performances of idiosyncrasy
and individuation, charismatic leadership and resistance to it, inclusiveness and
egalitarianism. The argument, again, is not that music represented these social
modalities, but rather that it instantiated them: in the course of musical performance some musicians "sang their own songs" while others "yanked" their collaborators into line. Significantly, such aspects of sociability were most in evidence
during moments of musical repair and infelicity—on occasions of obvious, rather
than subtle, participatory discrepancy (see Keil 1987).

The Littles' performance was a manifestation of both solidarity and individuation. Their harmony singing and rhythmic togetherness (the latter despite
Joe Little's tendency to vary rhythmic durations from chorus to chorus) was a
sounding-together that evidenced a history together.[25] At the same time, and
at the risk of stating something even more self-evident, their accord set them
apart from the members of the house band and from other coffeehouse attendees. Although they were outsiders in the North End, they were insiders when it
came to the twists and turns of their version of "Oh 'Twas Love." The performance
also established personal distinctiveness, and in a particularly corporeal way: Joe
Little's rhythmic idiosyncrasies required Audy and Menow to scramble to get back
in time with him (compare Clayton, Sager, and Will 2004: 21). At the coffeehouse,
rhythmically mediated personhood had a mental and somatic impact on fellow
musicians: when "the beat went upside down" (see Stirling Ranville's comment in
chapter 4) everyone had to somersault.

This is not to suggest that accompanists were always keen followers. In musical interactions, as in other arenas of Manitoban aboriginal social life, there was
some resistance to charismatic leadership. People admired compelling personas
but were averse to compromising their own sense of worth, consequentiality, or

autonomy. In keeping with this, leaders and accompanists alike often performed with a kind of easy indifference to one another, as if they were only contributing as they pleased. There was little in the way of deferential "following" or assertive "conducting" in ensemble situations. During the performance of "Oh 'Twas Love," for instance, there was minimal visual cueing between musicians. Certainly Albert Audy got up from his seated position during the first verse, positioning himself so that he could watch Joe Little's chord changes, and Juliet Little's eyes remained on her husband for most of the performance. Yet Nelson Menow remained in his chair behind the other musicians for the duration of the song, and Joe Little made no overt attempt to direct the other performers, except perhaps during the guitar solo.[26]

However atomistic this musical sociability might appear to outsiders, it was also a manifestation of inclusiveness. Although Menow and Audy preferred to play music that was metrically regular, they nevertheless supported the Littles and followed their lead. The coffeehouse could accommodate more than one metrical approach. This inclusiveness was characteristic of most of the aboriginal musical events I attended. Jam sessions, coffeehouses, and talent shows were immensely popular, and they were open to musicians of a range of abilities who played in an array of rhythmic styles. Even those who regularly railed against "bad timing" took part. Here too, organizers and musicians declined to say no to anybody who wanted to sing.

The musical sociability described here is in no way immutable; neither is it characteristic of all indigenous Manitobans. As argued throughout this book cultural practices come into being performatively, are negotiated, and change over time. It is not at all clear whether the participatory discrepancies explored here, or genres such as country and country gospel music, will continue to mediate collectivity and individuation for years to come. After all, many of the genres and forms of collaboration that were common when I did fieldwork were adopted rather recently in Cree and Ojibwe communities. It could be that certain ways of interacting will endure for some time, however, and that future musicians will continue to explore solidarity, individuation, authority, and egalitarianism in similar ways, but in other venues and through different musical practices.

Publicness and Its Limits

One reason discussion of these modes of musical sociability turns to the subject of their continuation is that they are distinct from, and to some extent problematized in relation to, ones that seem normative to the national public. The William Whyte coffeehouse hailed an aboriginal public whose members engaged with musical and social practices that, although similar to those in nonaboriginal communities, reflected indigenous cultural practices and experiences, including aboriginal experiences of colonialism. This public sang hymns, gospel songs, and choruses in a style similar to that of popular country music, but did so in Cree and Ojibwe as well as English, and often with considerably more metrical freedom. It was also a public that was "sober" in culturally specific ways: the coffeehouse was explicitly conceived as an environment where aboriginal people could find refuge from intoxicants, and it prioritized a tradition of devotional music closely associated with Native mortuary ritual. Further, as just discussed, it was a public whose members interacted with one another, musically and otherwise, in ways that extended or elaborated aspects of traditional northern Algonquian sociability.

One important—and distinguishing—aspect of this sociability was its inclusivity, and it is in part for this reason that Nelson Menow's words, "We don't want to say no to anybody who wants to sing," stand at the head of this chapter. At William Whyte, everyone was welcome to contribute, and taking part was not predicated upon expertise or professionalism. Accordingly, the first musician to interrupt the proceedings on the night of June 11 argued that perfection was not the point of the coffeehouse, saying, "It's for practice and [we're not] too serious on all of this."[27] And he emphasized the inclusivity of the gathering: it was "for people...like me, and that little spare over there, and Nelson, and all of you." These attitudes hold more broadly: participatory events such as jam sessions, coffeehouses, and talent shows thrive throughout the Manitoban indigenous public sphere. And it seems to me that this inclusivity is distinct from that which tends to hold in many nonaboriginal social contexts in North America. It is true that, there, less competent performers are often regarded with indulgent fondness, but more common is a kind of mild embarrassment, and the line between amateur and professional is in many cases brutally invigilated—consider, for instance, televised "idol" shows that juxtapose good singers and self-deluding no-talents.

Certainly there are aboriginal performance traditions that emphasize excellence (see chapters 3 and 6 in this volume and Nettl 1983: 309–10; 2005: 364). And many Native musicians whose professionalism and virtuosity is in no question have had mainstream success. But the contention here is that aboriginal public culture makes more room for participation and is not as likely to regard different or lesser competences as something to be ashamed of.[28] This is why, at William Whyte, apologetic and embarrassed performances were rare, and musicians such as Joe Little sang with charismatic self-assurance. These performers brought blessings to the venues they visited, and they moved their audiences, even those who considered themselves better musicians.

Distinguishing between what aboriginal and nonaboriginal Manitobans value in music is not an end in itself. Such differences are significant in contexts where publics overhear but do not necessarily understand one another. Warner's concept of counterpublicity is again helpful in explaining that some publics cast long shadows, having the power to characterize others as indecorous or otherwise problematic. Especially in contexts where so much of indigenous publicness seems familiar to other North Americans—country music, Christian song, and jam sessions in the school gymnasium, for example—aboriginal difference is too easily perceived as sameness done wrong.

* * * * *

Public spaces are, again, both intimate and imagining: although they present open invitations to all comers, they are also places of face-to-face engagement. The William Whyte coffeehouse was such an interstitial zone, but in a number of respects stood apart from other kinds of public spaces. Making acquaintances there quickly implicated one in relationships that involved more than mere voluntary association. I was rapidly integrated in networks of reciprocity and obligation and expected to do my part to support new friends. Although the coffeehouse was public-facing, then, it felt less oriented to imagined others than to persons known and knowable. There was a tendency toward intimacy, in other words. In this respect it reflected a more general characteristic of Manitoban aboriginal public culture: to place limits on "imagining" sociability and privilege face-to-face encounters. There was a disinclination to make public spaces empty zones, unperturbed by the smooth comings and goings of strangers. Rather, publicness was contained and public spaces were reenchanted as zones of intimate sociability.

In this respect, Nelson Menow's remark bears repeating a final time: "We don't want to say no to anybody who wants to sing, regardless of what, because that's the way Jesus wants us to be: to love one another, not to hate one another." The coffeehouse embraced strangers, engaged them in musical performance, and surrounded them with love. It privileged musical interactions that required performers to orient themselves to one another rather than to some publicly available concept of meter. This prioritization of intimacy merits attention as a strategy by which aboriginal communities translate (see Chakrabarty 2000: 47–71, 86–96) publicness into something amenable to indigenous sociability. It is accordingly to this subject that the final chapters of this volume turn.

6

Antipublicity

Family Tradition and the Aboriginal Public

Family Tradition at the Dance Competition

The Peguis First Nation holds its annual Treaty Days celebrations over the course of a week every July. The reserve is Manitoba's largest, with a population of over 7,200 Cree and Ojibwe people,[1] and its festival brings in aboriginal visitors from around the province and beyond. The community publicizes the event widely, and the ads inevitably burst with information about the range of musical, sporting, and gaming activities to take place. Regularly recurring events include a square-dancing competition, a Red River jigging contest, a powwow, a baseball tournament, a talent show, and a giant bingo.[2]

Traditionally, treaty-day celebrations mark the moment when First Nations people collect the annual payments promised them under the terms of treaties signed with the Crown.[3] Ceremony and festivity have often accompanied the disbursement: in the early twentieth century, a fully uniformed Royal Canadian Mounted Police officer made the payment in the form of brand new five-dollar bills (UMASC [1953]); in the community of York Factory, fiddle dances were typically held to celebrate the event (Beardy and Coutts 1996: 84–86). Today, treaty-day activities are typically organized by the First Nations concerned; they are an opportunity not just to have a good time, but also to celebrate the traditions, history, lands, and unique political status of First Nations communities.

On a hot Saturday afternoon in July, I drove up to Peguis from Winnipeg to see the square-dancing and jigging competitions held as one of the culminating events of the festival.[4] Arriving late, shortly after the square-dancing competition had begun, I hurried to the community dance pavilion, a rectangular structure with a corrugated metal roof and three sides open to the air. Two rows of bleacher-style seats ran along the long sides of the structure, and a raised stage was positioned at the rear wall. The pavilion was filled with enthusiastic attendees, a number of whom, like me, had brought video cameras to record the dancing. On stage Clifford Maytwayashing, an Ojibwe fiddler from Lake Manitoba First Nation, accompanied the proceedings with his band. The competition moved through four segments, for junior, intermediate, adult, and senior dance groups, each team performing two carefully choreographed dances. The participants had come from Peguis, Winnipeg, and several other communities, including Pukatawagan, some 900 kilometers (560 miles) away. After a few hours of dancing, the competition wrapped up, the judges announced their decisions, and prizes were distributed to the winners. There followed a long break, after which a Red River Jigging contest was to be held. During the interval I spoke with Ryan Richard (Figure 6.1), a square dancer and jigger in his early twenties whose acquaintance I had made the previous summer. He was considering staying for the evening tournament but was uncertain whether this would be possible since his ride home was leaving immediately. Excited at the prospect of watching him compete—many would have said he was the best dancer in the province—I offered him a ride back to Winnipeg so that he could stay.

During the hours between competitions, I wandered around the fairgrounds, bought some food in a tiny village of plywood concession stands, walked through a fairground midway, and watched part of a baseball game. The sights were in some ways similar to what one would find in any western Canadian community festival: the midway featured familiar rides and games of chance; the stands sold chips, soft drinks, candy, burgers, and fries; empty cups and wrappers blew

Figure 6.1 RYAN RICHARD, 2011. Photo by Bruce Chartrand.

around on the ground. Yet a number of things set the Treaty Days apart. The concession stands sold bannock burgers and Indian tacos. There was a distinctive sartorial mix: older attendees dressed in western wear while children and young adults wore urban fashions, a division that probably indicated who had grown up listening to country music and who listened to rap and R&B as well. Away from the midway were sites where campers had built shelters out of a mixture of contemporary and traditional materials, sometimes combining plastic tarpaulins with poplar and willow boughs. Still farther away were the powwow grounds I had visited earlier that week, comprising a stage, a large, circular wooden bower that offered shade to drum groups and the audience, and an open dancing area in the center. Other things seemed at once familiar and not. When I sat down to eat I met a young square dancer visiting from Skownan First Nation. He seemed worried and a little lonely, and he told me that some of the local boys had wanted to fight him because he wasn't from the reserve.

In the early evening, as I watched the baseball, a thunderhead began to roll in. It was nearly overhead by the time I realized that it was coming right at us. I went to my car to get my video camera and then ran for the dance pavilion, arriving just as the clouds burst. Many others took shelter as well. Rain pounded on the corrugated metal roof and blew in through the open sides of the building, pooling on the plywood dance floor. And then, almost as soon as they had arrived, the clouds rolled away, and the rain ceased. The setting sun was visible again, low in the sky, and the jigging competition was set to start.

When Manitoban aboriginal people talk about jigging, they most frequently mean a solo step dance called the Red River Jig. In the form seen most often in competition—and here it should be noted that practice varies widely—the jig has two parts, danced respectively to the alternating A and B sections of a fiddle tune, also called the Red River Jig. (For a thorough discussion of these steps see Quick 2008.) During the higher A section of the tune, the dancer does a basic step, often something like that in Figure 6.2.

During the lower B section, they do a fancy step. Some draw upon a repertoire of moves taught by family members and dance coaches others come up with new ones. Difficult and well-executed fancy steps are particularly appreciated. One time through the AB base step–fancy step pattern is called a "change"; in competitions, dancers are usually asked to do three. The Red River Jig is typically danced solo in Manitoba, except when integrated into square-dance choreography. At

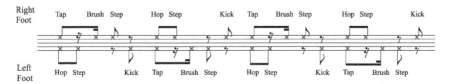

Figure 6.2 BASIC RED RIVER JIG STEP. Notated time values are approximate.

other times and in other places it has been danced in male-female pairs (see Begg 1871, Quick 2008). The jig is physically demanding, and a successful performance requires strength, but good jiggers have something else, too—a combination of control and ebullience. A good performance is, in sometimes startling ways, an embodiment of distinct and self-assured personhood.[5]

The tune that accompanies the dance has similar potential for individuation. Although it has become common in recent years for fiddlers to emulate Andy De Jarlis's version of the tune, fiddlers still play their own (see chapter 2; see also Lederman 1988: 210, 215, 216). Transcriptions of two such are shown: one

Figure 6.3 THE RED RIVER JIG (TRADITIONAL) AS PERFORMED BY CLIFF MAYTWAYASHING AT PEGUIS (I). Transcribed by the author. This is the version Maytwayashing played for the first male dancer in the jigging competition. It is included with Maytwayashing's permission. The barlines in the A sections indicate the presence of repeating motives and melodic groupings rather than metrical divisions; those in the B sections indicate apparent metrical groupings.

Figure 6.3 (Continued)

performed by Cliff Maytwayashing during the jigging competition discussed later (Figure 6.3), the other recorded by Garry Lepine, a Manitoban fiddler of Métis descent (Figure 6.4).

The jigging competition began around ten at night, a little after the sun had set. I was able to make a video recording of most of the event, and the following account draws upon this and my field notes.[6] As Table 6.1 shows, the contest had three divisions: men eighteen and over, women eighteen and over, and seniors (both women and men) fifty and over. The dancers came up one after another, performing two at a time in the women's and seniors' categories (in which there were more competitors) and singly in the men's category. Cliff Maytwayashing again accompanied the dancers, backed by an ensemble that included electric and acoustic guitars, bass, and drum machine, the latter likely cued by Maytwayashing himself. By the time the jigging competition started, the beloved fiddler and elder, who passed away in 2009, had already played for a full afternoon of square dancing; afterward he was scheduled to accompany a community dance until five in the morning.

Before the competition started, Ryan Richard, well-known around the province as a champion jigger, was invited to perform a dance exhibition. It seemed strange to me that the organizers extended this honor to him, since he had registered to participate in the following contest. This anomaly was the first of many. As Richard performed a series of virtuosic steps to the "Orange Blossom Special," he was joined on the dance floor by an uninvited local man, Tom Ross,[7] who proceeded to demonstrate his own, markedly less accomplished steps in his stocking feet. At one point Ross lost his footing on the rain-slicked floor and fell, to the audience's great amusement. When the two dancers returned to their seats, Ross proclaimed, seemingly oblivious to the impression he had created, "Well,

Figure 6.4 THE RED RIVER JIG AS PERFORMED BY GARRY LEPINE. Transcribed by Trent Bruner, BMus (Music Education) and BEd (Elementary), University of Saskatchewan, Canada; MMus (Ethnomusicology), University of Bergen, Norway. Reproduced with permission of both transcriber and performer.

they know I can jig now." When the actual contest began, Ross sat next to Richard and began repeatedly to ask to borrow his tap shoes. Richard declined. At first the appeals seemed earnest, although possibly devious. (If Richard lent out his shoes would he get them back? More worrisome, was Ross making an inappropriate request simply so that he could treat its refusal as a provocation? Complicating the interaction, Richard was not only an outsider at the event, but also openly gay, or rather two-spirited, the term he preferred I use when we discussed this account of the contest.) Later, when Richard took his turn as a competitor, Tom's demands got louder but also more playful.

Several more serious disruptions occurred during the men's eighteen-and-over division. One of the competitors was none other than Tom Ross, and when his

Table 6.1 **Jigging competition structure**

Section		Notes
Introductory events	Ryan's exhibition dance	These introductory events delayed the start of the contest until enough competitors could be signed up to take part
	Dance floor open for social dancing	
	Announcements	
Competition	1. Men (18 and over)	Competitors danced singly
	2. Women (18 and over)	Competitors danced in twos
	3. Seniors (50 and over)	Competitors danced in twos
	4. Women (18 and over) runoff competition	Featuring the best dancers from the initial women's round
Concluding events	Announcement of winners and distribution of prizes	

turn came, Susan Bird,[8] the woman who had been sitting beside him, began to yell, "My baby, don't fall down," and "Jig hard, my baby." Nor did he escape the attention of the emcee, who noted that this time Ross had "his jigging boots on," to much laughter from the audience. Ross danced in time to the music but didn't follow the canonical choreography for the Red River Jig. Most of his stepping seemed to involve stomping a single leg on the ground on the offbeats of the jig tune; he threw in a few thrusts of his pelvis and some air fiddling for good measure. Meanwhile, mirroring Ross's earlier transgression, Bird stepped out on to the dance floor and began to jig along with him. She also joined the next competitor—as did another audience member. Such behavior, however entertaining, was of course entirely outside of the bounds of contest protocol, and the frustrated emcee eventually asked the security guards at the event to prevent further interruptions.

Next was Ryan Richard's turn. But before he could begin, Susan Bird began to complain vociferously from the bleachers. Eventually the emcee acknowledged her from the stage, saying over the microphone, "I can't hear you; come up here and speak." She replied, "OK, I'm going to come up there [to] speak my mind." Meanwhile, Richard stood alone in the center of the dance floor, waiting to start. Bird went up on stage and had words off-microphone with the emcee, to the initial amusement and subsequent impatience of the audience. Soon people were yelling for the contest to start again. The emcee eventually announced over the microphone, "OK, I agree with her. She said we were going to give her five dollars the other night when she come and jigged. If I did that I'm sorry. I wasn't a judge and I didn't have the money, so ... I didn't look after that. All I do is I emcee." The competition resumed.

Richard danced with confidence, stylistic authority, and attention to detail. He did a more complicated version of the basic step than that performed by other dancers, and his fancy steps grew increasingly virtuosic as he moved through the three changes. In the first he tapped his free foot in front of and behind the weight-bearing leg; in the second he kicked out one foot and then the other in front of his body, tapping each twice very quickly; and in the third he performed his "ankle breaker," crossing his legs and rocking back and forth with the outsides of his feet supporting the weight of his body.[9] He finished with a bow to enthusiastic applause.

Figure 6.5 is a transcription of the version of the Red River Jig that Maytwayashing performed for Richard. The markings A, B, A′, B, A′, and B′

Figure 6.5 THE RED RIVER JIG (TRADITIONAL) AS PERFORMED BY CLIFF MAYTWAYASHING AT PEGUIS (II). Transcribed by the author. This is the version of the jig Maytwayashing played for Ryan Richard. It is included with Maytwayashing's permission. Again, the barlines in the A sections indicate the presence of repeating motives and melodic groupings rather than metrical divisions; those in the B sections indicate apparent metrical groupings.

Figure 6.5 (*Continued*)

indicate the music-structural shifts with which Richard synchronized his alternations between basic and fancy steps.[10] Comparing Figures 6.5 and 6.3 reveals that Maytwayashing played a significantly longer version of the tune for Richard than for the first dancer in the men's competition: section B′ is eight beats longer in Figure 6.5 than it is in Figure 6.3.[11] Such variations in length happened frequently, as Table 6.2 shows. Maytwayashing altered the length of the changes, but sometimes also the number of changes he played: twice he played two changes, nine times he played three changes, and twice he played four changes.[12] In this regard, Maytwayashing's approach was noticeably different from that of younger fiddlers, who tended to play the jig in exactly the same way every time.

When I mentioned to Maytwayashing in 2008 that he had varied the length of the tune from rendition to rendition, he was immediately aware there was a possibility for controversy. Even a hint of inequality can lead to complaints, including of contest fixing. All the same, he gave his permission to include transcriptions of his performances in this book, and his generosity and openness suggest to me that he had performed his role at the competition in good faith. When I asked him about the differences, he told me:

> I guess when you play for good dancers, eh, it makes you feel good . . . easy to play. Then after that a bunch of bad dancers come on, then—boy—I can't look at them at all. I gotta look away or look at the musicians, and try to keep myself in time, eh. [Laughs] So I start making mistakes.

Table 6.2 **Comparison of Maytwayashing's performances of the Red River Jig**

Dancers	First change		Second change		Third change		Fourth change		Notes
	A	B	A'	B/B'	A'	B/B'	A'	B'	
Women's competition									
Women 1, 2	20	22	20	22	20	27 (B')	–	–	
Women 3, 4	20	26	20	22	20	19 (B')	–	–	
Women 5, 6	20	26	20	22	20	22	20	19 (B')	
Men's competition									
Men 1	20	22	20	26	20	19 (B')	–	–	
Men 2	20	26	20	22	20	22	20	19 (B')	1.
Men 3	20	26	20	22	20	19 (B')	–	–	2.
Men 4	20	26	20	26	20	27 (B')	–	–	3.
Men 5	20	22	20	22	20	19 (B')	–	–	
Men 6	20	26	20	26	20	23 (B')	–	–	
Seniors' Competition									
Seniors 1, 2	20	26	20	22	20	11 (B')	–	–	4.
Seniors 3, 4	20	26	20	22	20	15 (B')	–	–	
Seniors 5, 6	20	26	20	19 (B')	–	–	–	–	
Seniors 7, 8	20	22	20	23 (B')	–	–	–	–	5.
Seniors 9, 10	20	22	20	Recording incomplete					

1. Ross dances; Bird goes up to dance with him, uninvited.
2. Bird and another uninvited person dance alongside competitor.
3. Ryan dances, but only after Bird finishes talking with the emcee.
4. Bird complains about "family tradition" before and after these competitors.
5. Bird dances in this round.

His answer suggests that his playing was an immediate aesthetic response to the kind of dancing he was seeing, with poorer performances causing mistakes. My recording offers some support for this explanation: in three of the four cases when Maytwayashing played more or fewer than three changes of the jig, the contestants were not following the canonical jigging pattern closely. All the same, I am not entirely sure I would dismiss all variations as mistakes. I wonder whether they might be characterized more broadly: as responses—perhaps evaluative responses—to the dancing he saw. Maytwayashing told me later in the interview:

> Dad taught me how to play music, and play with your feelings.... "Right from your heart," he used to tell me.... So that's the way I play as I watch the people dancing. They're happy and I get that happy feeling too.

Perhaps, then, some of his musical variations were positive reactions to the dancing: happy responses "right from the heart."

More drama was in store before the end of the evening. As the first competitors in the seniors' division went to have their numbers pinned on their shirts, Susan Bird yelled, "Take your family tradition!" and "We're sick of lies and b.s.!" When they had finished dancing, she shouted, "Pick your own family tradition; that's all you do anyways!" and "First place!" If Bird was predicting that one or both of them would come out on top, she was partly correct; one eventually took second place. Nor was Bird disinterested in the outcome of the contest: she was one of the entrants. When her turn came, she playfully started dancing before the music even started, again drawing laughter from the audience. Maytwayashing played a very short version of the Red River Jig for her and her co-competitor (again, in the seniors' rounds, two entrants danced at the same time). The curtailed musical performance did not seem to affect the judges' evaluation, however: it was Bird's co-competitor who eventually won first place.

Bird's remarks about "family tradition" were almost certainly allegations of nepotism. (I was only a visitor, so there could be another explanation, but no convincing one comes to mind.) She was contending that one or both of the first two competitors would do well because of family connections, perhaps to the chief, band councilors, emcee, or judges. My consultants have regularly characterized patronage as a determinant of favor at competitions, within the music scene, and more generally. There are frequent accusations that those with access to resources, or the power to vest honors upon others, prioritize kin and close friends. At least discursively, then, small-group "atomism" (Hallowell 1955) is a fact of community life. In this light, Bird's continual disruptions at the contest—including her demands early on for money—seem less capricious and more tactical and directed. This is not to say that the competition I saw at Peguis was fixed. It is rather to say that, in Manitoban aboriginal communities, fixing sometimes takes place, people widely believe it to be done, and, more broadly, resource distribution can be inequitable. Bird's complaints about favoritism, however particular, expressed very widespread concerns and tensions.[13]

Prizes were handed out at the conclusion of the jigging competition, and, to nobody's surprise, Richard took first place in the men's eighteen-and-over competition. Afterward we drove back to Winnipeg. A short way outside of Peguis we stopped at a gas station, and Ryan bought me a drink and offered to get me a pack of cigarettes out of his winnings. On the way home he told me that he was glad he had won the money, since it meant that he would be able to help his brother out; he had already given him and his girlfriend twenty dollars each, and now he would be able to give them more. This was one of many occasions when a consultant modeled for me the importance of giving and of looking out for one's relatives. We got back to Winnipeg around two o'clock in the morning, with just enough time to pick up a case of beer at the off-license before it closed. I dropped Ryan off at a friend's place.

On our way into the city, we had talked a little about the competition. When I asked him about Bird, Ryan told me that events like the one we had attended needed someone like that: a clown. Well, not exactly a clown, he didn't mean that, but something similar. His remark suggested that Bird's and Ross's behavior, for all its apparent inappropriateness, fell within the Anishinaabe tradition of trick-sterism.[14] Theirs was an altogether appropriate kind of inappropriateness. It was perhaps also for this reason that the emcee was compelled to attend to Bird's complaints—even though it meant halting the competition and allowing her to come up to the stage to give him a piece of her mind. This was not the only instance when an elder cowed a powerful person through behavior that, in nonaboriginal Manitoban communities, might have seemed dismissible.

Strict and Improvised Structures, Revisited

As chapters 1 and 2 suggest, public assembly inevitably involves some degree of intimacy: a print or radio advertisement may extend an invitation to an event to an audience of strangers, but the actual gathering assembles a concrete number of people in a specific time and place. The ensuing intimacies are often limited, of course, and may simply amount to collective, real-time affirmations or negotiations of the appropriate degree to which people should acknowledge or ignore one another.[15] In other cases, however, there is a transformation or reclamation of public space as community space that involves an insistence upon "deeper" forms of intimate interaction, more intensely participatory forms of collective engagement, and the specificities of local relationships and cultural practices.

Such prioritizations of intimacy and community were evident in a number of ways at the Peguis Treaty Days. In their most obvious form they involved the kind of "getting to know you" (compare Silverstein 1997) that visitors to festivals in many western Canadian communities might experience—but that nevertheless seem more heightened in First Nations communities (and at events such as the William Whyte coffeehouse). A number of visitors from outside of Peguis, probably the majority of them square dancers participating in the afternoon competition, had come to the festivities. During the course of the day, a variety of intimacies were initiated with them: strangers engaged them in conversation,[16] Ryan Richard was invited to give a dance exhibition (and asked for his shoes), another younger dancer felt threatened by local boys. In ways both exclusive and inclusive, the community accounted for them: as friendly acquaintances, disliked outsiders, honored guests, and so on.

The interactions at the jigging competition also privileged intimacy, but in more amplified ways. This was particularly evident in how various extemporized elements intersected with the formal structure of the event. As at the coffeehouse discussed in the previous chapter, social and musical interactions involved the simultaneous articulation of event structures of relative fixity and interactional formations of a more improvised character. (Table 6.2 above incorporates elements of both.) At the contest, however, fixed and free elements seemed to evidence different—and to some degree conflicting—social orientations. The official structure of the event exemplified a bearing toward a public, a kind of "competition publicness," whereas the freer interactions prioritized intimacy, sometimes in ways that threatened to compromise this publicness.

On the face of it, the contest established structural equivalence between participants: dancers from anywhere could come to the community, perform, and be judged on the same terms (like powwow dancers, they were given numbers to affix to their shirts, and judges did not even need to know them by name). Contest categories made allowances for gender and age: younger dancers competed against contestants of their own sex, and older ones vied against participants in their own age range. Everyone was to dance three changes of the Red River Jig played by the same fiddler. And the judges were to use the same bases for evaluating all participants. Hence competition publicness: a structure designed to give the same opportunity to all members of the public of potential participants. Yet, in the actual course of events, various actors undermined this smooth sameness: as has been related, members of the audience moved onto the dance floor during the turns of two competitors, and the music varied in length from dancer to dancer.

Even as they disrupted competition publicness, however, they affirmed other valued cultural practices. Bird's interruptions may have distracted judges and dancers and held up the competition, but they were also something the event "needed." She brought into play the part of the playful, upending trickster and through it posed questions about the fair distribution of wealth and honors. Maytwayashing's changing versions of the Red River Jig may have presented different affordances to different competitors, but they also affirmed a way of fiddle playing in which the tune changed from one iteration to the next (see chapter 2; see also Lederman 1988: 215–16; Rodgers 1980) and in which—I have suggested—musicians responded to dancers from the heart. In short, his playing prioritized interactive sensitivity rather than strict equivalence.

Interestingly, it was Bird who expressed concern that structural equivalence had never been a possibility at the contest—that winners would inevitably be selected on the basis of family connections ("That's all you do anyways"). Again, whether favoritism actually occurred is unimportant so far as the argument here is concerned. What is significant is the worry that those in power would "pick their own family tradition": that intimate ties would trump an ostensible commitment to the fair treatment of all. Bird understood the contest as an event geared toward clients in the community rather than a public of strangers.[17]

Thus, while fixed and extemporized structures of interaction were coarticulated at the Peguis competition, they suggested distinct social orientations. The more formal structures seemed oriented to a social imaginary, a public of potential participants whose members needed to be treated in the same way. The more improvised interactions frequently undercut this competition-publicness, and in ways that emphasized social intimacy. It was not simply that they weakened the structural equivalence of the competition, then, but rather that they prioritized the intimate, immediate, and face-to-face. Hence the interruptions on the dance floor were comical or contentious gestures directed toward other community members, while the variations in the music were responses to the dancers performing in the same room. The antecedence of intimacy was also evident in the motivations participants imputed to others. Bird characterized the competition as an excuse for those in charge to distribute awards and honors to their own kin, rather than to the best dancers. In her interpretation, it was all in the family.

The argument here is not that Manitoban aboriginal people are incapable of generating "proper" public culture or of taking part in the imagining sociability that enables it. It is rather that Native communities—and non-Native ones, too—are in the course of negotiating a balance between intimacy and stranger-sociability, between community and society. Culturally particular—and politically differentiated—indigenous modernities emerge in part through these ongoing negotiations. In the example above, various actors and groups asserted the priority of social intimacy, and of culturally particular practices, in ways that interrupted or undermined normative ways of being public. This goes on continually and is one instance of what is here called antipublicity: qualification of the orientation to a public, often through prioritization of the intimate. I have argued that publics and counterpublics emerge in part through the mass-mediated circulation of certain intimacies. Yet, and as the next section makes evident, some intimacies limit the emergence of publicness, while others seem to resist circulation.

Gift Giving, Patronage, and Wariness

Ryan Richard's presents to me and to his brother and his brother's girlfriend were a small example of the importance of gift giving in Manitoban aboriginal social life. Those he offered me likely acknowledged that, in providing a ride, I had enabled him to make some money in the dance competition. They reciprocated my own gift, in other words. His gifts to his brother and to his girlfriend exemplified the common expectation that relatives and friends should take care of one another. I witnessed many similar instances of prestation (Mauss 1990) between kin and close friends during my fieldwork and was myself frequently the beneficiary of gifts from consultants. In this way I became integrated in networks of reciprocity and support, since gift giving was also a way of establishing relationships. It was simultaneously, then, a manifestation of social closeness and the means of entailing it—to varying degrees, it both acknowledged and activated relationships (see Diamond 2008: 10).

Giving also had socially problematic aspects. My consultants, and various voices in the aboriginal public sphere, frequently claimed that members of reserve governments and indigenous political organizations looked after their families

and friends foremost, offering them the first opportunities when funding, housing, or honors were distributed. Preferential treatment was among a number of
unsavory practices designated by the pejorative category "politics." Yet allies and
enemies alike regularly expected politicians to dispense patronage. For insiders, it was one of the benefits of closeness; for outsiders, one of the sometimes
secret, sometimes flagrant misdeeds associated with power and material advantage. Even in cases where leaders were committed to fairness, it was frequently
expected that they would extend benefits and resources first to those closest to
them. One elder told me that he had been hired for a government job that put
him in charge of a significant budget. Torn between a commitment to be fair and
obligations to his relatives and friends, he had asked not to manage the money,
believing that he would be unable to say no to those who would inevitably come
to ask him for special assistance.

Patronage, real or imagined, played just as important a role in the realm of
music and dance. It was particularly in evidence at competitive events: talent
shows, dance contests, and awards programs, for instance, at which community
leaders and other important figures distributed money and honors. Vernacular
commentators regularly expressed doubts about whether these awards were mer-
ited, alleging favoritism. It is difficult to say how much actually occurred, but the
number of accusations was noteworthy. One friend claimed to have been implicated himself in an instance of unfair evaluation. He told me that he had been
asked to judge and emcee a talent show on a Manitoban reserve. Just before the
competition was to start, two late entrants were allowed in, both relatives of
important political figures in the community. My friend was informed that the
event organizers would be picking the second- and third-place contestants—as
it turned out, these happened to be the two late entrants—and that he would be
free to choose the winner. "They always complain when we choose the winner,"
they told him, to his great amusement.[18]

Although patronage was roundly criticized in the music scene, it was also courted.
Musicians aligned themselves with various political figures (or were believed to) in
the understanding that there were advantages to be had in terms of exposure and
material reward. After all, First Nations and Métis leaders were responsible for organizing some of the largest and most significant musical events of the year.

Thus, patronage, reciprocity, and commentary about them were bound up
in a number of ways with the articulation of social intimacies and imaginaries.
Gift giving both acknowledged and established bonds between social intimates,
even as it had the potential to distance them from outsiders, particularly those
who considered themselves thereby disadvantaged. In the same way, suspicions
were often an expression of social distance. So far as imaginaries were concerned,
patronage frequently stood in tension with ideas about how publics should function: it undermined public service in directing the ministrations of the powerful away from the public good and toward that of relatives and friends, and it
upset the ideal of impartial judgment. And yet, in moving away from nonspecific

stranger-orientedness, reciprocity and patronage also effected a reenchantment of sociability and a reprioritization of intimacy, kinship, and friendship (see Hasty 2005). They were not easily separated from the gift giving that remained important in other areas of social life.

Representing Patronage

Like the discussions of drinking in chapters 1 and 3, the foregoing account risks being perceived as propagating negative stereotypes, here of "corruption" and "nepotism" in aboriginal communities. It raises questions about how to represent practices that appear to play an important role in indigenous community life and expressive performance, but that are regarded as deeply problematic in national discourse. Complicating the matter is that many of these practices—especially certain forms of "politics"—are controversial within indigenous communities as well, although in culturally particular ways. A term such as "nepotism," familiar and seemingly transparent to the national public, does not quite capture the distinctiveness of patronage in Manitoban indigenous communities—neither the nuanced ambivalence with which it is regarded nor the abundance of strategies by which it is courted and contested.

The question of representation is particularly fraught because the Canadian government has regarded "corruption" in First Nations governments as grounds for legislation that would hold indigenous communities and governments more accountable to the federal government. In the early years of my fieldwork, Bill C-7, the federal First Nations Governance Act, threatened to extend federal surveillance and discipline even further into indigenous communities, infringe more significantly upon their sovereignty, and continue a legacy of assimilationist federal policies. It was vigorously protested by indigenous activists in 2002 and did not become law. As this book was in press, however, the federal government passed Bill C-27, which requires First Nations governments to publish extensive financial statements and schedules of remuneration, threatening severe penalties in cases of noncompliance.

During the leadup to the passing of the bill, Peguis First Nation, where the preceding ethnographic account was set, was regularly the subject of national media stories suggesting the community's elected officials were extravagantly compensated and had been mismanaging finances. This coverage was just one example of long-standing national discourses (for an older example see Morrison 1995) criticizing indigenous governments, expressing concern over how those governments spend their revenues (sometimes problematically characterized as the settler nation's tax dollars), and calling for increased federal intervention and oversight. John Provart, writing at the time of the First Nations Governance Act, describes national worries about First Nations governments and pressure on the federal government to "do something" about them (2003: 131).

Federal interventions are problematic for a number of reasons. As indigenous critics have argued, Bill C-27 subjects First Nations government to reporting requirements that are more stringent than in many other jurisdictions, threatens severe penalties for noncompliance, potentially undermines the competitiveness of band-owned businesses, and substantially increases paperwork burdens (Assembly of First Nations 2013). More broadly, Bill C-27 follow the path of previous problematic state measures in introducing ambitious legal initiatives not in response to requests from and consultation with aboriginal communities, but rather as a way to satisfy the concerns of the national public. Most significant of all, the legislation presumes the absence of structures of accountability within indigenous communities (compare Provart 2003: 163), extends federal control over them, and further limits their autonomy. It imposes an assimilatory regulatory regime across a range of indigenous groups rather than allowing those groups to refine and elaborate their own structures of governance and accountability.

It is clear, then, that indigenous patronage does not exist in a vacuum: it is observed by national audiences whose demands can have drastic consequences for Native sovereignty.[19] One response by advocates has been to argue that indigenous governments are no more troubled or corrupt than national ones. This approach is almost always compelling: in the early 2000s, the same federal Liberal government that had expressed concern about corruption in First Nations governments was itself shaken by an immense funding scandal; as this book goes to press, the Conservative government that passed Bill C-27 has been hit by an expense scandal.

Tara Browner makes an argument along similar lines in her discussion of nepotism at the 1989 Ann Arbor Pow Wow:

> Influential members of the Native community were selected as head veterans and judges, and the master of ceremonies was a friend of [the administrator in charge of organizing the pow-wow]. Nepotism and the dispensing of favors for relatives and friends is a common and often acceptable practice in most Native American cultures, and those in positions of authority are expected to do so. The practice is handled in the same manner in the dominant society. The greatest contrast between the two groups, however, is in the openness of the nepotism and the openness of complaining about it. (2002: 42–43)

Browner's contention is somewhat broader than this, however: she argues that while indigenous patronage resembles mainstream nepotism in some respects, it differs from it in the way it is performed and resisted. In short, she points to subtle but significant differences in cultural practice where outsiders might only see a familiar same.

Might the accounts of mid-twentieth-century anthropologists be at all helpful in exploring the question of patronage? As discussed in chapter 4, early ethnographers described northern Algonquian communities as low-integration societies in which personhood was highly individuated and in which little formal social organization existed beyond small, family-based trapping and hunting units. One of these authors, Leonard Mason, writing of a Cree community he visited in 1938 and 1940, remarked that, during an election, a number of community members had "objected [to the election of a particular individual] saying that he was in league with several councillors who were suspected of favouring themselves and their friends by an unequal division of the treaty supplies" (1967: 45). His account is reminiscent of present-day characterizations of reserve politics.

Older ethnographic accounts of the ways northern Algonquian people talked about powerful individuals share some interesting commonalities with present indigenous discourses about patronage. Mid-twentieth-century ethnographers described fears that those who were spiritually gifted would secretly use their abilities to harm rather than to heal and prolong life (see Hallowell 1955, Landes 1968, Rogers 1962; see also Angel 2002). The criticisms of prominent figures I heard while doing fieldwork tended to center on misconduct of a more secular sort—for instance, financial misappropriations or improper uses of political influence to extend honors and resources to family and friends or to punish enemies. Like the concerns described in the earlier literature, however, they often involved the improper or malicious doings, conducted secretly, of powerful figures (see Hallowell 1955: 146–47; Landes 1968: 11–12, 43, 57–67).

There have been important objections to the accounts of these early anthropologists. The idea that low-integration social organization was characteristic of northern Algonquian societies before European contact[20] was vigorously opposed by Harold Hickerson, who in a 1967 article argued that precontact northern Algonquians had instead been communal in organization and outlook. He went on to interpret social atomism as a symptom of the social "depression," "decay," "decline," and "decadence" (1967: 324, 337) that emerged during the European fur trade and was exacerbated under the reserve system (1967: 324–25, 338). He also argued that the behaviors anthropologists associated with atomism— including sorcery, suspicion, competitiveness, and jealousy—were unappealing to whites and could be marshaled rhetorically to justify colonialism in retrospect (1967: 323–24, 327). Yet Hickerson's line of argument was also problematic: it dismissed the often sympathetic representation of alterity in the anthropologists it criticized, and it characterized contemporary northern Algonquian society and sociability as decadent—in effect damning present-day communities to defend the supposed ones of the past (see Friedl's response in Hickerson 1967: 331–32).[21]

Again, are the early anthropological accounts at all helpful? Certainly any use of them needs to take into account their tendency to emphasize individuation and downplay community. As Michael McNally's rereadings of some of these early writings (and chapters 4 and 5 in this volume) demonstrate, collectivity has been a significant aspect of indigenous community life past and present. Individuation and small-group allegiance may be important aspects of northern Algonquian sociability, but that is far from the entire picture. I am hesitant to dismiss the literature altogether, however. It may be productive, for instance, to consider the possibility of connections between contemporary aboriginal criticism of leaders and the "suspicious" discourses about powerful figures that early anthropologists reported. In the past, as in the present, the powerful have often been regarded warily. It seems worth considering whether this carefulness evidences a certain persistent and productive ambivalence about power. Do widespread "complaints about nepotism" (to paraphrase Browner) represent not the absence of indigenous accountability but rather one of the very means by which the less powerful seek to effect it? Consider again the remarkable force that such complaints appeared to have at the dance competition described earlier.

Criticism does not always result in change, and it seems clear that there are winners and losers when scant resources are not equitably distributed in indigenous communities (see Provart 2003: 133). But it is important to take into account the nestedness of power structures. In a context where the state has extensive oversight of indigenous governments, it has often pointed to the apparent troubles of indigenous governments to justify the extension of its own power (see Herzfeld 1997). Given this situation, one way to frame the problem of representation is that it consists in finding ways of writing about indigenous differences, and speaking in favor of a just distribution of resources, that cannot easily be rallied in support of assimilative measures or the transfer of indigenous authority to the settler state.

* * * * *

Indigenous patronage has been represented in a variety of ways. Some have seen it, like low-integration sociability, as a troubled legacy of contact or colonialism. Others have presented corruption in aboriginal communities as a straightforward failure of Native governance and recommended that the state intervene to ensure accountability. Advocates have, in response, raised questions about the moral high ground from which dominant societies demand changes of aboriginal communities. Complicating the question of representation are additional concerns: that the impacts of colonialism and widespread poverty not be neglected, and that the position of the have-nots in communities where there is an unfair distribution of resources be remembered.

The account of patronage presented here is hesitant to dismiss it solely as a problem in indigenous governance, a legacy of the colonial encounter, or a symptom of poverty. Patronage in aboriginal communities is linked in complex ways to traditional forms of sociability and contemporary forms of reciprocity and can be one of the means by which public space is insistently remade to make room for intimacy. Nor is this to regard it through rose-colored glasses, since patronage is criticized and contested in indigenous communities. The point is that this is done in distinctive ways, and that the state and the national public often seem to overlook these or regard them as symptoms rather than potentially effective forms of redress. In short, they disregard the possibility that communities may be drawing upon, cultivating, elaborating, and inventing ways of insuring the accountability of their leaders. Here again is evident the dynamic of publicity and counterpublicity, in which difference is misheard as the wrong kind of sameness.

Secrecy and Reverence

The concept of antipublicity has been explored thus far as a prioritization of intimacy that qualifies or eclipses an imagining orientation to a public. But there are other examples of how aboriginal actors and communities place limits on publicness, and in particular the mass-mediated circulation or availability of song, knowledge, ceremony, and sacred items.[22] These include secrecy regarding matters of personal religious experience, the observance of protocols concerning sacred items and knowledge, and the insistence on respect and reciprocity in certain kinds of relationships.

The secrecy historically observed regarding sacred knowledge has clear implications for the limitation of publicness. As explained in chapter 4, in the past it was traditional for Saulteaux and Cree boys (and some girls) to go on a dream fast in which they sought encounters with other-than-human persons who granted special gifts and abilities (Brightman 1993: 78–79; Brown and Brightman 1988: 138–42; Hallowell 1955: 288, 1992: 87–88, 63–65). Neither the sacred encounter nor the other-than-human helper was spoken of boastfully or lightly, lest the gift be revoked. Hallowell writes: "[The] fasting experience was a sacred experience since direct contact with superhuman entities had been made. This was why the individual never referred to this experience lightly. Unless he were willing to lose his blessings he could not recount his dream in whole or even in part except under extraordinary circumstances" (1955: 360; see also Brown and Brightman 1988: 142; Hallowell 1992: 88–89; Landes 1968: 36–37).

In Landes's account, the Midéwiwin, the grand medicine society of the Ojibwe, also limited the circulation of sacred information. Midéwiwin patients attained certain privileged forms of knowledge in stages as they rose through the numbered grades of the society during the course of successive ceremonies, the commissioning of which required considerable outlay of resources (Landes 1968: 72–73, 78–81). Other forms of training and knowledge were provided specifically to midé officers, again often at a cost (Landes 1968: 76–78). Landes notes that "the general outlines of midé practices were common knowledge" but that certain types of information were guarded closely, including those required for curing and for "sorcery" (1968: 75).

Prohibitions on the circulation of knowledge continue to play a role in contemporary sacred and ceremonial activities. In early 2003 I attended the University of Manitoba's Elders and Traditional People's Gathering, a meeting of First Nations and Métis people. At the final session, an Anishinaabe elder began to relate a dream. He stopped at one point to ask that a video camera at the back of the auditorium be turned off, and this was done. Presuming that he objected only to the presence of video technology, I continued to take notes. Shortly thereafter a staff member came by to tell an academic colleague and me that it was rude to write while an elder related a dream. At the time the experience was both embarrassing and frustrating: after months of respectfully avoiding note taking, videotaping, and recording at events where I believed such activity would be improper, I had found myself in a situation where it seemed possible to undertake the observational aspects of my fieldwork with some degree of freedom. After all, I was at a university-organized and -funded event. Why shouldn't I be able to take notes during this plenary address, as I might have done in any other academic setting? Surely the information presented here was for the benefit of the public and could circulate freely?

But this was not the case: relating a dream was not a lecture or a speech.[23] Certain protocols prevented the capture of the dream on film and paper. Prohibitions against recording sacred material were very common while I did fieldwork, although reasons for these prohibitions were not always given. Explanations, when available, varied; they included concerns that recording took indigenous cultural and intellectual property from their rightful owners, and hints that recording risked insulting spiritual entities. It is therefore difficult to say whether the restrictions at the Elders and Traditional People's Gathering were meant to stop the public circulation of sacred materials. But even if they were not straightforwardly antipublic in intent, they were so in consequence: they kept the narration of the dream from being distributed to a public of strangers.

There was, generally speaking, reluctance to orient sacred knowledge and practices to a public. I rarely saw traditional ceremonies advertised or discussed in public forums, and video and audio recordings of such observances were rare.[24] There were exceptions: one rural retreat advertised on a website and regularly hosted nonaboriginal groups, who visited its sweat lodge to develop an awareness of Native traditions. And in Winnipeg a sweat lodge was constructed out in the open on the grounds of a downtown aboriginal community center.[25] The public ceremonies conducted at these places were controversial, however: some questioned the motivations of the ceremonialists involved, others their commitment and the extent of their traditional knowledge.[26] A woman involved with one of the lodges acknowledged in an informal conversation that there had been controversy about its publicness. In her opinion, however, the freedom to hold sweats openly marked a significant advance over the old days, when ceremonies had to be hidden from the Indian agent. Her characterization of the situation rendered secrecy an artifact of the colonial experience.[27] Yet the willingness of some to conduct public performances of northern Algonquian ceremonies should not obscure that many have strong misgivings about doing so.

During the early 2000s there were increasing efforts to incorporate traditional indigenous knowledge and practices in the curriculum of Manitoban educational institutions, particularly those with significant Native populations. These generated discussion and disagreement. My Ojibwe professor Roger Roulette told me that a course on traditional aboriginal music had run at a Manitoban institute of higher education, but that the way it was conducted had worried him. On the one hand, he found it distressing that powerful ritual articles were being treated as secular musical instruments. He told me he had asked a faculty member, "Have you ever seen a rosary made of macaroni? Have you ever seen a toy confessional?" On the other hand, he worried that the young people using these instruments would summon something they would be unable to cope with (see also J. Brown 2003: 13–14). It was not safe to let just anyone handle them.

Similar arguments were in evidence at a gathering sponsored by the Manitoba First Nations Education Resource Centre in the spring of 2003. Organizers had invited a range of elders and educators to discuss the possibility of incorporating knowledge about aboriginal medicines in grade-school curriculums. During a breakout session for Ojibwe participants, a number of attendees expressed trepidation about the teaching of traditional medicines in a school setting. Two of them emphasized the need for caution and respect. Olga McIvor reported:

> An elder was concerned that if you teach young children medicine . . . they might poison themselves or not treat the medicine with respect and [could] thereby harm themselves. It may be better for an elder to identify which children are the gifted ones who have an interest in medicines. (McIvor 2003: 1)[28]

The elder's concerns had a significant spiritual component: it was not only that children might poison themselves, but also that they might show disrespect to the medicine and thereby come to harm.[29] These apprehensions resonated with traditional beliefs concerning affronts to spiritual beings: a person who offended one of these other-than-human persons was believed to invite retribution and harm.

The second part of the elder's response—namely, that elders should identify the children with gifts and teach them—also merits consideration. Like a number of the statements made at the gathering, it affirmed a traditional Ojibwe idea that individuals are blessed with specific gifts. It also suggested medical pedagogy should be offered at the discretion of the teacher. In this understanding of teaching, elders monitored children for evidence of giftedness, receptiveness, and reverence, and excluded disrespectful or unsuited pupils from inappropriate pursuits. This is a long way from classroom pedagogy, in which knowledge is disseminated to all, regardless of attitude or aptitude. Here education does not address an unknown public of aboriginal students, but rather particular individuals identified in the course of interpersonal engagement.

Speakers emphasized the importance of intimacy not only in traditional pedagogy, but in the harvest and exchange of medicines as well. They suggested, in short, an intimate and reciprocal relationship with nature. One stressed the importance of offering tobacco before gathering medicine, and of taking only what was needed. Others criticized the exploitative and ecologically damaging undertakings of the province's lumber and hydroelectric industries. Yet another was concerned that people who did not have the gift of healing were "commercializing the medicine and making it a business" (McIvor 2003: 2). These statements together modeled a reciprocal relationship between Anishinaabeg and nature, in which payment was given for medicines taken. And they contrasted this relationship with the straightforward exploitation by large corporations of natural resources.

To sum up, traditional people placed limits on publicness in a number of ways. Most preferred not to allow recordings to be made of traditional ceremonies and knowledge. Many were uncomfortable with the idea of such things being advertised, sold on the market, or made available to the general public. These limitations on the circulation of the sacred may be related to older customs of tactful silence regarding sacred encounters and knowledge. Also evident was a prioritization of intimacy and personal interaction. It was important that traditional knowledge be imparted only to those who had an aptitude for it and would display an appropriate reverence toward it, persons who could only be identified through personal engagement. This precaution, like others, points to a privileging of yet other intimacies: sacred knowledge, songs, and ceremonies could not be distributed to just anybody, for this would risk offending other-than-human intimates.

Economics, Colonial History, "Politics", and the Prioritization of Intimacy

Publicness is transformed by the realms of cultural practice it encounters. It is not simply the content of publicness that changes—although publics are constituted through, and distinguished by, the circulation of different kinds of performances and publications—but its workings as well. In short, "imagining" forms of acquaintanceship, like other globalizing phenomena, change as new groups of people engage with them. An analogy can be made with Dipesh Chakrabarty's theory of global capital. The historian argues that capitalism is not and cannot be universal, for everywhere that it spreads it encounters particular "pasts"—or what might here be called cultural practices. It is consequently continually being qualified by the particularity of the contexts it enters: "Even in the very abstract and abstracting space of the factory that capital creates, ways of being human will be acted out in manners that do not lend themselves to the reproduction of the logic of capital" (Chakrabarty 2000: 66–67).[30] Similarly, publicness is not reproduced everywhere in the same way; it is instead qualified by the kinds of communication and behavior that constitute it, and by the practices that resist it. I have suggested that Manitoban aboriginal people shape and circumscribe publicness in part through certain practices that prioritize intimacy. A number of further instances of resolute intimacy are here examined. They reveal how communities and actors "re-enchant" (Hasty 2005) economic and political imaginaries, downplay "imagined communities" (Anderson 1991), and emphasize face-to-face ones.

Chris Beach told me that after the Manitoban success of singles from his independently produced *Opportunity* album (2002a), he was courted by a record label specializing in aboriginal music. The owner of the label offered him a national distribution deal, but he turned it down, unhappy with the financial terms. In 2004 he released two new albums, again independently, and undertook the business of distributing them himself. A couple of years later, on a trip with Beach and his sister to attend a festival on a northern reserve, I got to see firsthand how he did business. During the long drive northward we stopped, not only to buy fuel, but also to see if there might be an opportunity to sell recordings in the stores attached to the gas stations.[31] Once we arrived in the community, Beach headed to the festival grounds and walked around with a large box of CDs, selling discs to whoever was interested. He took time to chat with his customers and occasionally autographed a CD. At one point he met up with the chief of the reserve and hinted that he would not mind performing at the festival (he mentioned to me that he had sometimes won a last-minute booking simply by showing up). The chief declined, explaining that there were simply no additional funds with which to pay him. Still, CD sales were brisk, and, as I remember, Beach easily managed to cover the cost of the trip with the money he made.

When Beach rejected the record company's offer of nationwide distribution, he told me, he did so in part because he would have received only a small royalty for each CD sold through its distribution network. He also would have had to pay a high unit price for any discs he wished to sell himself. Beach did most of his business in person, in the manner just described, and this was what made the record deal unattractive to him. His decision, however, limited his market in many respects to the area he himself could cover.[32] In some ways, Beach did orient his music to a public or market of unknown listeners: he campaigned to have his songs played on NCI FM, for instance, and indeed in one of them celebrated the popularity of his music on that station (see chapter 3). All the same, his decision about the distribution deal confirmed face-to-face encounters as a central aspect of his life as a performer. It suggested a preference for transactions with known and knowable persons, and a lesser concern for imagined markets. And it reproduced something not quite the same as the logic of capital.

A number of talented aboriginal musicians gave regular public performances but, unlike Beach, were hesitant about recording. They regularly engaged with audiences, but face to face rather than via the mass media. Here, too, a potential relationship to a social imaginary was precluded. One acquaintance was wary of being recorded live and regularly checked to ensure that my minidisc recorder and video camera were turned off when he performed. He expressed concerns on occasion that others would sell copies of his performances and that he would miss out on the financial benefits of his own efforts. Yet his hesitation concerning recordings extended well beyond concerns about bootlegging. On at least two occasions, I heard him relate how he had been offered a very substantial sum of money to go to Nashville to promote and possibly put to disc one of his own songs. He declined the offer, and the song remained unrecorded.

Another was Percy Tuesday, one of the more charismatic and entertaining singers on the country and blues scene when I began fieldwork in Manitoba in the early 2000s. Tuesday had a knack for finding songs that suited his voice and personality and then making them his own. (It is now Tuesday, rather than Freddy Fender, whom I associate with "Wasted Days and Wasted Nights," and I still laugh when I remember his sly take on Merle Haggard's "Okie from Muskogee.") He had a particular gift for connecting with audiences, and I didn't doubt him when he told me he had "brought the house down" at impromptu performances in blues clubs in Minneapolis and Memphis. So it was remarkable to me that he had done little to court a wider, mass-mediated audience. As he explained to me in a 2002 interview, he had in fact had chances to do so. In the late 1960s he was a member of the Feathermen, an aboriginal band that performed regularly around Winnipeg. This was a time of possibility for Manitoban musicians: Neil Young and the Guess Who were moving into the international spotlight, and Ray St. Germain, a Métis singer, had become well established on the national pop scene. Tuesday told me that at one point Don Hunter, the manager of the Guess Who, had wanted to put his band on a local television station and set up an audition for them. But the band ended up getting drunk the night before, and that was the end of that. In 1979, a decade later, Tuesday and his brother traveled down to Nashville on a whim. He got up on the stage to sing at a nightclub in the city, and afterward some people from a major label came over to talk, suggesting that there might be possibilities for him. He "chickened out," he told me, and did not follow the opportunity up. More recently, in the late 1990s, he made a basement recording but didn't like the sound of his voice, and he didn't release it.

Tuesday clearly enjoyed playing for audiences in person, but his remarks attributed his decision not to chase after a wider, mass-mediated audience to something more than the prioritization of face-to-face encounters. He drew connections between his hesitation to seize opportunity and the colonial conditions that had shaped his early experiences. It was only during his own lifetime that First Nations people had been allowed to vote in federal elections and freed from prejudicial restrictions on alcohol consumption. His generation and that of his parents had been forced to leave their home communities to attend residential schools, where the government tried to strip them of their languages and cultures. As a consequence, he told me, many aboriginal people still have difficulty with self-esteem.

Tuesday's remarks suggest that colonialism and the widespread derogation of indigenous people and cultures that attended it have had a weighty impact on not only intimate but also imagining forms of aboriginal acquaintanceship. The self-doubt that colonialism engendered, his words suggest, plays a part in the disinclination of some musicians to address a public. And this points to a somewhat broader definition of antipublicity, as something more than the contemporary consequences of ancient tradition. The "pasts" that shape aboriginal publicness are also shared, colonial ones, and the cultural practices that place limits upon it are of complex and sometimes relatively recent origin. Speech and silence alike are entangled with the colonial legacy (see Spivak 1988; Stokes 2010: 96).

A final vignette returns to the subjects of patronage and the problematized realm of "politics." In the early 2000s a large Native political organization held a divisive election, with two closely matched candidates vying for the presidency in an acrimonious race. Both campaigns recruited musicians for support, and for a time musical life became highly politicized. This was a worrying development for some: as already noted, indigenous political organizations provide many performance opportunities, and there was concern that whoever won the election would reward those who had supported them during the campaign. One singer told me that he believed he had experienced retribution for his political allegiances. During the campaign he spoke out in public support of one of the candidates in a radio advertisement. Shortly afterward he was invited to perform at a benefit concert organized by the other candidate (a fund-raiser for a radio program). He showed up and sat through the event until it ended at two in the morning, but was not called up on stage. He returned home, convinced that he had been intentionally humiliated. His mother, a formidable woman in her seventies, was incensed. The following Monday she set out with a picket sign for the office of a politician connected to the offending candidate and began to protest that the former stole money from his own people. Evidently rattled—he had recently faced widely publicized accusations of sexual harassment and had had his office picketed by a group of around seventy protesters—he invited her in to talk. They quickly got to the root of the problem: the slight to her son. He phoned the candidate and put the mother on; she gave him a piece of her mind and eventually hung up on him. The candidate immediately phoned the singer to apologize, saying among other things that the last thing he had wanted to do was offend his mother.

Politics, in the account I heard, was only tangentially about the public good; it had much more to do with personal allegiance and antagonism, patronage and punishment. A protest sign was involved, and the issue of fiscal mismanagement of the people's funds was raised, but these were secondary concerns. Indeed, they were brought to bear tactically in order to exact recompense for a perceived personal humiliation. The episode ended once the singer and his mother got in touch with the apologetic candidate, and to my recollection there was no discussion of her protest in the media. Politics was here an arena for the negotiation of relationships between intimates (and in this sense very much in keeping with the vernacular usage of the term).

Throughout this book I have argued that circulating intimacies are the stuff of publicness, but in this chapter I have been interested in pointing to other possibilities, especially those where the intimate or interpersonal seems dramatically to eclipse the imaginary. Such insistent prioritizations of intimacy—which clearly occur in many cultural contexts, and not only among aboriginal Manitobans—are an important consideration, since they suggest one of the ways in which existing cultural practices shape and qualify capitalist economics and the seemingly universal structures of public culture.

More broadly, of course, even these resolute assertions of intimacy have the potential to circulate publicly. Monitored and discussed in dominant spheres of discourse, they are often characterized as failures to be normatively public. It is accordingly worth considering how such apparently parochial affirmations of intimacy are in fact enmeshed in the cultural politics of the nation state.

Conclusion

Publicness is increasingly available as a mode of acquaintanceship, yet it is not the same everywhere. Wherever it goes, it is qualified and transformed by the particularities of culture (what Chakrabarty calls "pasts"). These have implications for the practices and discourses that, in circulating, performatively constitute social imaginaries, but also at deeper levels: for instance, in the degree to which actors orient or calibrate practices and discourses to imaginaries in the first place.

In Manitoban aboriginal contexts, this is most evident in straightforward cases of antipublicity, where various factors discourage the mass-mediated circulation of sacred things. The disinclination to record, publish, or broadcast certain songs, rituals, dreams, and knowledge seems related in part to much older traditions of tact and secrecy regarding the sacred. As noted at a number of points, in the past it was very rare to speak openly of one's encounters with powerful spirit helpers, for instance. All the same, antipublicity should not be understood simply as the set of restrictions imposed by primordial tradition. Some of those who oppose the public circulation of such knowledge voice their objections using very contemporary concepts—for instance, the idea of intellectual and cultural property. And other forms of antipublicity are closely connected to the deeply damaging legacy of colonialism and to present-day prejudice and inequity. Antipublicity must be understood as a contemporary phenomenon.

Somewhat more complicated than prohibitions on mass mediation are those instances where the socially immediate and intimate take priority over the socially imagined—or where "family tradition" eclipses publicness. The jigging contest described at the beginning of the chapter is one such instance. It made use of the basic format of a public-facing competition, but this was qualified in significant ways during the event: through, on the one hand, musical interactions that preferred immediate responsiveness rather than exact repetition, and, on the other, unscripted interruptions that engaged inventively with the participants and the context of occurrence, but that disturbed and delayed performances. More generally, such competitions were often held to be compromised by patronage, with community leaders allegedly making use of them to distribute honors and awards to kin, friends, and allies. In short, social intimates were often perceived to take precedence over the public of potential competitors at such events.

Here, too, links can be drawn to cultural practices: variations of the fiddle tune affirmed an older, more flexible approach to playing, while the uproarious interruptions of certain participants connected to a tradition of tricksterism. Complaints about family tradition, meanwhile, contributed to the rich set of discourses that surround patronage. As these examples suggest, some of the ways immediacy and intimacy are privileged are highly specific, culturally speaking. To cite another instance, some Ojibwe elders practiced a respectful and reciprocal personal relationship with the medicines they harvested and for this reason found problematic the idea that general audiences should be taught about them, or that commercial enterprises should harvest them in bulk and sell them on the market. Other ways of advantaging intimacy seem relatively similar to ones that can be found in nonaboriginal contexts in North America. After all, patronage and personal antagonisms shape politics in aboriginal and nonaboriginal communities alike (not to mention academic institutions and nation-states). Insistent prioritizations of intimacy are in no way unique to indigenous groups. All the same, it is important not to characterize all of these as the same thing. To see only corruption, for instance, may ignore the links between contemporarypatronage and the very significant role that reciprocal giving continues to have in indigenous communities.

The prioritization of intimacy is not necessarily, then, a bulwark of tradition against a tide of modernity: it often takes social imaginaries into consideration. The mother in the vignette of the aggrieved singer was above all concerned with the offense to her son; she was not particularly interested in addressing the political debates circulating in the Manitoban aboriginal public sphere during a tense election campaign. All the same, she clearly took this discourse into account. She cannily chose as the object of her protest a man around whom public controversy was swirling, and who could little afford another protest at his door. This was a case in which intimacy clearly took precedence over imagining—the protest was a ploy to get through to the offending candidate—yet was in no way ignorant of it.

I have suggested that the interactions explored in this chapter—competitions where the set music changes, instances and allegations of patronage, performers who limit their audiences and markets—represent qualified publicness. All the same, the complex ways in which imagining sociability is impacted by culture do not translate well, and nonaboriginal observers often simply perceive publicness done wrong. This of course can contribute to the fraught relationship between the aboriginal and national publics, perhaps nowhere more so than in debates concerning corruption and nepotism in First Nations governments.[33] Here again, aboriginal intimacies and imaginaries are bound up in the dynamics of counter-publicity: the ongoing awareness of the eye of the national public, and of its interest, concern, disdain, or even hostility.

7

Circulation Controversies

Sacred Practice in Public Performance

As remarked in earlier chapters, the fairs and exhibitions held in Manitoba in the early twentieth century welcomed not only members of the settler public but also aboriginal people, the latter attending as both performers and, apparently, interested spectators. A colonial logic typically informed such events, with indigeneity displayed in unflattering opposition to Euro-Canadian civilization. All the same, aboriginal attendees seem to have attempted to make positive use of these occasions. For instance, Manitoban Dakota held a war dance each year during the Brandon exhibition, after which a ceremonialist named Wanduta would "announce...the number of spirits that he had seen" (Pettipas 1994: 119, quoting Wilson Wallis 1947: 126). In 1902 the same conductor presided over a "Hay Dance" or "Grass Dance" in Rapid City (Pettipas 1994: 119). Whites from the town paid Dakota to hold a dance and then charged admission; the event seems to have been a traditional giveaway ceremony, with a number of horses and merchandise bestowed (Pettipas 1994: 119). Hence the Brandon and Rapid City events incorporated traditional religious practices under the guise of entertainment for non-indigenous audiences.[1]

Many early public performances of aboriginal drum song and dance in Manitoba appear to have involved Dakota people from the southwest of the province.[2] Newspapers report a number of such events in the 1900s and 1910s (discussed in Dueck 2005: 150, 152, 159, 169–70), and they may have occurred as early as the late nineteenth century, if the caption the Archives of Manitoba gives to the photo in Figure 7.1, "1886 Pow-wow in Virden," is accurate. That Dakota communities should have been involved in these performances is perhaps to be expected, given the historically important role of Plains peoples in the history of the powwow (Powers 1990: xvi). Manitoba's Cree and Ojibwe communities do not seem to have been as active in this respect.

A significant exception was the Manitou Rapids Reserve (present-day Rainy River First Nation),[3] where the Ojibwe ceremonialist Maggie Wilson organized public performances of her Union Star Dance (Landes 1968: 207–12). Wilson received the dance in 1914 over the course of several vision sessions; during

Figure 7.1 "1886 POW-WOW IN VIRDEN." Archives of Manitoba, Indians 17 (N7569). Photo reproduced with the permission of Archives of Manitoba.

these the Thunders taught her songs and dances and gave her designs for ceremonial objects, including a drum, ceremonial staffs and pipes, and regalia (Landes 1968: 208). Wilson held the dance in order "to aid the tribe and other Canadians in the Great War.... At first she called the undertaking the Star Dance, from its heavenly origin; then she called it the Union Star Dance because the United States joined Canada [in the war] and so could also enjoy [the dance's] patronage" (Landes 1968: 207–8). The dance was originally held in the fall and spring, but later the Thunders told Wilson to commercialize it, and she began to hold it more often, on the ball ground near Fort Frances, Ontario (Landes 1968: 212). Wilson's dance appears to have been a public ceremony in at least two respects. Most obviously, it was performed in a public space, and anyone who paid a fee could attend. Perhaps more interestingly, it undertook a spiritual intervention *on behalf of* a public: namely, the Ojibwe, Canadian, and American soldiers, known and unknown, fighting in Europe, and those who hoped for their safe return.[4]

In the present day the most familiar public event to incorporate sacred elements is the powwow, a large gathering, often taking place over more than one day, incorporating contributions from drum groups and dancers, the former typically made up of several members who sing while playing a large drum, the latter usually specializing in one of a variety of solo dance styles, each with its own regalia and choreography (see Browner 2002). Although contemporary powwows, particularly competitive ones, do not have the thoroughgoingly sacred character of many traditional ceremonies, they incorporate many spiritual elements: sacred songs and dances, moments of prayer, and ritual items and instruments. The jingle-dress dance and its associated regalia are a good example.[5] In the version of the origin story Tara Browner relates, the dance and regalia come from the Ojibwe community of Whitefish Bay (Browner 2002: 54) in western Ontario, close to the Manitoba border. They first appeared to a man who, concerned for the poor health of his daughter, had sought out help in a dream. In the vision he was given instructions concerning the dance and regalia; he and his daughter obeyed these, and she was healed. Later in life she inaugurated a society of jingle-dress dancers to help propagate the dance. Eventually the dance and regalia were incorporated in the powwow (Browner 2002: 54–58).[6]

Although powwows are frequently public events, widely advertised and open to all comers, other, more sacred, ceremonies are often kept out of the public eye (see chapter 6). So it was that an August 2009 episode of CBC Radio's *ReVision Quest* (CBC Canada 2009) discussed Christianity alongside traditional practices such as the sweat lodge, but while Christian songs were heard during the program, none of the sounds of the sweat lodge were, the narrator explaining that it would not be appropriate to record or transmit them. His remarks accorded with my own early fieldwork experiences: while recording country gospel singing posed few problems, recording what went on in a sweat lodge was out of the question. Indeed, even some of what goes on at public powwows may be veiled from the public. Browner remarks that the very act of dancing in a jingle dress "constitutes a prayer for healing, and often spectators, musicians, and other dancers will make gifts of tobacco to a dancer and request that she pray for an ill family member while she dances." She calls it "an example of hidden spirituality and ritual within a public forum," adding, "There is little fanfare and no public announcement when the Jingle Dance is performed as a healing prayer, only a quiet circulation of family members from dancer to dancer, a whispered request, and a quick nod of thanks by both parties" (2002: 53).

So, while sacred ceremonies have occasionally been presented publicly, they are in the present day typically guarded as intimate (but not necessarily small) community events. All the same, the existence of variation points to the dynamic and negotiated aspect of their publicness. Various agents have different and sometimes conflicting ideas about what kinds of music, dance, and sacred activity can circulate appropriately in the public sphere, and the publicness of traditional practices is subject to debate and historical change.

Enclaving, Diverting, and Honoring: Public Circulation and Propriety

The hesitation to hold ceremonies in public in some cases seems to evidence traditional attitudes of tact, caution, and reverence regarding sacred knowledge and experiences (see chapter 6). It may also reflect a reluctance to suffer attendees who are disrespectful or dismissive—or adventurers in search of cultural differ-ence.[7] However strong antipublic feelings are, there have also been incentives to orient ceremonial life to a public. As the accounts above indicate, even during the years when the federal Indian Act forbade sun dances, potlatches, and give-aways (1896–1951), ceremonial events were conducted in public spaces. This may have been in part for material reasons: nonindigenous audiences would pay to see traditional Native dancing and singing, and this was no little inducement for aboriginal people living in poverty. Indigenous people also sought to get around legal prohibitions on ceremonial life, and settler audiences eager to see traditional dancing provided opportunities to do just this (Pettipas 1994: 139–41, 178–79). It is true that such ceremonies tended to omit elements the government deemed particularly problematic (see Pettipas 1994: 136–39); nevertheless, participants still held them. After all, they were a means of cultivating relationships with one another and with other-than-human persons, and of improving health and giving thanks for such improvements (see Pettipas 1994: 183–85). Furthermore, they provided opportunities to intervene on behalf of relatives and of the national public, as the case of Maggie Wilson's Union Star Dance suggests.

These incentives meant that communities made public certain sacred practices that might otherwise have occurred in much more restricted contexts of interac-tion. Similar reorientations go on in the present day, albeit perhaps more contro-versially (see chapter 6). One way to characterize these changes of trajectory is to speak of *diversions* of sacred practices and knowledge from social *enclaves*, using terms related to those Arjun Appadurai introduces in his anthropological work on the exchange and circulation of commodities (1986).[8] These terms will be helpful in the remainder of this chapter, which explores transmissions of sacred practices and knowledge; the roles, relationships, and networks—intimate and imagin-ing—these transmissions help to instantiate; and the advantages that accrue to those who divert or control the transmissions.

As has been established, the circulation of spiritual knowledge and sacred rit-ual is subject to cultural constraints. Within certain cultural regimes, some things can be legitimately passed on only to certain persons. For instance, as discussed in the preceding chapter, some northern Algonquian elders regard it as irrespon-sible to impart knowledge of sacred medicines to those who are ungifted or irrev-erent. Other kinds of information, for instance, the contents of certain sacred dreams, have in the past been transmitted only very rarely. In short, then, certain kinds of information are enclaved within particular social networks or even as personal secrets.[9] (It can be added that transmissions stand in complex entail-ing relationships with social roles and networks. It is not simply that one shares certain things only with certain kinds of persons, but rather that sharing is a per-formative act that helps to constitute relationships and roles, creating the kinds of persons one shares with.)[10]

Neither enclaves nor the social prohibitions that enforce them are incontro-vertible in actual practice, however. Objects, practices, and knowledge are often diverted from one network to another—including, in the examples given above, from socially intimate contexts to public ones. As those examples also suggest, diversions are often undertaken because they seem advantageous. Still, and especially if there are prohibitions on their transmission, these changes in trajectory can have serious social and spiritual ramifications. People who make sacred ceremonies available to the general public may face disapproval from members of their communities, while those who display disrespectful attitudes toward other-than-human persons may experience supernatural retribution.

Ownership and Theft of Secular Music and Dance

Outside the spheres of traditional and sacred music I sometimes encountered controversies concerning who might legitimately perform particular songs or dances. It was not unusual for performers to make use of choreography or music that other performers considered their own. At the jigging contest described in chapter 6, for instance, Ryan Richard and another male competitor both deployed the "ankle breaker" as one of their three fancy steps. It was a move that, so far as I knew, Richard had introduced to competition jigging. Richard laughingly observed that the young man had stolen it from him. Similarly, in square dancing, troupes sometimes took choreography from one another. Edward Guiboche occasionally remarked that square-dance groups across the province performed his routines. He and Richard were nonchalant about such appropriations, an attitude that perhaps reflected a confidence in their own gifts as innovators from whom others had to borrow.[11]

Musicians also appropriated one another's songs or performances and benefited from them from time to time, or suspected that others were up to such behavior (it was not uncommon for musicians to assume that I was asking to record their performances so that I could sell copies for my own financial benefit[12]). Such encroachments were fair cause for confrontations and grudges. Yet it often seemed that grievances had more to do with respect than money: they could arise in situations where little of financial worth was at stake, and their resolution did not necessarily involve repayment. One friend told me that he had given a country-rock band his blessing to perform one of his songs. Eventually the group recorded the song and released it on an album, but without crediting him in the liner notes as the songwriter. Unhappy, he confronted the lead singer, who apologized and promised to give him credit in the future. And that was the end of the question so far as my friend was concerned: the issue was not monetary compensation but rather appropriate acknowledgment.

Questionable appropriations of songs, dances, and profits were problematic, then, but in ways that seemed to differ subtly from what was normative in middle-class nonaboriginal practice. This was true of other kinds of "stealing," too. One year when I was making a Christmas visit to some elderly friends, one of them told me that her son had recently attempted to take a decorative knick-knack from her. He had mentioned several times while visiting with his partner and children that he liked it (this was a common way of hinting that you would like to be given something) and, accordingly, when it had gone missing, she had suspected him of taking it. Her suspicions were, in her opinion, confirmed when, after she remarked to him that the object had gone missing, it quickly turned up again. My friend clearly considered her son's behavior wrong, yet gave no indication that she thought it deeply unbecoming (similar behavior in the community I grew up in would have been regarded as unworthy of an adult son and father, and probably would not have been admitted so casually to a friend). Theft was bad, but one had to expect that others, even loved ones, might pursue things they wanted by such means.

The point is not that aboriginal people are more untrustworthy than nonaboriginal people (colonial and postcolonial history suggests very much the opposite!), but rather that social practices of ownership and appropriation and ways of discussing and understanding them differ in subtle ways from those that are considered normative in settler society. Stealing was undoubtedly problematic for my consultants, but in ways that differed from how middle-class whites viewed it. It is important to acknowledge that such differences were in no way universal or static. They were nevertheless common enough to be notable and for this reason merit consideration—not least because they have implications for how the national public perceives and problematizes its indigenous other.

The foregoing accounts open a space for those that follow, which, like them, seek to unmoor concepts such as "ownership" and "theft" from narrow and culturally specific meanings. Together they additionally suggest that "diversions" occur frequently, coming up in domestic interactions, in appropriations of intellectual and cultural property, and in many other instances. Accordingly, discussions of property and protocol need to take diversions into account, as abnormalities that are in many respects rather normal.

Circulation Controversies

Disagreements concerning the appropriation of dance moves or the sale of recorded performances might be considered exemplars of a general category of *circulation controversies*: disputes regarding the acquisition and transmission of songs, rituals, knowledge, instruments, and so on. Such controversies occur in many North American indigenous contexts, but their stakes seem particularly high where the materials being enclaved or diverted are traditional or sacred, as a number of recent published accounts suggest.

Anna Hoefnagels (2002) has discussed the controversies that attend breaches of protocol in the performance of powwow songs in southwestern Ontario. She suggests that as the recording of powwow songs has become more common, songs have begun to move more freely between performers. There appears to have been an attendant increase in the number of contraventions of protocols concerning who is allowed to perform songs, what performers must do before singing a song that belongs to someone else, and in what context certain songs may be sung (2002: 130, 132–33). Perhaps in part because the powwow is a relatively recent arrival in southwestern Ontario, these protocols are not as widely known or practiced as they might be, and it is occasionally necessary to address inappropriate behavior, as the following quotation from an interview Hoefnagels conducted with Vydel Sands suggests:

> When you take a song from out west by recording or whatever, you have to know...that song was made for a reason. It was either made for Grass Dancers or it was made for an Honour Song for somebody, and you might have recorded an Honour Song, and it wasn't made necessarily for dancing. And you come over here and you start singing that thing, [someone is] going to come over here and say "hey!"...And you're going to get admonished. They might take your drum away. (Sands in Hoefnagels 2002: 133)

Sands explains that some songs should not be used for dancing but that certain drum groups (perhaps because they are somewhat new to powwow) do so anyway. He goes on to suggest what can happen to such drum groups: other, more knowledgeable, people may criticize them or even take away their drums, keeping them from performing. In short, he addresses what I have called enclaving (the fact that certain songs are to be performed only in particular circumstances) and diversion (the fact that some performers nevertheless perform these songs) as well as the consequences of the latter (the steps more senior or knowledgeable musicians take to try to keep such transgressions from recurring).

Another article, by Klisala Harrison (2002), explores customary limits on song performance amongst the Kwakwaka'wakw, an indigenous group from the northwestern coast of North America, and how these stand in conflict with Western concepts of copyright law. In traditional Kwakwaka'wakw practice, Harrison explains, songs and song genres are often owned by individuals or groups (2002: 141–45). They may have been given to them by songmakers or by supernatural beings; ownership can also be transferred by inheritance or as a dowry (Harrison 2002: 141–44). Complicating matters, however, it is not necessarily the song's owner who sings the song, but frequently an entirely different person. There are, furthermore, strict rules regarding the performance of songs associated with the potlatch (a ceremony traditionally central to social and economic life in northwestern indigenous groups): singers must know who owns the potlatch songs they will perform, obtain permission to perform the songs from them, and then do so only in their presence or that of their family members (Harrison 2002: 145). As Harrison points out, neither the Kwakwa̲ka̲'wakw concept of ownership nor its performance protocols are enshrined in copyright law: accordingly, the Kwakwa̲ka̲'wakw do not have legal recourse to halt or seek compensation for performances such as the 1993 touring production by the American Indian Dance Theater that incorporated their songs and dances (Harrison 2002: 140). At the time Harrison wrote the article, members of the Kwakwa̲ka̲'wakw advocated change to copyright law and urged singers and entrepreneurs to respect Kwakwa̲ka̲'wakw precepts and protocols until this could take place (Harrison 2002: 146). The article highlights the distinctions between traditional indigenous ways of enclaving performance and state-sanctioned legal enclaves.

These accounts suggest that to the concepts of enclaving and diverting might be added another: *honoring*. While doing fieldwork I frequently heard this word used to designate proper comportment with respect to elders, ancestors, and spirit beings. It is used here to indicate the observance of indigenous protocols relating to the circulation, exchange, enclaving, and diversion of music.

Two theoretical emphases underlie the terms "enclaving," "diverting," and "honoring." One is the dynamic and social nature of ownership and diversion. Enclaving, for instance, is made manifest through performative acts that continually entail its social reality: for instance, assertions and ratifications of musical ownership, unopposed uses of songs and ritual instruments, socially sanctioned silencings, and exclusions of those held not to have rights to certain songs. A second theoretical concern is a comparative representation of concepts of ownership that "provincializes" (Chakrabarty 2000) more familiar Western terms. Insisting that both Western copyright law and Kwakwa̲ka̲'wakw song protocols are forms of enclaving places them within the same frame, even as the comparison emphasizes the gulf that separates them in terms of their power to restrict the actions of others.[13]

A Circulation Controversy: The University of Winnipeg Pauingassi Collection

Again, the stakes of controversies over enclaving and diverting are often higher when they concern traditional and sacred materials. This seemed to be the case in a 1999–2002 disagreement involving items deaccessioned from the University of Winnipeg's Anthropological Museum.[14] In the early 1970s, an archaeologist at the University of Winnipeg collected items from Pauingassi, an Ojibwe First Nation in eastern Manitoba, for his department's museum (J. Brown 2003: 626–27; Singleton 2002: 6). They included a number of sacred instruments that had once belonged to the medicine man Fair Wind (J. Brown 2003: 626–27). In 1995, according to Jennifer Brown, at the time professor of history at the University of Winnipeg, the institution hosted a special event, inviting Charlie George Owen, the grandson of Fair Wind and the "senior elder" at Pauingassi, to view these items and to give a talk in Ojibwe:

> After his visit, he set on record his view that the items were well cared for there and that they should stay; there was no safe place for them in Pauingassi....He gave us a mandate to photograph them and record their stories from him and other elders, and wanted us to write a book about the people connected with them. As he said, the stories and artifacts together would serve to teach young people in both Pauingassi and the university. (J. Brown 2003: 627)

According to Brown, university employees attempted to carry out Owen's commission, but were unable to do so because some of the most important items had been irregularly deaccessioned from the collection. They subsequently came into the possession of persons associated with the Three Fires Society (see J. Brown 2003: 627–28; Singleton 2002: 12–14). The society practices a form of the traditional Midéwiwin; it is based in Wisconsin but has members in both the United States and Canada (Kruzenga 2001; see also Nelson 2002a, 2002b; Three Fires Midewiwin Lodge 2012).

University employees, descendants of Charlie George Owen, and others made requests for the items to be returned to the university but were unsuccessful; a battle eventually ensued in print. Terrance Nelson (former chief of the Roseau River Anishinaabe First Nation) argued that the removal of the items was an act of repatriation at a time when thousands of indigenous artifacts and bones remained in Canadian museums and universities (Nelson 2002a, 2002b). He suggested that the objects had been doing no good where they were and implied that the people of Pauingassi were too Christianized and too alienated from traditional practices to make appropriate use of them themselves. He added that the items had begun a new work (Nelson 2002a):

> A sacred item has a spirit that works for the healing of the people. What good does a sacred item have sitting in a museum? An item that has sat for a long time may also be cleansed and imbued with another working spirit. The drums and other items received from the University were cleansed and worked with in ceremony. They have begun a new work. It may be that they can be returned to do work in Pauingassi, the question remains who is prepared to care for these items and are they capable of working with the sacredness of these items. Who today in Pauingassi is trained in Mediwiwin ceremony? Are the Christian priests in Pauingassi prepared to respect the right of Ojibway people of Pauingassi to return to their Mediwiwin beliefs and forsake the Christian way of life? (Nelson 2002a)[15]

Len Kruzenga reported in an article in *The Drum* that members of the Pauingassi community, including Joe Owen and Moses Owen, successive chiefs and themselves descendants of Fair Wind, had called for the return of the items. Joe Owen asked those responsible to respect "Charlie George Owen's right to determine how the objects...which are so meaningful to us should be used." Kruzenga quoted Margaret Simmons, a supporter of Pauingassi's attempts to reclaim the ritual objects, as saying that community members regarded the loss of these items as theft. And he suggested that members of the Three Fires Society had tried to "discredit Charlie Owen and the Pauingassi community at large as unworthy of the use or benefit of the artifacts" (Kruzenga 2001). Media attention grew, and the province's auditor general was commissioned to write a report on the release of the items from the museum.

Eventually, Eddie Benton-Banai, Grand Chief of the Three Fires Midewiwin Lodge, returned some of the most important sacred items—two water drums and two drumsticks—giving them to a grandson of Fair Wind in an invitation-only ceremony (J. Brown 2003: 627–28n; Nelson 2002b). Terrance Nelson reported that Benton-Banai had said that the spirits of the drums had asked to go home, and that contrary to a previous report the drums had not been used in ceremonies (Nelson 2002b; compare J. Brown 2003: 629n).[16]

Additional framing statements help to clarify what was at stake for those involved in, or commenting upon, the controversy. Jennifer Brown wrote in an article in *Canadian Historical Review* that people who had a close relationship to Fair Wind's ritual items considered it inappropriate to use such articles once they had been retired. Of a large drum that at one time belonged to Fair Wind, now in the care of the Red Lake District Museum, she remarked:

> Some people in Red Lake and elsewhere have suggested, that the drum be repaired and played again, and perhaps returned to Poplar Hill. But those who knew it in Poplar Hill told us that its present home is acceptable; it is "in retirement" and should not be used. Their ancestors had the spiritual knowledge, power, and blessings to conduct its ceremonies, but they have passed on; and, further, the drum would risk disrespectful treatment there, whether by the followers of evangelical Christianity or by those involved with alcohol and solvent abuse. In any case, as they and others told us, modern ceremonial practitioners should receive their own blessings and be gifted to make their tools through their own dreams and visions. They could, in fact, be harmed by using other people's powerful materials improperly, without being adequately taught by them or receiving their authorization. (J. Brown 2003: 625)

She noted that museums and indigenous communities are increasingly working together to care for historical indigenous materials in ways that observe both traditional protocols and institutional practices (J. Brown 2003: 629–30) and emphasized the importance of preserving such materials for those who will have an interest in them in the future:

> No matter what anyone does with them now, the materials gathered[17] need to be looked after somewhere (ideally, in more than one place) and held in trust for those who may need and want them most tomorrow or further into the future. They should be kept safe and yet accessible, not kidnapped away by institutions or individuals for their own private purposes. (J. Brown 2003: 631)

A very different framing of the controversy was presented in an article by Brian Rice published in the *Grassroots News*, an aboriginal newspaper. Rice described walking through Chicago's Field Museum and being aggrieved to see indigenous artifacts on display like "war trophies that had been taken from communities after they had been physically, spiritually and culturally assaulted.... I wanted to break the glass and take the items out and give them back to the people [to] whom they belonged" (Rice 2002). He asked himself what his reaction would be if he learned that the originary community of the items had voluntarily given them up and allowed them to be put on display:

> What would I do if the people had become Christian and didn't want them anymore? What if I gave them back and they were simply put on display like at the museum in Chicago as some kind of artifact...? I thought to myself that this would be even worse.... I felt perplexed by the situation because I knew I would never give them back to the museum.... I probably would look for an Aboriginal group or society who were trying to hold on to the Aboriginal ways of belief and might find value in them. At least they would be in safe hands from being further desecrated I thought, although in my heart I would want to give them back to the community... where they belonged. (Rice 2002)[18]

The disagreement differed in some important respects from the circulation controversies previously described. It involved one-of-a-kind items rather than reproducible, mass-mediated performances or publications, and these items were kept in a physically situated public space (a museum) rather than disseminated to imagined publics. It nevertheless seems appropriate to explore the controversy in this chapter, in part because it was publics that were the potential beneficiaries of the ritual objects, and in part because the case demonstrates so clearly the dynamic and contested nature of enclaving and diverting.

As Table 7.1 shows, there were several diversions and enclaves, some characterized in very different ways by those who commented upon the controversy. The most striking differences concerned the second enclave and diversion. For Brown and, apparently, for Charlie George Owen and other descendants of Fair Wind,

Table 7.1 **Enclaves and diversions in the University of Winnipeg Anthropology Museum controversy**

Circulation stage	Characterization A *Brown, members of the Pauingassi community as reported by Kruzenga*	Characterization B *Nelson, Rice (speaking before final return)*	Characterization C *Nelson (after final return)*
Enclave 1 Items no longer used following death of Fair Wind	Items were in "retirement," but there was "no safe place" for them.		
Diversion 1 Items acquired by University of Winnipeg			
Enclave 2 Items kept in University of Winnipeg Anthropology Museum	Owen considered the items "well cared for" and thought they should remain at the museum.	Items kept "like war trophies" [implied] and "desecrated."	
Diversion 2 Items irregularly deaccessioned	Removal of items did not respect Owen's right to determine how sacred items were cared for. Some members of the community considered it "theft."	The removal of the items from the collection was a "return."	
Enclave 3 Items in keeping of Three Fires Society	Contemporary ceremonialists should "be gifted to make their tools through their own dreams and visions."	Items to begin "a new work" for an "Aboriginal group or society" or "the people" more broadly. Items "in safe hands from being further desecrated."	Items "nourished" and "smudged" but "never used...in ceremonies."
Diversion 3 Items returned to descendant of Fair Wind			Drums had asked to go home.

the Anthropology Museum was a good, safe place for the items. Having finished their first, ritual life,[19] they had begun a second one, as materials to be employed in the instruction of "young people in both Pauingassi and the university." As various people quoted in Len Kruzenga's article suggest, the subsequent deaccessioning of these items was perceived as theft and as an act of disrespect to the descendants of Fair Wind.

Nelson, in his initial remarks, on the other hand, characterized the museum as an enclave that kept sacred objects from helping "the people," and Rice compared the display of sacred items at one museum to "war trophies." For Nelson, turning the artifacts over to the Three Fires Society was "returning items belonging to First Nations people back to their rightful place within Ojibway culture" (not necessarily to the actual community of origin, apparently, but to other Anishinaabe people who practiced traditional ways). It allowed the items to begin "a new work." For Rice, removing the items from the museum meant keeping them "from being further desecrated."

So, on the one hand were the wishes of the descendants of Fair Wind, who had personal links to the items and were familiar with the protocols surrounding them. On the other hand were the concerns of other First Nations people, all too aware of the poor track record of museums with respect to indigenous sacred items, and eager to reclaim materials related to their spiritual heritage. One side perceived a legitimate enclave disrespectfully breached; the other, the freeing of illegitimately locked-up items. Nor were these the only ways of framing the matter: there were hints that another framework might be brought to bear. The auditor general's report on the controversy mentioned that the deaccessioned articles might "be classified as Group II objects as defined by the Canadian Cultural Property Control List, and thereby objects which are subject to the provisions of the Act in respect of their export from Canada." It also stated that the act allowed "proceedings to be undertaken to recover artifacts which may have been exported in contravention of the Act" (Singleton 2002: 15). According to the report, in other words, moving the items outside of Canada to the United States may have been illegal, and there may have been grounds to take steps to get them back. In the theoretical terms employed here, Canadian law understood national boundaries to constitute a privileged enclave when it came to the movement of certain valued objects. A fourth and final framework defining legitimate custody, this one of a sacred nature, is evident in Nelson's article, which reports that Benton-Banai had said that the spirits of the drums had asked to go home.

In sum, a number of agents asserted the legitimacy of some enclaves or diversions while declaring others to be invalid (the passion felt and expressed by the parties on the different sides of the issue should not be underestimated). It is not simply that their legitimacy was contested, moreover, but that it was negotiated and established through these discussions. For a variety of reasons—including the intervention of Maureen Matthews of CBC Radio, who spoke personally to Benton-Banai about the people of Pauingassi (CBC Manitoba 2002a)—it became more and more difficult to sustain the argument that it was appropriate to keep the drums in Wisconsin. That enclave eventually lost its social—and, from another point of view, spiritual—legitimacy.

It is notable, so far as the themes of this volume are concerned, that two of the perspectives just explored justified certain diversions and enclaves in part because they promised benefits for a public. Brown, discussing the contemporary, postcolonial missions of museums, spoke of "those who may need and want [access to traditional artifacts]...tomorrow or further into the future." Nelson wrote, "A sacred item has a spirit that works for the healing of the people."[20] In both cases there was a sense the items should be available for the good of a general body of others. Yet, since the items were specific, one-of-a-kind things, making them available to a public inevitably and paradoxically necessitated ensconcing them in some sort of enclave. Keeping them in a museum meant they would be supervised by caretakers, subject to institutional regulations, and available only at certain hours and in specific capacities. Similarly, integrating those items in an aboriginal institution meant they would be held by certain persons, subject to certain protocols, and available only in certain contexts. Here is evident another distinction between social imaginaries and public places: whereas mass-mediated items circulate freely amongst a public of strangers, one-of-a-kind objects necessitate certain forms of institutional intimacy.

Ethnographic Diversions

As the foregoing discussion suggests, certain kinds of academic work—including establishing a scholarly collection of sacred artifacts—can be understood as instances of diversion and enclaving. The term "diversion" also seems appropriate for describing scholarship that draws upon ethnographic methodologies. Ethnomusicologists have regularly taken songs, narratives, and objects from intimate contexts of community life and oriented them to publics of strangers. Indeed, many of the preceding chapters do just this: describing, transcribing, and interpreting performances, narratives, and interactions that came into being in socially intimate contexts, for the purpose of publication.[21] Nor does diversion begin and end with the publication of the intimate. In some cases it also involves channeling music and discourse from one public into another. In this respect even some of the public performances described in this volume might be understood to have been diverted: the music that fills the Manitoban indigenous public sphere is here described for an audience partially made up of people unfamiliar with it. (There are also in-between cases: does everyone who puts out a CD, phones a community call-in show, publishes a blog, or posts without privacy filters on a social networking site really understand himself or herself to be hailing a public?)

A model of enclaves and diversions places "scholarly" and "vernacular" practice on the same playing field. Yet while it suggests that, at some level, scholars engage in practices similar to those of the people they study, it in no way claims that diversions and enclaves are all the same. Even when ethnographic diversions can be justified in terms of ethnographers' own values—for instance, when they contribute to a more thorough and nuanced understanding of musical practice—such diversions may not be considered defensible by the persons or groups they study, or by all persons or factions within these groups. Ethnographic inquiry will indicate that some enclaves and diversions are more legitimate and suggest ways of honoring them. Still, as the preceding account suggests, legitimacy is viewed from different perspectives by different agents, inflected by interest, and circumvented by a variety of strategies. So while ethnographic inquiry will probably suggest contextually appropriate ways to honor, even these may not rule out controversy.

The genres of music and dance that are the main focuses of these chapters—fiddling, country music, gospel song, and jigging—are practices that indigenous Manitobans perform publicly without controversy, and accordingly my investigations and recordings were generally unproblematic. It is probably not surprising, then, that they play such a central role in a book concerned with indigenous public culture. On the other hand, traditional sacred practices are frequently ensconced out of public view, and my consultants never seemed entirely comfortable with the idea of my writing about them (compare Whidden 2007: 76 and Diamond 2008: 9). It seemed proper to honor those aspects of my fieldwork experience, and accordingly this book focuses on elements of Manitoban indigenous expressive culture that are not closely guarded. So, while I discuss antipublicity at length, I do not describe traditional sacred observances, except where information about these has already entered public circulation in works by other ethnographers. This is emphatically not to say that those who write about such things do a dishonor: there are clearly authors who receive permission and encouragement to do so. And in any event, this volume undertakes a fundamentally similar kind of work, since it too orients indigenous intimacies to a public.

8

Conclusion

The ethnographic accounts and analyses in this volume affirm and elaborate arguments by Berlant (2008), Stokes (2010), Warner (2002), and others that intimacy is central to social imagining. Its precedence is evident in instances such as the NCI Jam discussed in chapter 3: in its 2002 instantiation, that event addressed and constituted an indigenous public through musical performances that reflected on romantic, domestic, and community relationships, as well as the sentiments associated with them. This was in no way unusual: although publicness is often thought of in terms of the circulation of rational and critical discourses, there is almost always more music than talk on Native radio stations, and the most significant events in aboriginal community and public life incorporate—or are built around—dance and song. Expressive practices are fundamental to social imagining, and this seems particularly true as far as indigenous publicness is concerned.

The intimacies explored in this volume include not only sung reflections on relationships and rural communities, but also and especially occasions of social, musical, and choreographic interaction. The preceding chapters have examined a variety of these, including how singers and communities extend comfort to the bereaved at funerary wakes, how musical performances at coffeehouses and jam sessions bodily instantiate the individuality of participants, how the comfortable negotiation of twisting, turning fiddle tunes can reflect a life of making music together, and how performances and competitions create opportunities to extend and contest patronage. These intimacies also help to constitute indigenous imaginaries.

The foregoing chapters follow previous authors in understanding social imaginaries to be plural, and to stand in relationships of primacy and subordinacy. The plurality of publicness is apparent in the way certain broadcasts, performances, and publications hail specifically indigenous audiences, for instance through the use of aboriginal languages. It is also evident in the way some venues and public spaces draw audiences made up almost entirely of aboriginal people, whether for gatherings that seem distinctively Native, such as powwows, or for activities that appear similar to ones in which nonaboriginal people are typically in the majority, for instance country music talent shows.

Even when the musical practices that fill Manitoban aboriginal public spaces overlap with those that circulate more widely, they are often implicated in establishing distinctively indigenous modes of intimacy and imagining. Musicians use popular forms to reflect upon aboriginal communities and histories. Gospel musicians interact in ways that instantiate northern Algonquian ways of performing selfhood and negotiating leadership. Step dancing competitions and talent shows present opportunities to perform—and express opposition to—patronage. And gospel jamborees and so-called Indian bars articulate competing "wet" and "dry" forms of indigenous corporateness.[1]

Publicness is not only plural, however, but stratified, and some forms of publicness seem problematic from the perspective of other, dominant ones—hence the distinction between publics and counterpublics discussed by Warner (2002) and Hirschkind (2006), among others. Such stratification was especially evident during the colonial era, when the Canadian national public regarded the indigenous population as its uncivilized other, but it continues in the postcolonial present. For the contemporary settler public, Native crime, intoxicant use, unemployment, and patronage constitute troubling forms of publicness—as do, in other ways, demands for political and economic redress. Indigenous publicness has likewise been considered musically problematic: in the colonial era, dancing was restricted or prohibited and drum song was often heard as meaningless noise. In the present, the unpolished or rhythmically irregular performances frequently heard in aboriginal venues may be perceived as a sonic homology of social abjection.

Significant for the relationship between publics and counterpublics is a cognizance on the part of counterpublics that some of the practices that distinguish them are regarded as problematic: a rueful recognition—Herzfeld (1997) calls it "cultural intimacy"—of national concern and disapprobation. Aboriginal Manitobans hear the concerned and critical opinions that circulate in the national public sphere regarding (for instance) indigenous intoxicant abuse and reserve corruption, and their own discourses and expressive performances reflect an awareness of them.

This is not to say that counterpublics are constituted only through national discourses that speak about them, for counterpublics also speak back. This was particularly evident during the Idle No More demonstrations of late 2012 and 2013, a momentous series of protests that brought First Nations people from across Canada together in response to federal legislation that threatened indigenous sovereignty and environmental protections. At the rallies in Winnipeg, demonstrators spoke out against the legislation, but they also sang and danced: on December 31, 2012, hundreds gathered at the junction of Portage Avenue and Main Street (see Map 2) to take part in an immense round dance. Less obvious forms of resistance have also been evident, for instance the adoptions of western wear and cowboy songs that, beginning in the middle of the twentieth century, disrupted the cowboy-Indian opposition so widespread in popular representations of the North American west.

Existing writing on intimacy and imagining and on publics and counterpublics has been useful in framing some of what I observed while doing fieldwork, but it tends to privilege mass-mediated performances and publications. My own field-work, in contrast, has prioritized "face-to-face"[2] encounters. It has accordingly been necessary to seek out theoretical starting points that are amenable to dis-cussing intimate musical and social interactions without losing sight of how they are related to larger social formations. The search has led to some productive ways of thinking about musical intimacies and imaginaries, involving closer attention to venues, modalities or styles of sociability, and embodied practices. It has also identified some of the ways that Manitoban aboriginal people (and probably most groups) qualify or challenge publicness: through antipublic prohibitions on circu-lation, on the one hand, and prioritizations of intimacy, on the other.

Much of my fieldwork has taken place in public venues—coffeehouses, festi-vals, concerts, powwows, taverns, contests, talent shows, and so on—and such sites accordingly appear frequently in the preceding chapters. Theories of social imaginaries often emphasize stranger-sociability and virtual spaces—the public as a "social space created by the reflexive circulation of discourse," for instance (Warner 2002: 90)—but most of my fieldwork was situated and emplaced, involv-ing interactions with identifiable persons rather than with an unknown public. It became evident that theories of publicness—especially if they are to be use-ful to those who practice common kinds of participant observation—could account more explicitly for venues. To this end I have proposed that public spaces be understood to exist at the interstices of imagining and intimacy: oriented to publics of strangers, yet simultaneously sites of face-to-face interaction between known and knowable persons.

During the course of my fieldwork it also became evident that the details of social and musical interactions were important, in part because they instantiated distinctive aspects of northern Algonquian sociability. For this reason a number of chapters have explored the nuances of such interactions, inspired by the close analytical approaches of scholars such as Goffman (1967, 1974), Monson (1996), and Silverstein (1997). Considering these interactions has suggested how selves and groups emerge performatively, and how leadership is ratified and resisted, in the course of northern Algonquian musical performance. The close focus in these analyses is not meant to privilege the microsocial to the exclusion of its broader social context, however. Such interactions occur in public spaces and thus extend a particular manifestation of indigenous sociability into the public sphere. In affirming certain ways of being musical and sociable, they also affirm certain ways of being public, in sharp or subtle distinction to those that are considered normative by other publics.

During the initial period of my fieldwork I was new to many of the prac-tices I investigated—including fiddling, square dancing, and powwow danc-ing—and a good deal of my time was spent learning their rudiments, often in the company of other beginners. These experiences drew my attention to particular aspects of publicness. Certainly, musical publics are constituted in part through the reflexive circulation of mass-mediated performances, broadcasts, and publications, and in part through practices of listening and viewing—but they also come into being as musicians and dancers train their minds and bodies to interact competently with other, as yet unknown participants. Publics emerge through processes of physical and mental discipline, in other words: through careful calibrations of our embodied comportment to that of imagined others. Few of the people who help to extend publics in this way have opportunities to contribute to the widely disseminated performances and publications that are the most frequent objects of musical scholarship, yet they play a vital role in propagating publicness all the same. This has implications for how social imaginaries are conceptualized and investigated. At the very least it necessitates the acknowledgment that musical publics include many, many "hidden" (Finnegan 2007) yet actively attuned participants—students, amateurs, and others—who have regularly been ignored. Additionally it suggests that the pedagogical sites where publics are extended may offer especially rich opportunities for the ethnographic exploration of everyday intersections between intimacy and imagining.

Although my experiences during fieldwork offered insights into the relationship between face-to-face interactions and social imaginaries, they also pointed toward some of the ways that aboriginal communities shape and qualify publicness, one of which is through antipublic prohibitions on the recording, broadcasting, and publication of certain kinds of sacred knowledge and ritual observance. As comparisons with other indigenous groups suggest, such restrictions belong to a much larger group of practices of social enclaving that limit the exchange, transmission, and circulation of culturally privileged information, practices, and things. When practices of enclaving come into contact with the structures of publicness, they necessitate culturally specific translations and elaborations of them. Social groups impose a variety of limits on what can circulate publicly; it is in part the nature of these limits—their what, how, and why—that distinguishes imagining modes of sociability from one another.

Publicness is also qualified when it is eclipsed by social intimacy, and during my fieldwork this happened in many different ways. Performers who sang or played with minimal reference to metrical structures often seemed more interested in making a musical contribution to an immediate social context than in making sure that their contribution conformed to dominant standards.[3] Similarly, at many coffeehouses, jam sessions, and talent shows, egalitarian participation was more valued than (what the general public might have judged to be) competence or excellence. In some other cases, musicians preferred face-to-face engagement with audiences and customers to the anonymity of mass mediation and the market. In still others—musical and otherwise—obligations to social intimates conflicted with the duty of public-facing persons and institutions to be impartial.[4]

Of course, intimacies take precedence over imagining in all kinds of social contexts; it is how and why and the degree to which they do so that particularize public cultures. In my experience Manitoban aboriginal people tend to prioritize relationships with known and knowable persons, preferring "non-imagined" communities to "imagined" ones (Anderson 1991), and in this respect they are probably similar to many other groups. But they also privilege certain relationships and in certain ways. Antipublic protocols prohibiting the circulation of sacred knowledge, for instance, demonstrate a respectful orientation to other-than-human intimates: dream visitors, sacred medicines, and the spiritual beings who take part in sacred ceremonies.

Paradoxically, then, it is these unique ways of privileging intimacy that help to make the aboriginal public sphere special and distinct. Perhaps most significant, in my experience, is the emphasis on egalitarian participation—the disinclination to say no to anybody who wants to sing. The Manitoban aboriginal musicians and organizers I have met engage in creative work that addresses an indigenous public, but they do so in no small part by cultivating spaces where singers, instrumentalists, and dancers of a wide range of abilities can make music together, face to face.

Notes

1. My description refers to the recording of the song I purchased in 2002 (C-Weed 2000). There are no backing vocals in this version, although I have heard another recording in which additional voices join in on the chorus.
2. The honor song is in the "incomplete repetition" form characteristic of much powwow music (see Browner 2002). At the beginning of the track, the repeated incipit and the first statement of the main body of the honor song are heard. At the conclusion of the track, the honor song gradually fades up again, and the second statement of the main body of the song is heard. The song also makes a brief appearance in the middle of the track.
3. Lyrics here and elsewhere are quoted from the original CD booklet with the following changes: I have added capital letters at the beginnings of lines, shifted line breaks to reflect the underlying meter of the song, and added punctuation. Lyrics appear by kind permission of Ben's Buddy Publishing.
4. Other concerts included Manitoba Night, sponsored by the provincial government, and Sounds of the Red River, sponsored by the City of Winnipeg.
5. "Games Chairman Realizes a Dream," *Winnipeg Free Press*, July 28, 2002, A4.
6. See for instance "Running Keeps Him on Track," *Winnipeg Free Press*, July 29, 2002, C1. The article focuses on a Métis long-distance runner who overcame his problem drinking through running.
7. "Games Show Promise of a Better Future," *Thunder Voice News*, August 2002, 2. It can often seem as though news coverage of aboriginal Winnipeggers centers mainly on gang and criminal activity, but during the Games the papers were full of stories of aboriginal successes.
8. I have changed all names.
9. Ranville described his gigs at the Westbrook for me in an interview a few days later:

   It's like the last couple of weeks ago when I was playing at the Westbrook, singing at the Westbrook, with all my heart and all my soul: little, dingy little bar in a little town in Canada, an obscure little town in Canada and, *God*, what a place to be. Thank God. Thank God, what a great place to be. Really touching two or three or four people that are not too hammered to miss it. That's my concert; that's my venue; that's my success.

10. Thus I speak of "imagined communities" in a different way to that employed by David Samuels (2004: 261).
11. That it is a listenership is significant: this aboriginal public is imagined in relation to not only political experience, aspiration, and sentiment, but also sound.
12. A connection might also be drawn with what Etienne Wenger (1998) calls "engagement."

13. Thanks to Luis-Manuel Garcia for a thought-provoking discussion of the meaning of the term "intimacy." My own use of the word should be understood not as a definition, but rather as a creative deployment that strays in a number of respects from its vernacular sense.

14. The pictorial representation of overlapping modes of sociability in Figure 1.2 is indebted to Georgina Born's helpful diagrams of "nesting" and "zoning" in her presentation "On the Publicization and Privatization of Music," given April 19, 2008 at the University of Cambridge. My thinking on public assembly as a space between imagining sociability and face-to-face interaction was clarified by hearing Andrew Eisenberg's paper "Soundly Placed Subjects: Resonant Voices and Spatial Politics in Mombasa Kenya" at the 2007 meeting of the Society for Ethnomusicology in Columbus, Ohio (Eisenberg 2007).

15. In part this happens through the responsive aspect of publicly oriented performances, which inevitably privilege some previously circulating performances over others.

16. That attempts to prioritize or enclave intimacy can themselves end up as the stuff of publicity certainly complicates things, as chapter 7 suggests.

17. For a general theory regarding participatory modalities of musical performance, and the musical characteristics that often seem to attend them, see Turino 2008, especially 23–51.

18. In this case, intimacy and imagining exist in a dialectical relationship that very much resembles the one between privateness and publicness perceived by Habermas.

19. Indigenous rap has become increasingly prominent in recent years, with the group Winnipeg's Most receiving national airplay and attention.

20. By extension, one might speak of the "listenerships," "viewerships," and so on enabled by other forms of mass mediation.

21. There are notable exceptions: see Berlant and Warner 1998, Garcia 2013.

22. Acknowledging this distinction, while at the same time moving the focus of investigation back and forth between imagining and intimacy, may be another way to explore culture as simultaneously "something that can be separated from persons and sold in a capitalist economy and something that is read through embodied practices, affective experiences, racially identified persons, and the performativity of everyday life" (Bigenho 2012: 10).

23. Turino 2008 also uses the term *intimacy* to characterize face-to-face musical interactions.

24. The concepts of publicity and antipublicity may have some bearing on questions explored in literature on the powwow. One early view of the powwow was that its historical emergence signaled the beginning of a general North American indigenous ethnicity and the ending of local, tribal particularities (see Howard 1955). This idea was vigorously opposed by William Powers, who argued that broader "intertribal" senses of indigenous identity complemented tribal particularities that continued to endure (Powers 1990: 86–110). More recent authors similarly acknowledge how the powwow enables translocal and intertribal forms of affiliation even as it acknowledges local, tribal, and regional specificities and they discuss the concepts, practices, and material culture that make music and dance particular to specific populations (see Browner 2002 and 2009, Scales 2007, and the various contributions in Ellis, Lassiter, and Dunham 2005). The sphere of North American powwow performance can be understood as a public (constituted as indigenous singers and dancers orient their musical and choreographic practices toward those of unknown others). But it may also be worth asking what antipublic elements are evident at powwows, and what aspects of the contemporary powwow privilege intimates and intimacy above indigenous imaginaries. Is the mass-mediated circulation of certain elements restricted? And do various communities take steps to prevent certain kinds of traditional music, knowledge, or material culture from appearing at powwows in the first place?

25. See Silverstein 2004 (especially informing this statement is page 622n). Similar approaches to culture and genre seem evident in work by Turino (2008) and Berlant (2008). Berlant sets forth a model of limited performativity: "what we have called the 'performativity' of personality usually produces variations *within* a conventional expectation of self- and world-continuity, rather than mainly providing dramas of potential frame breaking alternativity" (2008: 4).

26. "Enmusicalization" is an awkward neologism, but it gets around referring to music as a text, which might strike some readers as problematic and would probably necessitate a long discussion of the meaning of the latter term in metapragmatic writing.

27. Bill C-31 reversed a long-standing law that any Indian woman who married a non-Indian man lost her own status (non-Indian women who married Indian men, in contrast, gained Indian status). It also extended Indian status to many Métis people who had lost it, including women who had married non-Indians and the children of these unions. Consequently many people who were once considered Métis are today registered as Indians (see Dickason 2002: 313).

28. The term "Saulteaux" distinguishes Canadian Ojibwe, who made a historical migration westward via a route that skirted the Great Lakes by the north, from American Ojibwe, who migrated westward via a southerly route. The term "Chippewa" is more common in the United States. In the Ojibwe language, people identify themselves as Anishinaabeg (sing. Anishinaabe).

29. See Friesen 1987: 45–54. Both French and English traders made use of the Hudson's Bay until the signing of the Treaty of Utrecht in 1713, at which point the French ceded the Bay to the English (Friesen 1987: 51–52). French Canadian trade through the south continued even after New France fell to the British in 1763 (Friesen 1987: 56–57).

30. These musical genres, dances, and instruments came with both British and French-Canadian traders. The French Canadian connection to indigenous fiddling is evident insofar as French Canadian and aboriginal fiddlers both make use of foot-tapping patterns when they play. Cf. Lederman 2001: 406.

31. A number of agreements were signed at a later date in more northerly regions of the northwest (see Dickason 2002: 254).

32. It was in fact possible for First Nations people to become citizens; however, Indians who became enfranchised were required to give up the special rights accorded to them under the terms of the treaties.

33. "Citizens Plus" was the title of the "red paper," the official response of First Nations to the white paper (Dickason 2002: 378–79).

Chapter 2

1. Thanks to Sarah Quick for identifying this tune. In Manitoba many aboriginal fiddlers call it "Flaming Arrow," the title it bears on Cliff Maytwayashing's album of the same name, but it is better-known to others as the "Buckskin Reel."

2. Thanks to numerous commentators on various versions of this chapter, including José Martins, for pointing out the similarity between the performance and a Suzuki violin recital, with students arranged in rows and playing by heart. The resemblance was certainly compounded by the similarity between the opening of "Red Wing" and Robert Schumann's "The Happy Farmer" (the latter is included in the first volume of the *Suzuki Violin School*).

3. Alongside a summer festival called Folklorama, Festival du Voyageur was one of two annual cultural festivals to emerge in 1970 amidst intense arguments (in the late 1960s and early 1970s) concerning how Canada was to be imagined politically. The question was whether the country would understand itself as a multicultural nation (the ideology that informed Folklorama) or as a bicultural polity founded by two European groups (the ideology that informed the early Festivals du Voyageur); see Dueck 2005: 73–146.

4. For a comparative discussion of two other Winnipeg festivals, see Pauline Greenhill's 1999 work on Folklorama and the Winnipeg Folk Festival. For a consideration of the relationship between Manitoban public festivity, the striation of cultural difference, and Canadian national imaginaries, see Dueck 2005: 73–146, 188–206.

5. Confusingly perhaps, many First Nations and Métis Manitobans have French surnames and French-Canadian ancestors.

6. Note that in some areas Métis musical practices may diverge significantly from those of other indigenous groups; this appears to be the case on the Turtle Mountain Chippewa Reservation in North Dakota (Bakker 1997: 123–24).

7. Thanks to Virginia Gluska and Blaine Klippenstein for clarifying this history in email exchanges in 2008 and 2009.

8. Email communication, September 2009. Original question: "Am I right in understanding that at some of the larger jamborees or get-togethers, young fiddlers from different communities will in fact meet each other or play together for the very first time?" Original answer: "The Division probably covers one of the largest geographic areas in Canada, if not in the world. It runs schools from Southern Manitoba to Churchill MB so it is difficult to get students together from different communities. Many of the communities are isolated fly-in communities so yes it probably is the first time that students are getting together like this."

9. Name changed.

10. So-called limping meters are one interesting exception to the structure diagrammed in Figure 2.2; see Lerdahl and Jackendoff 1983.

11. This was also true of some performers in the second category. Again, see the transcription of Cliff Maytwayashing's performance of the Red River Jig in chapter 6.

12. There was a hint that this was in part because the musicians who played alongside him objected when he did not stay within metrical bounds.

13. The fiddling and jigging contest at Festival du Voyageur seemed to fall between these two extremes—hence, perhaps, its duality as an event oriented to a broader middle-class public and as a node in the network of annual festivals that articulate a largely working-class aboriginal publicness.

14. Other characteristics included short bow strokes, a soft sound, a tendency to "double string"—that is, to play double stops and drones—and to hold the violin in a nearly vertical position (Lederman 1988 and 2006).

15. I transcribed "McAuley's Creek Breakdown" from a compact disc entitled *Emile Spence's Reel* (ca. 2001). Ivan Spence's original guitar part is augmented on the remastered version by newly added guitar parts contributed by Jim Flett.

16. Nevertheless, during this time Manitoban aboriginal musicians were already participating in the "imagining" sociability that is characteristic of public culture. For example, Victor Courchene, born on a rural reserve in 1927, told me that he had bought his first guitar for five dollars when he was a young man. In his youth he made music with a fiddler he knew, but he also accompanied himself while singing country songs popularized by such singers as Ernest Tubb and Jimmie Rodgers.

17. Again, the minimal metricality and asymmetrical phrasing of many aboriginal fiddle traditions is not associated with any particular aboriginal group or subgroup. Although elements of the style have sometimes been closely associated with the "historical Métis" (as Annette Chrétien notes in Chrétien 1996: 104), they can in fact be found in many other aboriginal traditions.

18. Consider, for example, Emile Lavallee's metrically irregular "Drops of Brandy" and Red River Jig and compare these with his other, much more metrically regular selections, all on the Gabriel Dumont Institute compilation *Drops of Brandy*.

19. At this time Morisseau worked closely with a group of fiddlers from St. Laurent, Manitoba. The group was not officially connected to the Frontier Fiddlers program, since the town of St. Laurent was not part of the Frontier School Division; nevertheless, the local fiddling chapter was in regular contact with the others and participated in group assemblies of fiddlers from different communities (personal communication, Mark Morisseau). Morisseau was my main source of information about the Fiddlers. I did not have regular contact with any particular Frontier Fiddlers chapter, although I saw groups perform publicly on numerous occasions and spoke with and interviewed fiddlers and instructors who were involved in the program.

20. I have emphasized synchrony here, but acknowledging the embodied practices of others does not necessarily mean replicating them: publics form around more and less stable practices.

21. Musical collaborations increasingly involve not simply small ensembles consisting of a guitarist and a fiddler, but larger four- and five-piece bands that include electric bass and drums. Metrical and formal regularity also facilitates interactions between newer, larger groups of musicians.

22. Not all of these musicians evidence the same melodic and metrical freedom as some older performers, but aspects of the traditional style are nonetheless present in their playing.

23. Arcand's Fiddle Fest Web site <http://www.johnarcandfiddlefest.com/> (accessed June 2006 and May 2012).

24. Some refer to the Red River Jig as "the Métis national anthem," but it has a prestigious place in many First Nations communities as well. On the controversy surrounding its "anthem" status see Chrétien 1996: 104.

25. In such contexts, indigenous fiddling is more often rendered as "Métis" fiddling, in a way that obscures the important role that fiddling plays within First Nations communities.

26. This is to say, inexact or nonstandard tuning as seen from the dominant Western perspective. I have not investigated tuning in traditional or appropriated genres of northern Algonquian music and cannot comment on whether it presents evidence of an indigenous tuning system or its vestiges.

27. Some may wonder to what degree the aboriginal public described here is a space of indigenous politics, and to what extent it is what Berlant calls a "juxtapolitical" space: "a loosely organized, market-structured... sphere of people attached to each other by a *sense* that there is a common emotional world available to those individuals who have been marked by the historical burden of being harshly treated in a generic way and who have more than survived social negativity by making an aesthetic and spiritual scene that generates *relief from the political*" (2008: 10; emphasis in original). Martin Stokes presents a more optimistic reading of the political work done by sentimental public culture, arguing that in Turkey popular music has been an important force in sustaining public life and transforming public discourse for the last sixty years (2010). I perceive political import in the pronounced ruralness of aboriginal music and dance traditions, yet I wonder about the absence of the overtly political in much of the music that circulates in the indigenous public sphere. This may itself be a kind of politics—not simply relief from the political, but a refusal of it. Some refusals of politics might be understood as rejections of certain ongoing aspects of colonialism, including its determination to draw aboriginal people into deeper and deeper engagement with the nation-state.

28. As Berlant (2008: 4–6) points out, performances and publications almost inevitably engage with sets of generic expectations that they help to reproduce, however ambivalently. Radical breaks are rare.

29. Turino has observed that "presentational" and "participatory" modalities of performance have different objectives and are judged by distinct criteria by those who practice them (2008). To this I would add that there can be serious social consequences when a dominant public views the participatory practices of a subaltern one as failed presentational performances (a mistake that is easy enough to make when both publics share the same songs and genres).

30. It is to be hoped that the concepts of publicness and intimacy developed here complement the concepts of "Pan-Indianism" and "ethnic group formation" as developed by Christopher Scales (2004: 13–33). In its insistence that publicness and intimacy are continually contested, the theory advanced here resonates with Scales's acknowledgment that ethnic groups constitute themselves around a diverse and continually negotiated assortment of practices and ideologies (2004: 26–28). And like Scales's approach, it lends itself to an examination not simply of the spaces that are created through "imagining" forms of sociability, but also of the ways this imagining intersects with quotidian practice (2004: 26).

Chapter 3

1. This is not to say that all classic country singers have small vocal ranges and shy away from melismatic passagework; George Jones is a case in point.

2. Jourdain performed the piece in D major (the key in which Rimes performs) rather than B-flat major (the key of the Prince original) and employed vocal ornaments very similar to Rimes's at the end of the second and third choruses.

3. "It's My Time," the choice of the second-place singer, Galvin, stood more squarely in the new-country camp.

4. The first phrase in each verse moves past the dominant to a kind of cadence on the sub-dominant, employing a harmonic structure that is much more characteristic of rock than of classic country.

5. The country version of "Purple Rain" was probably unknown to many in the audience; although it appeared on LeAnn Rimes's *Sittin' on Top of the World* album, it was never released as a single.

6. As the winner of the competition, Jourdain's live performance would be broadcast one hundred times the following year on NCI, and I heard it often enough to become familiar with it. Listening under less charged circumstances, I was struck by how little it reflected what I remembered. At Country Jam, it had seemed that Jourdain was entirely on top of her performance. On the radio I heard tuning problems and vocal strain—a young singer struggling with a difficult piece.

7. For instance, the year before the competition in question NCI had begun to broadcast a hip-hop program.

8. Band offices are the offices of First Nations governments.

9. In the 1950s federal and provincial governments began to establish Friendship Centers in urban urban areas with large aboriginal populations. These community centers allowed indigenous people to come together for purposes of mutual assistance, fellowship, and entertainment.

10. This is not entirely accurate. It is true that in 1980 the institutions targeting the aboriginal public were not nearly as successful and visible as they are today. Nevertheless, some of them, such as Sunshine Records and NCI, were well established before Ranville had his first hit. In fact, later in the same interview Ranville mentioned Sunshine Records as a long-standing Manitoban aboriginal music institution. He also acknowledged Manitoban aboriginal musicians who had influenced him, including Ray St. Germain and Alex Parenteau.

11. Michael Warner says, of the relationship between publics and counterpublics, that "a counterpublic maintains at some level, conscious or not, an awareness of its subordinate status" (2002: 119). The word "subordinate" is important, not only because it identifies a differential power relationship, but also because it acknowledges the connection between publics and counterpublics.

12. Dakota communities still play an important role in the vitality of the Manitoban powwow.

13. The Manitoba Sioux communities mentioned in the article were founded by Wahpeton Dakota people, who fled to Canada following a conflict with American settlers in 1862 (Dickason 2002: 245). The North and South Dakota communities mentioned also have populations of Wahpeton Dakota.

14. Just a few years after this newspaper article was published, the Ojibwe ceremonialist Maggie Wilson organized a Union Star Dance to assist Ojibwe and Canadian soldiers fighting in the First World War (see Landes 1968: see also chapter 7). This is an even clearer example of an articulation between traditional indigenous life and national public culture.

15. When Menow told me, "People wouldn't favor anybody," he did not initially indicate the terms that might have dictated favoritism in such contexts; his response emphasized geography rather than race. He may have been thinking about how some judges favor local musicians. Nevertheless he did say, during the 2003 interview and in a later (2008) one, that there was no racism at the *Western Hour*.

16. Ray St. Germain came to prominence in the Canadian popular scene in the 1960s, hosting a nationally broadcast variety show called *Music Hop* (St. Germain 2003 liner notes: 2–3). He continued to host nationally broadcast music programs for over twenty years.

17. The long-standing inclusiveness of the scene complicates the discussion of "aboriginal country music" in the province. It is difficult to say, for instance, whether there is a

"nonaboriginal country-music scene" (outside of "alt-country" musicians, who are, by and large, middle-class nonaboriginals).

18. "Cowboy" is, of course, a shorthand term for a diverse array of white hero figures, including lawmen and pioneers, who epitomize justice, bravery, physical strength, and cunning.

19. In an interview conducted in the summer of 2008, Menow was a little more critical of the racism that manifested itself in mainstream representations of indigenous people.

20. Thanks to Josh Pilzer for drawing my attention to the economic context for Menow's remarks.

21. No aboriginal consultant has ever suggested to me that the appropriation of cowboy songs and fashion was a conscious act of resistance. But the meanings of sartorial style and musical taste are not always straightforward or explicit. The fashions and listening habits associated with punk and the folk-music revival were hardly transparent to many of those involved (see Hebdige 1979, Cantwell 1996); why should the aboriginal cowboy code be any more obvious?

22. Herzfeld's discussion of "cultural intimacy" tends to focus on how "rueful self-recognition" is mobilized between social intimates; I am more concerned here with how it shapes imagining modes of sociability (1997: 3–4). In general, I use Herzfeld's expression "rueful self-recognition" more often than "cultural intimacy," since "intimacy" has a very specific meaning in this book. For another exploration of cultural intimacy in relation to popular music, see Stokes 2010.

23. The title of the article evokes the colonial idea that cultures civilize only gradually, over the course of decades or centuries. The idea seems to be that allowing "Indians" to drink has set them backward on the civilizational path to the drinking patterns of the fur-trade era—that is, before the time when the state intervened. Gray seems to be drawing upon an understanding of culture, civilization, and change that has been criticized by Johannes Fabian as "allochronism" (Fabian 1983; see also Chakrabarty 2000).

24. The article subsequently shifts tone and goes on to describe normative beer-parlor etiquette in humorous terms. In a sarcastic passage that suggests discomfort not only with Native drinking, but also with normalized white middle-class intoxication, the author suggests that beer-parlor conversation "must be kept at a standard 150 decibels lower than that of the average cocktail party."

25. In 1971 a case was brought against the Marlborough Hotel alleging defamation and discrimination. The manager of the front office of the hotel had distributed a memorandum to his staff that ordered them to keep aboriginal guests out of the hotel ("Court Rejects Indians' Charge," *Winnipeg Tribune*, [June 16, 1971], clipping without page number consulted at University of Manitoba Archives and Special Collections).

26. Although Ranville does not condemn drinking in the interview excerpts quoted here, he regularly discussed the harmful effects of alcohol at the time we spoke.

27. For a much more critical description of aboriginal drinking, generalized to encompass drinking behaviors across Canada, see Thatcher 2004: 15–27.

28. One worrisome aspect of literature that examines aboriginal drinking is that it tends not to compare indigenous drinking patterns to those in other economically disadvantaged populations (cf. Thatcher 2004, Saggers and Gray 1998).

29. It could perhaps be said that it is precisely because of permeability that publics and counterpublics are differentiable. Publics hear and see one another, and this allows some to stigmatize the practices of others even as those others know themselves to be stigmatized.

30. Of the thirty songs performed by Country Jam competitors, twenty were love songs, nine of them by aboriginal songwriters; four celebrated rural homes, three of them by aboriginal songwriters about their home communities; and seven mentioned drinking, three of them by aboriginal songwriters.

31. Tichi (1994) identifies the celebration of the rural home as part of a larger sentimental complex that juxtaposes this home with "the road," the space of adventure and danger away from it. In this fourfold complex, song originates when the singer is in one space and yearns to be in another: from the road, home seems like a space of safety, happiness, and

completeness; from home, the road seems like a space of adventure, economic gain, and freedom; from the road, the road seems cold, lonely, and dangerous; and from home, home seems personally and economically stifling.

32. Barbara Ching (2001: 8–25) discusses this hinterland but focuses on how the concept functions as a metaphor for social class.

33. Written by Marty Brown, Richard Young, and Stan Webb.

34. Norway House received diesel generators in 1963 and was connected to the power grid by power lines in 1973 (Manitoba Hydro 2009). As Bradburn and many of his listeners would have been aware, roads, bridges, and hydroelectric power lines came to Native communities much later than to others in Manitoba.

35. The exception to these negative depictions of alcohol consumption was Loretta Crane's "The Barrows All-Stars Tribute," which depicted a group of friends happily drinking and making music together.

36. Richard did not place in the 2002 competition, but he recorded and released the song as a single, and it went on to receive considerable airplay on NCI in 2003.

37. Lest there be any confusion, the actual rhythms of traditional indigenous life often involve stretches of intense labor, self-discipline, and abstinence.

38. There are notable musical similarities, too: the verses of Richard's song have almost exactly the same harmonic structure as the verses and choruses of Williams's song (Richard's song is in C rather than E, however). Richard was almost certainly familiar with "Family Tradition," which is regularly covered by bar bands on the aboriginal country scene.

39. To call Hank Williams Jr.'s song "mainstream" is not to deny its status as "outlaw country" or "hard country" music, distinct from country music oriented to a pop audience.

40. Fourteen of the twenty love songs performed by competitors expressed sadness or heartbreak.

41. Shannacappo did not place in the competition, but he subsequently recorded and released "Never Be a Cheatin' Heart," which won NCI's award for Single of the Year in 2003.

42. In 1996 over 30 percent of aboriginal parents were single (Canada and Manitoba 2000: 90–91, 110n), compared to 14.5 percent of nonaboriginal parents (Canada 2005). David Schneider and Raymond Smith (1973) suggest that marital instability is connected to financial insecurity in North American kinship; their observations may not be generalizable to indigenous families.

43. The term "single parent" obscures the diversity and depth of the social networks in which "single aboriginal parents" and "children in one-parent aboriginal families" are actually located.

44. Nevertheless, bearing David Samuels's arguments in mind (2004), such songs should not be understood to constitute the only "true" Manitoban aboriginal country music. A great deal of what makes music indigenous involves the people who mobilize it and the contexts in which it is enmusicalized.

45. People also affirmed social closeness in highly visible ways—not only by speaking well of social intimates, but also through prominent displays of financial and social support. These displays were further revisited in conversation for others, so that they too were witnesses to these affirmations of allegiance.

46. See Mason 1967: 6; compare Hallowell 1955: 277–90.

Chapter 4

1. They used a contemporary reprint of the 1927 edition of Rev. J. A. Mackay's *Psalms and Hymns in the Language of the Cree Indians of the Diocese of Saskatchewan, North-West America*.

2. When I discussed the opening of this chapter with Audrey Guiboche, she reminded me that one of the groups that had participated in the wake was made up of singers from Easterville (Chemawawin Cree Nation) under the leadership of Hubert Thomas, whose singing is discussed in the preface to chapter 5. It is altogether possible that what I have represented as two groups of singers was actually three groups, from Sapotaweyak Cree Nation, Moose Lake, and Chemawawin Cree Nation.

3. I do not know who composed this song. Two consultants suggested that it came from northern Manitoba; another had heard someone claim that it came from Alberta. My copy of the lyrics was photocopied from a photocopy used by Mary and Kendra Sinclair. The lyrics were presented on a single page in two columns, the first in Cree, the second in English.

4. The capitalization, spelling, and punctuation of the Cree lyrics is as in the Sinclairs' copy (see previous footnote) except that a doubled "A" was removed from the beginning of the third line of the first stanza at the recommendation of Nelson Menow. The capitalization, spelling, and punctuation of the English lyrics are as in the original except that I have changed the word "I" to "I'll" near the beginning of the second line of the fourth stanza. Nelson Menow translated this excerpt rather differently when we discussed it in the summer of 2008:

> This very night
> You came to sit with me
> I have left peacefully
> Do not weep for me
> Do not be lazy
> You have to let go of me peacefully
> Do not weep for me
> For I have left and gone peacefully.
> Don't feel pity for me
> For I will never leave thee.

5. Again, social and musical intimacy should not be understood as privacy; indeed, the funerary rites discussed herein are in some cases community-wide events.

6. Menow grew up in Norway House Cree Nation, but he also lived for a time in Peguis, which has a population of both Cree and Ojibwe people, and in Winnipeg, where his circle of acquaintances included Cree, Métis, and Ojibwe people. Given his familiarity with aboriginal people from a variety of backgrounds, it seems appropriate for him to comment upon the wake.

7. Aboriginal mortuary observances are similar in many ways to nonaboriginal ceremonies I have attended in Manitoba. After death, the body is taken to a funeral home, embalmed, and prepared; a viewing event or events—the wake—follows; there is a subsequent and separate funeral service, sometimes at a church; and this is followed by the burial and a communal meal (compare Metcalf and Huntington 1991: 196). It is the length of aboriginal wakes that distinguishes them from others. Accordingly they are often held in places that can accommodate all-night gatherings and singing: family homes, or the Aboriginal Funeral Chapel in Winnipeg's North End, for instance.

8. Since my closest acquaintances in the aboriginal community were teetotalers, I did not witness any examples of this "opposite way" of running a wake.

9. A number of Ojibwe hymnals were published beginning early in the nineteenth century in the United States (McNally 2000: 51–54); Canadian Ojibwe hymnbooks appear to have drawn upon these as well as the Ojibwe-language work of James Evans (McNally 2000: 53).

10. In 1989–93 the First Nations homicide rate in Manitoba was twice as high as the national average; during the same period the suicide rate among young men aged fifteen to twenty-four was 126 per 100,00, more than five times the national average; for young women aged fifteen to twenty-four it was 35 per 100,000, more than seven times the national average (see Dueck 2012, Canada and Manitoba 2000: 36–39).

11. How to interpret this gesture? As a manifestation of "northern Algonquian individualism": of an iconoclast who saw no reason to hide his impatience for the sake of those grieving inside? As evidence of postcolonial anomie: of standards of comportment so weakened by colonialism that disrespectful behavior is common, even at moments of communal sadness? As an example of the deep resentment many feel for the church in the wake of residential schooling? Or as a gesture that paradoxically underlined the collectivity of the event, bringing attention to the fact that some members of the community (probably including some nonchurchgoers) were cut off from the activities going on inside the church, and that they were ready to move on to the parts of the ritual in which they too could participate?

12. As noted in previous chapters, many aboriginal people live far from their communities of origin, and travel home can be time-consuming or prohibitively expensive, particularly in the case of isolated fly-in reserves.

13. Regarding regulation, Durkheim writes, "When the individual feels firmly attached to the society to which he belongs, he feels morally bound to share in its grief and its joy" (1995: 403). Of integration, he says, "People cry together because they continue to be precious to one another and because, regardless of the blow that has fallen upon it, the collectivity is not breached.... To commune in sadness is still to commune, and every communion of consciousnesses increases social vitality, in whatever form it is done" (1995: 405).

14. This is not always the case, of course. For example, some believe that those who have not accepted Jesus as their personal savior will go to hell, and some believe that those who commit suicide are damned. I discuss some of these eschatological divergences in Dueck 2012.

15. The metaphor as elaborated here is not explicit in Marsden's reply: he does not say that it is singers who give comfort ("coffee") to mourners. This extension of his actual words does seem justified, given the context.

16. A connection can be drawn here with Turino's exploration of the social efficacy of "dicent indices" (see especially 2008: 42–44). Marsden's coffee metaphor suggests that music is (understood by the bereaved to be) a dicent index of the community's comfort, and that it is a convincing and effective sign of consolation because of its iconic resemblance to embodied experiences of being comforted and warmed.

17. At least insofar as insofar as music, emotion, physical feeling, and social experience can be distinguished from one another (compare Turino 1999: 241).

18. In Peircean semiotics, indexicality is a semiotic relationship of copresence, in which a sign points to another existing object that is its referent (on indexicality see Peirce 1960: 143; Parmentier 1994: 6–7; Turino 1999: 227). Understood in this respect, the icons discussed earlier are ones that index something else: for instance, songs at the wake are icons that index the support and comfort of the community. But "indexicality" as used here draws upon Michael Silverstein's bi-directional conception of the term. In this understanding, indexicality works in two directions: on the one hand, sign activity indexically presupposes other elements of its context; on the other, it indexically entails, or brings into existence, elements of this context (1993: 36 and 1998). Social action is thus not only contingent but also consequential; it both presumes and produces.

    Scholarly accounts of indexical iconicity in music have often focused on the "presupposing" aspect of indexicality. They discuss music as an icon that points to some other aspect of culture or to experiences in the past. So, for instance, Thomas Turino in a foundational article outlining "a Peircean semiotic theory for music" describes how music can be indexically iconistic of social relations (Turino 1999: 234). And David Samuels examines musical performances and hearings as feelingful indexical icons of past performances and hearings (see Samuels 2004: 139; compare McNally 2000: 190 and Turino 1999: 235–36 on "our song"). Neither author uses the term indexicality in Silverstein's second sense; that is, to describe how musical performance is consequential within its cultural context (Silverstein 1997). This is most emphatically *not* to say that either author is unconcerned with the entailing, performative aspects of musical performance. Indeed, Turino discusses "creating" and Samuels "triggering" in their discussions of indexical iconicity. The point here is rather to clarify that the term "indexicality" as used here differs in certain important respects from conventional Peircean usages in music scholarship. Thanks to Vicki Brennan, whose remarks in a 2008 email helped me to develop the framework of my argument here.

19. Individualism should be understood not as an absence of sociability, but rather as a manner of relating to others.

20. Northern Ojibwe did communicate about such dreams in various indirect ways, however, which helps to explain the similarity of accounts of them, and also how anthropologists came to learn about them. Notably, elders would sometimes draw upon their dreams when they imparted a name to a baby in a naming ceremony (Jenness 1935 quoted in McNally 2009: 16).

21. Hallowell interprets northern Ojibwe "sorcery" as a sublimation of impulses to actual physical aggression, and fear of the magic of others as a cultural constraint on behavior that might express overt hostility or invite overt retribution (1955: 277–90).

22. Hallowell relates how, according to his consultants, there was a time when midé men and conjurers "were constantly trying one another out" (1955: 289). He transcribes a story of one such contest, between an arrogant midé leader named Pàzαgwígabo and a quiet healer named Owl. The duel is in large part undertaken to determine whose personal power is greater: Pàzαgwígabo, perhaps jealous of Owl's powers but hubristic enough to consider himself more powerful, bullies Owl into a duel, in part by insulting Owl's healing abilities. He tells him, "You think you are a great man. But do you know that you are no good? When you want to save lives you always bring that stone along. I don't believe it's good for anything." When the two meet up next, after Owl's magic has brought Pàzαgwígabo near death, Owl lets his rival know that he is the victor and the stronger "conjurer" and warns him against overestimating his power: "You know who Owl is now! I was only playing with you this time. I did not intend to kill you. But I never want to hear again what you said in this place [i.e., Pàzαgwígabo's remarks about Owl's powers and paraphernalia].... Don't think you are such a great midé! [i.e., leader of the Midéwiwin ceremony]" (Hallowell 1955: 289).

23. Such a dramatic reversal is described by R. W. Dunning in the community of Pikangikum in the second half of the twentieth century, although in this case, the author seems to suggest, the upset marked a significant social shift, as traditional "medico-magical" power was undercut by the increasing power of the Canadian government (Dunning 1959: 181–86).

24. Accordingly, this volume tries to avoid terms that have sometimes been used to characterize aspects of indigenous sociability but carry negative associations, including "suspicion," "lawbreaking," and "nepotism."

25. To reiterate a point made in chapter 1, I understand cultural practice as something that has some fixity or stickiness but is nevertheless subject to ongoing contestation and transformation. See Silverstein 2004.

26. Again, some readers may wonder whether these rhythmic characteristics simply manifest a lack of musical competence. The short answer is no. At any rate, the legitimacy of these musical interactions is beside the point I am making here, which is that they evidence a distinctive mode of musical sociability in which individuality is dramatically realized and, for fellow musicians, made somatically palpable.

27. It seems to me that the individuation Marsden describes can be distinguished from the Western ideology of the emergence of the "unique artistic voice," although he makes use of familiar tropes. "Western liberal individualism" and "low-integration indigenous sociability" are not the same thing, although they certainly intersect and have borrowed from one another.

28. At a very basic level of repertorial distinction were differences codified in hymnbooks and other song collections. Typically, members of church groups and informal associations of singers shared common songbooks; these facilitated collaborations with in-group singers while potentially limiting interactions with out-group musicians.

29. Using Turino's (2008) Peircean terminology, a musical leader's demands of her musical accompanists might be characterized as a "dicent index" of her uniqueness.

30. Here, unfortunately, I interrupted Ranville.

31. This notwithstanding the complaints of certain practitioners quoted earlier. As I have suggested, these musicians make music together with the very musicians they complain about.

32. This is particularly evident in the long analysis undertaken in chapter 5. I should add that this is in no way to suggest Turino is unaware of divergences from his general model; see 2008: 36.

33. Indigenous people have long incorporated nonindigenous elements in traditional expressive practices; the use of snuff cans to construct the jingles for jingle dress dance regalia is a good example (see Browner 2002: 54). And if a mass-produced industrial product can be integrated in Ojibwe ceremonial life, it seems reasonable to suggest that European hymns and American gospel songs can be incorporated in northern Algonquian expressions of

communality and individuality. Still, the incursion of nonindigenous musical forms in indigenous life is anything but culturally equitable. Traditional modes of indigenous social and musical interaction have been sharply impacted by the interventions of settler society and by the near ubiquity of mass-mediated musics of nonindigenous origin. Even today, unique musical practices and aspects of traditional ceremonial life remain under threat, and the situation is dire for many North American aboriginal languages. So while it should be acknowledged that hybrid expressive practices manifest (and constitute) unique, contemporary indigenous identities, aesthetics, and forms of sociability, this should not obscure their origins in contexts of unequal power relations. Nor should it veil contemporary structures of power that threaten even the unique musical translations considered in this chapter.

34. It is not that these performances symbolize in abstract form these modes of sociability, but rather that they are spaces in which community and individuality are experienced and by which they are socially engendered (compare Stokes 1994: 2; Turino 1999: 241).

Preface to Chapter 5

1. As the wording of this sentence suggests, I do not know Thomas well, having only met him briefly. Thomas is from Chemawawin First Nation.

2. I give the first two words of the Cree hymn as the title; the title given on *Cree Hymns Vol. 1*, is "Son [*sic*] of My Soul."

3. The 1927 volume is an expanded edition of a hymnal first published in 1891. On *Cree Hymns Vol. 1*, Thomas clearly announces the numbers of most of the hymns before he begins to sing them. These numbers and the lyrics correspond to those in the reprint of the 1927 edition.

4. A few hymnbooks containing Cree or Ojibwe songs feature a very limited amount of musical notation; most have none whatsoever. In certain Manitoban communities nonaboriginal clergypersons and missionaries may have referred to hymnals with notation in them when singing hymns for or with aboriginal singers. As much seems evident given the 1958 edition of the *United Church of Canada Cree Hymn Book*, which contains an index matching Cree hymns to their counterparts in the *United Church Hymnary* and Sankey's *Sacred Songs and Solos*.

5. Silverstein's theory has informed work in anthropology, ethnomusicology, and English; see for example Baumann 1996, Herzfeld 1997, Monson 1996, Warner 2002.

6. In Peircean semiotics, indexical signs stand in relationships of cooccurrence with their referents (Peirce 1960: 143; see also Parmentier 1994: 6–7; Turino 1999: 227; Turino 2008: 8–10). As explained in a previous footnote (see chapter 4, n. 18), Silverstein's theory of language and culture understands this indexical cooccurrence dually: indexes do not only point to things that already exist, but also bring things into being (see Silverstein 1993: 36).

7. Often in ways that do not involve conscious thought or intention on the part of the actor.

8. On iconicity see Peirce 1960: 143; Parmentier 1994: 6–7; Turino 1999: 226–27; Turino 2008: 6–8. As Turino notes, musical iconicity allows listeners to perceive musical repetition (and, at larger levels, form). Iconicity here refers to all kinds of similarities, and not simply visual ones.

9. A text, in metapragmatic analysis, is a cohering structure of interaction emerging in real time: although the term might suggest otherwise, a text need not involve writing or even words. Rather, it is what emerges as two or more persons interact with one another, or as a person engages with a song, book, recording, etc. Hence the terms "entextualization" and "enmusicalization," which suggest the coming into being of a coherent interaction.

10. It can be added that signs often regiment reflexively: they characterize themselves in addition to the signs around them (see Silverstein 1993: 50–52). A cadential formula, for instance, signals the close of the very phrase of which it is a part.

11. Moreover, all of the important harmonic, melodic, and structural events in the song coincide with downstrokes rather than upstrokes. For a discussion of the musical features by which listeners infer a metrical structure, see Lerdahl and Jackendoff 1983: 74–85.

12. As Lerdahl and Jackendoff explain, harmonic shifts tend to occur on metrically strong beats (1983: 74–85). It seems evident that the reflexive regimentation of sign activity regularly occurs across harmonic, rhythmic, and melodic "domains."

13. Note that the thick barlines in the score do not in fact signal units of this hypermetrical structure; they coincide rather with line breaks (as consideration of other songs in the hymnal makes clear).

14. In other words, to use Lerdahl and Jackendoff's (1983) helpful distinction, Thomas's performance articulates an all-encompassing grouping structure but a more minimal metrical structure.

15. I am not sure that Thomas's performance is an example of the common musical phenomenon in which musicians pay less attention to meter or rhythm at the ends of phrases, allowing it to fade or "thin" there (on "thin" and "thick" meter see Rockwell 2009b). At the same time, it would be difficult to prove that Thomas is mobilizing metrically patterned musical materials in ways that engender structures of metrical expectation in some listeners but have no similar effect upon him. A clearer instance of minimal metricality can be found in the performance by the Littles considered in chapter 5.

16. In the liner notes for *Cree Hymns Vol. 1*, Thomas writes, "I hope these songs will touch and inspire your hearts like they did for my family and me."

Chapter 5

1. These eastern European immigrants had come to Canada following the introduction of a new federal policy on immigration in 1896; see Hiebert 1991: 59–75.

2. In short, middle-class Winnipeggers still think of the North End as a problematic neighborhood, but their concern is now more likely to focus on aboriginal than eastern European people.

3. When I showed this chapter to Audrey Guiboche in 2012, she emphasized that the coffeehouse was not oriented solely to its immediate neighborhood: it was additionally conceived as a place where people from all over could come to sing.

4. These recordings ran the gamut from the professional to the DIY: some were produced at substantial cost by Sunshine Records, others were done at smaller studios in the Winnipeg area, while still others were desktop published using home computers and other affordable technologies. Singers supplemented their income by selling their recordings, typically at the going rate for store-bought CDs.

5. Including the minor supertonic (ii) and submediant (vi) and various "sus" chords.

6. Whether this will continue to be the case remains to be seen. It could be that there will be pressure from nonaboriginal Manitobans to secularize. It could also happen that the question of sacred observance will become increasingly fraught owing to disagreements between those who practice traditional observance and those who are exclusively Christian in their expressions.

7. Michael McNally makes a similar point regarding the Minnesota Ojibwe (2000: 15–16); he notes that the emphasis on practice is evident even in the term for Christians in the Ojibwe language, *Anami'aajig*, which translates into English as something like "those who pray" or "how we pray." This is not to say that indigenous Christians do not think theologically, or that they do not have theological disagreements. Nevertheless, in my experience discussions of theology tended to focus on its practical implications. For instance, one consultant criticized Catholic doctrines on suicide because they added to the misery of families of children who killed themselves. Other friends criticized the preaching of a "health and wealth" evangelist because they perceived him to be enriching himself at the expense of others.

8. For discussion of a comparable opposition see Mass-Observation 1987: 155–67.

9. These analyses are indebted to Michael Silverstein's (1997) investigation of "the improvisational performance of culture" in real-time "getting-to-know-you" conversations.

10. Originally composed by Ira Stanphill and popularized by Elvis Presley, among others.

11. Inclusiveness is clearly not the same thing as equal treatment (equal treatment typically necessitates some form of inclusiveness, but inclusiveness does not necessitate equal treatment). Nevertheless it seems to me that inclusiveness was practiced at William Whyte because it was a manifestation of equal treatment, which was valued.

12. The William Whyte coffeehouse (like many similar jams and coffeehouses that drew aboriginal participants) could perhaps be understood to enact what Turino calls "sequential participatory music," a form of collective musical sociability in which participants alternately occupy roles as performers and listeners (2008: 48–51). That music popularized by country stars is particularly popular at such gatherings suggests something similar to what Turino notes about American karaoke events: that they are instances of participatory music making that allow singers to play the role of the presentational star. Connected to one to another here are two rather different forms of interaction. On the one hand is an intimate and participatory form of musical engagement in which there is little overall distinction between audience and performer (since anyone may occupy either role), and in which the overall economic interaction is one of exchange. Yet there is simultaneously an engagement with a social imaginary (country music) and a capitalist market via the emulation of voices and songs that circulate on recordings distributed by the Nashville music industry. My focus in this chapter is on participants' interactions with one another, what these accomplish within the intimate space of the coffeehouse, and the way these are oriented outward toward an aboriginal public. For the present I bracket how this is additionally connected to international imaginaries and markets. The discussions in chapters 1, 2, and 3 should make it clear that these broad kinds of "imagining" sociability are also in play.

13. This seems probable given that when she did eventually sing, she repeated a song she had performed earlier in the evening.

14. It is not my intent to suggest that indigenous sociability is thoroughgoingly self-interested and agonistic. Negotiations of status and privilege are hardly unique to indigenous interactions. There are unique aspects of indigenous sociability, however, including robust social mechanisms that qualify authority and privilege.

15. "The Lord is with us. He loves us," Menow told us. "Think about it when you get home. That's why I do a lot of crying. I'm not ashamed to cry. Because I know God loves me."

16. The following analysis is indebted to Ingrid Monson's discussion of the Jaki Byard Quartet's 1965 recording of "Bass-ment Blues" (1996: 174–82). Like that reading, it draws upon Silverstein's metapragmatics, examines interactional sociality by analyzing the details of a recorded musical event, and gives close consideration to moments that some listeners might dismiss as infelicities, understanding them rather as important moments in the mutual creation of (what is here called) musical intimacy.

17. The song is titled "Oh, 'Twas Love of God to Me"—in English—on a self-released cassette by the Littles (Little and Little n.d.). Martha Stockton composed the hymn, also known as "Wondrous Love," in 1871 (Julian 1925: 1591; Goodenough 1931: 465). According to one unsubstantiated source (Taylor 1989: 50), she was inspired to write the hymn by a Native American woman's description of how a missionary brought the gospel to her husband's village. Thanks to Dick at the Cyber Hymnal (<www.cyberhymnal.org>) for helping me to find this account in Gordon Taylor's *Companion to the Song Book of the Salvation Army* (Taylor 1989).

18. None of the hymnals I consulted contained a version of "Oh 'Twas Love" that matched exactly what the Littles sang, and it may be that their version features unique Oji-Cree elements not transmitted elsewhere. My spelling follows the version with which the song seems to have the most in common, from the Northern Canada Evangelical Mission's 1980 *Cree Hymns* ([Northern Canada Evangelical Mission] 1980). This is true for all the words but "Ispimihk e gii otohtet / E wii." "Ispimihk" and "otohtet" come from the Northern Canada Evangelical Mission's 1979 *Moose Cree Gospel Songs* ([Northern Canada Evangelical Mission] 1979). Nelson Menow recommended "e gii," and "E wii" is a guess, based on what I hear on the recording.

19. Menow translated the third line as "Above, which he came from" and the fourth line as something like "For he came to save me." He did not object to my suggested "Above, which he came from / In order to save me." The English version of the chorus as sung by the Littles differed significantly from Stockton's original, which follows:

> Oh, 'twas love, 'twas wondrous love!
> The love of God to me;
> It bro't my Saviour from above,
> To die on Calvary (Baird and Reden 1872: 58).

It seems probable that the Littles' English-language chorus is a retranslation of Cree lyrics into English, rather than a variant of Stockton's original. The similarities between their English-language chorus and Menow's translation of the Cree-language one make this even more likely.

20. In 2008 Audy did not recognize the song until I quoted the words to him—and this after we had watched a video recording of the performance. Accordingly, I wonder whether he recognized the song when he accompanied it in 2003.

21. This pattern established both a country sound and a metrical structure.

22. Menow's responsorial approach more easily accommodated the Littles' rhythmic style.

23. On "role" in conversation see Silverstein 1997.

24. The formula articulates a descent from B through A to G, embellished by figuration, chromaticism, and decorative "cover tones" in parallel thirds above the main melody.

25. Variations in duration are also evident on the Littles' recording of "Oh 'Twas Love of God to Me" (Little and Little n.d.).

26. On one occasion I mentioned visual cueing to a reasonably prominent Métis country musician, who found the idea ridiculous. He moved in any number of ways on the stage, he told me. How would another musician ever be able to judge when he was cueing them? Notably absent was any consideration that he might *want* to cue other performers.

27. Turino, discussing American karaoke performance, suggests that two frames are typically in play: a participatory frame in which all are encouraged to take part, and a more karaoke-specific frame of non-serious "play" (2008: 51). The musician's words suggest a similar framing, although in my experience singers and musicians at the coffeehouse tended to take themselves and the music seriously.

28. Nettl, perhaps simplifying his position in a textbook chapter for an undergraduate audience, writes: "The rather athletic view of music taken in Western culture, where star performances by individual composers and performers and their ability to do very difficult things is measured, is replaced in Native American cultures by quite different values" (2008: 346).

Chapter 6

1. The population figure is taken from the community's Web site, <http://www.peguisfirstnation.ca/> (accessed 9 August 2012).

2. The square-dancing competition is typically advertised more prominently than the powwow and is given pride of place as a weekend event (the powwow takes place in the middle of the week).

3. Nowadays many people live off-reserve and receive their payments through other channels.

4. My experiences at Peguis were as a visitor and an outsider; I attended the festival as a member of the public responding to an advertised invitation to "come out for a week of fun." I have obscured a number of facts that would help to identify certain participants because of the nature of what they say. I have not indicated the year in which the competition took place, and I have invented names for those participants with whom I did not establish an interviewing relationship. I interviewed Ryan Richard and Cliff Maytwayashing.

5. The jig is increasingly performed in choreographed unison by square-dancing troupes, however. In such instances it is not as personal or individual an expression.

6. At the end of the competition, a number of the female dancers who had scored well performed again so that a winner could be determined. By this time, my camera had run out of battery power.

7. Not his real name.

8. Not her real name.

9. During the competition, Ryan noted that another contestant had stolen this signature move and incorporated it in his routine.

10. A' is distinguished from A, and B' from B, by musical function. A appears at the beginning of the piece but A' cannot, since it begins with a sort of elision that ties it to the end of B. B can occur between instances of A and A' (or between those of A' and A') but B' can only appear at the end of the piece.

11. The total number of beats was obtained, here and in Table 6.2, by counting from the beginning of section B' to the downbeat of the concluding chord.

12. The length of the A and A' sections of the jig stayed constant from performance to performance: twenty pulses each time. The B sections were either twenty-two or twenty-six pulses in length, while the final B' sections ranged from eleven to twenty-seven pulses in length. The length of the B' sections depended on how many times Maytwayashing repeated the twisting, four-pulse figure evident in mm. 44–45 of Figure 6.5.

13. Thus my concern here is not to establish whether judges at the contest gave preferential treatment to any of the dancers, or to rally evidence about how or how often patronage occurs during competitions, but rather to explore the tensions between aboriginal publicness and various forms of "special treatment" (acknowledged, unacknowledged, and alleged). Other productive approaches are possible. Chris Goertzen (1996) presents convincing evidence of local favoritism in the judging of an old-time band competition in North Carolina; this is complemented by a perceptive (and sympathetic) reading of the judges' decision.

14. For a discussion of the importance of comicality in Ojibwe myth and sociability see Gross 2002: 445–49, 452–58.

15. Does one enter the conversation frame with the strangers seated beside one in a concert hall, for instance?

16. As Richard and I waited in the dance shelter for the jigging competition to start, the elderly man and woman seated next to us struck up a conversation with us. By the end of the evening, I had learned about his broken arm, her former job as a chemical dependency counselor, and their recent triumph at the Treaty Days waltz competition. They also learned about us.

17. The expression "family tradition" suggests a referent in popular culture: a song of that name by Hank Williams Jr. (see Williams 1993). It was a song familiar to many Manitoban aboriginal country fans.

18. My friend related this story to several others and me. After he told it, he looked over at another singer and told him that he should have come up to compete. The implication was that, as the judge in charge of picking the first-place winner, he could have made sure that his own friend took home the prize.

19. In this respect it bears noting that the new legislation opens up the account books of indigenous communities to even further scrutiny by a national audience, potentially increasing populist calls for interference by the state in indigenous governance.

20. See Hallowell 1955: 119–20 (Hallowell uses the expression "social atomism" on p. 147); Landes 1968: 4–5. The claim that social atomism existed before contact with Europeans posed a challenge to an idea championed by Karl Marx and W. H. R. Rivers among others: namely, that hunter-gatherer societies were necessarily communal in organization (see Hallowell 1955: 241, 415n; Hickerson 1967: 313–16).

   Landes and Hallowell present a somewhat static view of culture, despite Hallowell's interest in acculturation. A more historically dynamic understanding of northern Algonquian culture, taking greater account of the impact of European contact, emerges in the later decades of the twentieth century (see Francis and Morantz 1983: 95–97 for a discussion of some of this literature).

21. Nevertheless, Hickerson, like other writers from the second half of the twentieth century, helped to create a more historically dynamic picture of northern Algonquian cultures.

22. For discussion of issues involved in mediating sacred songs and knowledge to a public, see Diamond 2008: 9; Diamond, Cronk, and von Rosen 1994: 2.

23. One explanation of the difference is that the very presentation of sacred knowledge requires attendees to behave differently from how they might at an academic talk. The presentation of a dream is a revelation of the sacred that recruits all in its hearing to participatory roles as respectful witnesses. These roles are mandatory, since the dream both requires and creates a total sacred or ritual space in which all present are implicated. Documenting and transcribing are refusals of these roles and for this reason are problematic. On the "obligations and responsibilities" associated with traditional knowledge, see Diamond 2008: 9; on the injunction to engage in participatory social and musical practices, see Turino 2008: 28–30.

24. There are at the time of this writing a few videos of indigenous sweat lodge ceremonies, sun dances, and shaking tent ceremonies available on YouTube—a very small number when compared to the number of videos that can be found of powwow singing or dancing, for instance. Those that do depict ceremonies often refrain from including particularly sacred moments, and remarks in the comments section suggest that many people are troubled to find that videos of these ceremonies are publicly available.

25. See "Sweat Lodge Makes History," *Winnipeg Free Press*, August 27, 2002.

26. It is not my intention to criticize these publicly oriented lodges or the people associated with them. In fact, one of the two lodges mentioned was particularly welcoming to me and introduced me to traditional aboriginal ceremonial observance in the first place.

27. I have suggested that the hesitation to make ceremonies public is probably related to precolonial practices of concealment. Nevertheless, the woman's explanation of its origins needs to be taken into account, since others too attributed the secrecy of contemporary ceremonial life to the colonial experience.

28. I draw these points from my field notes, compiled after the event, and from a summary of participants' contributions compiled by Olga McIvor during the afternoon discussion session that she chaired and I attended.

29. When I discussed the inclusion of this material in the chapter with McIvor in 2012, she suggested that elders were concerned that students would be disrespectful because many of them had been brought up in Christian environments and were accordingly out of touch with indigenous traditions.

30. Stokes (2002) has previously drawn upon Chakrabarty's insight in an exploration of the economics of musical practices. Compare Turino (2008: see especially 77), who suggests that participatory musical traditions can hinder the emergence of commodity forms.

31. Highway 6, the road we took for most of our journey, is a major artery for aboriginal travel in Manitoba. Residents of Grand Rapids, Cross Lake, Norway House, and other northern communities take the route when traveling to Winnipeg and back. It thus made good sense for Chris to sell his CDs in shops along the way.

32. "The market" is also an imaginary, as Benedict Anderson (1991) suggests through the formulation "print-capitalism."

33. Note the nesting: insistent prioritizations of intimacy become a concern for the national public.

Chapter 7

1. Although the settler public was eager to view such events, their government was keen to suppress them. Wanduta was sentenced to four months of hard labor for his participation in the Rapid City dance (Pettipas 1994: 119). Public demand was high for performances of indigenous dancing throughout much of the period when it was obstructed by Canadian federal law, and many such performances were organized despite misgivings in the Department of Indian Affairs. See Titley 1986: 171–83.

2. The town of Brandon in the southwest of Manitoba (an area where there is a large Dakota population) was a particularly important center for such performances.

3. Located in western Ontario close to the Manitoban border.
4. Wilson's own son-in-law was one of the soldiers who fought in the war (Landes 1968: 208).
5. Many central elements of the powwow come from Plains traditions (Powers 1990: xvi, 18–19, 29; Browner 2002: 19, 34), and these and the powwow itself are new arrivals in many northern and subarctic Algonquian communities (see Whidden 2007: 113–15). The jingle-dress dance and associated regalia are perhaps the most prominent northern Algonquian contribution.
6. It is interesting to observe similarities between contemporary jingle dresses and the dance regalia for Maggie Wilson's Union Star Dance. Compare Browner 2002: photograph 8 with Landes 1968: plate 4.
7. Such problematic attitudes were evident even in the early decades of the twentieth century: Manitoban newspaper articles expressed a fascination with deep cultural difference on the one hand, and derision of indigenous people who "weren't Indian enough" on the other (see Dueck 2005: 169–72).
8. Jennifer Brown's "Doing Aboriginal History: A View from Winnipeg," quoted extensively below, also draws upon Appadurai's *The Social Life of Things*.
9. Indeed, certain forms of publicness also involve a kind of enclaving, even though public-oriented performance addresses an unknown and unspecified audience of strangers. Manitoban indigenous publicity construes an aboriginal audience, while an expression such as "my fellow Canadians" construes an audience of Canadian citizens. Public address is simultaneously inclusive and exclusive.
10. For an account of the relationship between roles and things in Melanesia, see Strathern 1988.
11. It may also have reflected acceptance that such borrowing was common in the dance scene, and that sooner or later their unique contributions would be absorbed as part of a common fund of choreographic possibilities.
12. Ethnomusicologists can receive substantial material rewards for the work they do in the field, but typically in the form of salaried employment.
13. Christopher Scales relates a fascinating example of how musicians themselves relativized a normally powerful legal enclave—namely, contract. Arbor Records, a Winnipeg record label, attempted for a time to bind powwow groups to long-term recording contracts (Scales 2004: 249–57). Eyabay, a popular powwow group, signed such a contract with Arbor but then broke it to record a CD with another label (garnering a significant advance in the process). The group escaped the potential legal fallout of their actions because Arbor was hesitant to sue them. Scales writes: "There were few palatable options. Eyabay was in clear breach of contract. Arbor could sue but the end result would simply be that Eyabay would likely never do another recording with [the head of Arbor Records] and Arbor Records would quickly become known as the record label that sues powwow groups. It would spell the end of the company. All [the head of the company] could do was cut his losses, rip up Eyabay's contract, and try to negotiate another deal with the group" (Scales 2004: 251). Eventually, Scales reports, the label stopped signing musicians to long-term contracts (Scales 2004: 255).
14. I began my fieldwork after most of the events in this episode had already occurred. I met a number of people who publicly opposed the removal of the sacred items from the University of Winnipeg collections. I did not meet or interview any of the people who publicly supported the removal of these artifacts.
15. Nelson's original spellings and punctuation are maintained here.
16. "'We feasted the grandfather water drum and the little boy water drum,' said Benton Banai. 'We nourished them, smudged them, but contrary to what was reported we never used them in ceremonies. We never sounded their voice'" (Nelson 2002b).
17. In the immediate context in which it appears, "materials gathered" might refer to photographs, writings, and radio programs. But given the larger context it should probably be understood to refer to indigenous artifacts.
18. Rice's original spellings and punctuation are maintained here.
19. See also J. Brown 2003: 14n. Landes, writing of items associated with the Midéwiwin, seems to suggest a similar attitude; see Landes 1968: 81–84.

20. The Three Fires Ojibwe Culture and Education Society is at the time of writing a public-facing organization, with status as a public charity in the United States.

21. For a discussion of some of the ethical issues that surround the mediation of traditional knowledge, items, and sounds to a public, see Diamond, Cronk, and van Rosen 1994: 1–2, 13–14.

Chapter 8

1. To claim that the aboriginal public is distinctive is not to say it is culturally homogeneous or static. Consider again Courtney Jourdain's winning performance of a countrified version of "Purple Rain" at the 2002 NCI Jam, which epitomized a number of shifts taking place in aboriginal popular-music performance at the time, among them the increasing prominence of female singers, a lesser dependence upon the musical structures of classic country, and an increasing diversification in indigenous musical tastes.

2. Again, "face-to-face" refers to interactions that involve actual co-presence as well as those conducted with the help of telephonic, televisual, or teletextual technologies. The key distinction is between such personal interactions and performances and publications oriented to audiences of strangers.

3. In other cases, of course, performers seemed to understand exactly such "crookedness" as something a public might enjoy.

4. These privileged intimacies can become the stuff of publicness: patronage rarely remains a family secret. The national public may interpret prioritizations of intimacy, musical or otherwise, as evidence of parochialism, backwardness, or a failure to be properly modern. In this respect, even antipublic behavior can contribute to the public-counterpublic dynamic: the process by which the national public distinguishes itself from a problematic indigenous other.

Bibliography

Aboriginal Justice Inquiry. 2008 [1991]. *Report of the Aboriginal Justice Inquiry of Manitoba.* Originally published 1991. Consulted at <http://www.ajic.mb.ca/volume.html> (accessed 26 February 2008).

Abu-Lughod, Lila. 1986. *Veiled Sentiments: Honor and Poetry in a Bedouin Society.* Berkeley and Los Angeles: University of California Press.

Adorno, T. W. 1941. "On Popular Music." With the assistance of George Simpson. *Studies in Philosophy and Social Sciences* 9/1: 17–48.

Althusser, Louis. 1971. "Ideology and Ideological State Apparatuses (Notes towards an Investigation)." In *Lenin and Philosophy*, translated by Ben Brewster: 127–86. New York: Monthly Review Books.

Anderson, Benedict. 1991. *Imagined Communities: Reflections on the Origin and Spread of Nationalism.* Revised ed. London: Verso.

Angel, Michael. 2002. *Preserving the Sacred: Historical Perspectives on the Ojibwa Midewiwin.* Winnipeg: University of Manitoba Press.

Appadurai, Arjun. 1986. "Introduction: Commodities and the Politics of Value." In *The Social Life of Things: Commodities in Cultural Perspective*, edited by A. Appadurai: 3–63. Cambridge: Cambridge University Press.

———. 1996. *Modernity at Large: Cultural Dimensions of Globalization.* Minneapolis: University of Minnesota Press.

Asch, Michael, ed. 1997. *Aboriginal and Treaty Rights in Canada: Essays on Law, Equity, and Respect for Difference.* Vancouver: UBC Press.

Assembly of First Nations. 2003. *Charter of the Assembly of First Nations.* <http://www.afn.ca/index.php/en/about-afn/charter-of-the-assembly-of-first-nations> (accessed 8 May 2013).

———. 2013. "Bill C-27: First Nations Financial Transparency Act." <http://www.afn.ca/uploads/files/parliamentary/analysisbillc-27.pdf> (accessed 25 May 2013).

Baird, E. T., and Karl Reden, eds. 1872. *The Voice of Praise: A Selection of Hymns and Tunes for the Sabbath School, Prayer Meeting, and Family Circle.* Richmond, VA: E. Thompson Baird.

Bakker, Peter. 1997. *A Language of Our Own: The Genesis of Michif, the Mixed Cree-French Language of the Canadian Métis.* Oxford: Oxford University Press.

Bauman, Richard. 1996. "Transformations of the Word in the Production of Mexican Festival Drama." In *Natural Histories of Discourse*, edited by Michael Silverstein and Greg Urban: 301–27. Chicago: University of Chicago Press.

Beardy, Flora, and Robert Coutts, eds. 1996. *Voices from Hudson Bay: Cree Stories from York Factory.* Montreal and Kingston: McGill–Queen's University Press.

Beaster-Jones, Jayson. 2007. "Sounds of the Past Selling the Future." Paper given at the 2007 meeting of the Society for Ethnomusicology in Columbus, OH.

Beaudry, Nicole. 2001. "Subarctic Canada." In *The Garland Encyclopedia of World Music. Vol. 3: The United States and Canada*, edited by Ellen Koskoff: 383–93. New York: Garland.

Becker, Howard S. 2008 [1982]. *Art Worlds*. Updated and expanded. Berkeley and Los Angeles: University of California Press.

Begg, Alexander. 1871. *Dot It Down: A Story of Life in the North-West*. Toronto: Hunter, Rose.

Benedict, Ruth. 1989 [1946]. *The Chrysanthemum and the Sword: Patterns of Japanese Culture*. With a foreword by Ezra F. Vogel. Boston: Houghton Mifflin.

Berlant, Lauren. 2008. *The Female Complaint: The Unfinished Business of Sentimentality in American Culture*. Durham, NC: Duke University Press.

Berlant, Lauren, ed. 2000. *Intimacy: A Special Issue*. Chicago: University of Chicago Press. This book is a republication of *Critical Inquiry* 24/2 and includes articles cited elsewhere in this bibliography.

Berlant, Lauren, and Michael Warner. 1998. "Sex in Public." *Critical Inquiry* 24/2: 547–66.

Bhabha, Homi K. 1994. "The Other Question: Stereotype, Discrimination and the Discourse of Colonialism." In *The Location of Culture*, 66–84. London: Routledge.

Bigenho, Michelle. 2012. *Intimate Distance: Andean Music in Japan*. Durham, NC: Duke University Press.

Bird, S. Elizabeth, ed. 1996. *Dressing in Feathers: The Construction of the Indian in American Popular Culture*. Boulder, CO: Westview Press.

Bohlman, Philip V. 1988. *The Study of Folk Music in the Modern World*. Bloomington: Indiana University Press.

Bolton, David. 1961. "The Red River Jig." *Manitoba Pageant* 7/1. <http://www.mhs.mb.ca/docs/pageant/07/redriverjig.shtml> (accessed 12 January 2009).

Born, Georgina. 2005. "On Musical Mediation: Ontology, Technology and Creativity." *twentieth-century music* 2/1: 7–36.

———. 2008a. "On the Publicization and Privatization of Music." Paper given 19 April, 2008, at the Centre for Research in the Arts, Social Sciences and Humanities at the University of Cambridge.

———. 2008b. "Anthropological Musicologies." Paper presented at the Dent Medal study day, 29 November 2008, on the occasion of the awarding of the Dent Medal to the author. Draft emailed by the author.

Bourdieu, Pierre. 1977. *Outline of a Theory of Practice*. Translated by Richard Nice. Cambridge: Cambridge University Press.

Bowsfield, [Hartwell]. 1956. *Manitoba Pageant April 1956*. <http://www.mhs.mb.ca/docs/pageant/01/manitobaname.shtml> (accessed 21 April 2009).

Brennan, Vicki. 2008. "'Straight to Heaven': Music, Ritual and Performance in Yoruba Churches." Paper given at the 2008 meeting of the Society for Ethnomusicology in Middletown, CT.

Brightman, Robert. 1993. *Grateful Prey: Rock Cree Human-Animal Relationships*. Berkeley and Los Angeles: University of California Press.

Brown, Jennifer S. H. 2003. "Doing Aboriginal History: A View from Winnipeg." *Canadian Historical Review* 84/4: 613–36.

Brown, Jennifer S. H., and Robert Brightman. 1988. *"The Orders of the Dreamed": George Nelson on Cree and Northern Ojibwa Religion and Myth, 1823*. Manitoba Studies in Native History III. Winnipeg: University of Manitoba Press.

Brown, Michael F. 2008. "Cultural Relativism 2.0." *Current Anthropology* 49/3: 363–83.

Browner, Tara. 2002. *Heartbeat of the People: Music and Dance of the Northern Pow-wow*. Urbana: University of Illinois Press.

———. 2009. "An Acoustical Geography of Intertribal Pow-wow Songs." In *Music of the First Nations: Tradition and Innovation in Native North America*, edited by Tara Browner: 131–140. Urbana: University of Illinois Press.

[Burlot, Guy, compiler?]. 1953. *Ayamihe-Masinahikan e Nehiyawastek*. [Winnipeg]: Éditions de la liberté.

Bussidor, Ila, and Üstün Bilgen-Reinart. 1997. *Night Spirits: The Story of the Relocation of the Sayisi Dene*. Winnipeg: University of Manitoba Press.

Calhoun, Craig. 2003. "'Belonging' in the Cosmopolitan Imaginary." *Ethnicities* 3/4: 531–53.

———, ed. 1992. *Habermas and the Public Sphere*. Cambridge, MA: MIT Press.

Canada. 1971. *Indian Treaties and Surrenders, from 1680–1890* [i.e., 1902]. 3 vols. Originally printed Ottawa: B. Chamberlin, Printer to the Queen's Most Excellent Majesty, 1891. Reprinted Toronto: Coles Publishing.

———. 2005. "Canada at a Glance." Pamphlet published by Communications Division, catalogue 12-581-XPE. Christian Carbonneau, project manager. <http://dsp-psd.tpsgc.gc.ca/Collection/Statcan/12-581-X/12-581-XIE2004001.pdf> (accessed 1 September 2009).

———. 2009. "Women's Right to Vote in Canada." <http://www2.parl.gc.ca/Parlinfo/compilations/ProvinceTerritory/ProvincialWomenRightToVote.aspx> (accessed 1 September 2009).

Canada and Manitoba. 2000. Aboriginal People in Manitoba 2000. Prepared by Bruce Hallett of Human Resources Development Canada (HRDC), with research assistance from Myrna Nemeth (HRDC), Harvey Stevens (Manitoba Family Services and Housing), and Donna Stewart (Manitoba Aboriginal Affairs Secretariat). <http://www.gov.mb.ca/ana/apm2000/apm2000.pdf> (accessed 22 January 2006).

Cantwell, Robert. 1996. *When We Were Good: The Folk Revival*. Cambridge, MA: Harvard University Press.

CBC Canada. 2009. "Jesus vs. Nanabush." *ReVision Quest*, Episode 8. Broadcast 17 August 2009.

CBC Manitoba. 2002a. "Fair Wind's Water Drum." Investigative report by Maureen Matthews. Broadcast 19 April, 2002.

———. 2002b. *Original Citizens*. Nine-part radio series broadcast on CBC [Canadian Broadcasting Corporation] Manitoba. <http://winnipeg.cbc.ca/features/originalcitizens/> (accessed 21 February 2004).

Chakrabarty, Dipesh. 2000. *Provincializing Europe: Postcolonial Thought and Historical Difference*. Princeton, NJ: Princeton University Press.

Chrétien, Annette. 1996. "'Mattawa, Where the Waters Meet': The Question of Identity in Métis Culture." Master's thesis, University of Ottawa.

Clayton, Martin. 2007 [1997]. "Metre and Tal in North Indian Music." *Music, Time and Place: Essays in Comparative Musicology*: 7–27. Delhi: B. R. Rhythms.

Clayton, Martin, and Laura Leante. 2013. "Embodiment in Musical Performance." In *Experience and Meaning in Music Performance*, edited by Martin Clayton, Byron Dueck and Laura Leante. Oxford: Oxford University Press.

Clayton, Martin, Rebecca Sager, and Udo Will. 2004. "In Time with the Music: The Concept of Entrainment and its Significance for Ethnomusicology." *ESEM Counterpoint* 1 (Autumn 2007). <http://ethnomusicology.osu.edu/EMW/Will/InTimeWithTheMusic.pdf>.

Ching, Barbara. 2001. *Wrong's What I Do Best: Hard Country Music and Contemporary Culture*. Oxford: Oxford University Press.

Coates, Ken, and Fred McGuinness. 1985. *Pride of the Land: An Affectionate History of Brandon's Agricultural Exhibitions*. Winnipeg: Peguis Publishers.

Cooke, Peter. 1986. *The Fiddle Tradition of the Shetland Isles*. Cambridge: Cambridge University Press.

Day, Richard J. F. 2000. *Multiculturalism and the History of Canadian Diversity*. Toronto: University of Toronto Press.

De Jarlis, Andy. 1961. *Andy De Jarlis' Canadian Fiddle Tunes from the Red River Valley*. Book 2. Toronto: Berandol Music.

Diamond, Beverley. 2002. "Native American Contemporary Music: The Women." *World of Music* 44/1: 11–39.

———. 2008. *Native American Music in Eastern North America: Experiencing Music, Expressing Culture*. Oxford: Oxford University Press.

Diamond, Beverley, M. Sam Cronk, and Franziska von Rosen. 1994. *Visions of Sound: Musical Instruments of First Nations Communities in Northeastern America*. Chicago: University of Chicago Press.

Dickason, Olive Patricia. 2002. *Canada's First Nations: A History of Founding Peoples from Earliest Times*. 3d ed. Oxford: Oxford University Press.

Doffman, Mark. 2013. "Groove: Temporality, Awareness and the Feeling of Entrainment in Jazz Performance." In *Experience and Meaning in Music Performance*, edited by Martin Clayton, Byron Dueck, and Laura Leante. Oxford: Oxford University Press.

Douglas, Mary. 2002. *Purity and Danger: An Analysis of Concepts of Pollution and Taboo.* London: Routledge.

Dueck, Byron. 2005. "Festival of Nations: First Nations and Metis Music and Dance in Public Performance." Ph.D. diss., University of Chicago.

———. 2006. "'Suddenly a Sense of Being a Community': Aboriginal Square Dancing and the Experience of Collectivity." *Musiké 1: Music and Ritual*: 41–58.

———. 2007. "Public and Intimate Sociability in First Nations and Métis Fiddling." *Ethnomusicology* 51/1: 30–63.

———. 2012. "No Heartaches in Heaven: A Response to Aboriginal Suicide." In *Aboriginal Music in Contemporary Canada: Echoes and Exchanges*, edited by Anna Hoefnagels and Beverley Diamond: 300–322. Montreal and Kingston: McGill–Queen's University Press.

———. 2013a. "Civil Twilight: Country Music, Alcohol, and the Spaces of Manitoban Aboriginal Sociability." In *Music, Sound, and Space: MP3, Recordings, and Tuning in to the Contemporary World*, edited by Georgina Born: 239–256. Cambridge: Cambridge University Press.

———. 2013b. "Rhythm and Role Recruitment in Manitoban Aboriginal Vocal and Instrumental Music." In *Experience and Meaning in Music Performance*, edited by Martin Clayton, Byron Dueck and Laura Leante. Oxford University Press.

Dunning, R. W. 1959. *Social and Economic Change among the Northern Ojibwa.* Toronto: University of Toronto Press.

Durkheim, Emile. 1995 [1912]. *The Elementary Forms of Religious Life.* Translated and with an introduction by Karen E. Fields. New York: The Free Press.

Eisenberg, Andrew. 2007. "Soundly Placed Subjects: Resonant Voices and Spatial Politics in Mombasa Kenya." Paper given at the 2007 meeting of the Society for Ethnomusicology in Columbus, Ohio.

Elias, Norbert. 1994. *The Civilizing Process: Sociogenetic and Psychogenetic Investigations.* Translated by Edmund Jephcott. Revised ed. Edited by Eric Dunning, Johan Goudsblom, and Stephen Mennell. Malden, ME: Blackwell.

Ellis, Clyde. 1990. "'Truly Dancing Their Own Way': Modern Revival and Diffusion of the Gourd Dance." *American Indian Quarterly* 14/1: 19–33.

Ellis, Clyde, Luke Eric Lassiter, and Gary H. Dunham. 2005. *Powwow.* Lincoln: University of Nebraska Press.

Evans, James. 1954 [1841]. *Cree Syllabic Hymn Book.* Text in Cree syllabics and English. Introduction in English by Margaret V. Ray. Translation by Raymond B. Horsefield. Facsimile of original 1841 edition, printed at Norway House, Hudson's Bay Territory. Toronto: Bibliographical Society of Canada.

Fabian, Johannes. 1983. *Time and the Other: How Anthropology Makes Its Object.* New York: Columbia University Press.

Faulkner, Robert R., and Howard S. Becker. 2009. *"Do You Know...?": The Jazz Repertoire in Action.* Chicago: University of Chicago Press.

Feld, Steven. 1990. *Sound and Sentiment: Birds, Weeping, Poetics, and Song in Kaluli Expression.* 2d ed. Philadelphia: University of Pennsylvania Press.

Fiddler, Chief Thomas, and James R. Stevens. 1985. *Killing the Shamen.* Moonbeam, Ont.: Penumbra Press.

Finnegan, Ruth. 2007 [1989]. *The Hidden Musicians: Music-Making in an English Town.* New ed. with preface added by the author. Middletown, CT: Wesleyan University Press.

Fox, Aaron A. 2004. *Real Country: Music and Language in Working-Class Culture.* Durham, NC: Duke University Press.

Francis, Daniel, and Toby Morantz. 1983. *Partners in Furs: A History of the Fur Trade in Eastern James Bay, 1600–1870.* Montreal and Kingston: McGill–Queen's University Press.

Freud, Sigmund. 1961 [1920]. *Beyond the Pleasure Principle.* Translated and edited by James Strachey. New York: W. W. Norton.

Friesen, Gerald. 1987. *The Canadian Prairies: A History.* Toronto: University of Toronto Press.

Frost, F. 1937, ed. *The Ojibway Church Hymn Book: Being a Collection of Hymns Gathered from Various Sources for Use in Divine Worship and in the Home.* London: Society for Promoting Christian Knowledge.

Gabriel Dumont Institute of Native Studies and Applied Research. 2002. *Drops of Brandy: An Anthology of Métis Music.* Saskatoon: Gabriel Dumont Institute.

Garcia, Luis-Manuel. 2013. "Crowd Solidarity on the Dancefloor in Paris and Berlin." In *Musical Performance and the Changing City: Postindustrial Contexts in Europe and the United States*, edited by Carsten Wergin and Fabian Holt: 227–255. London: Routledge.

Geertz, Clifford. 1973. *The Interpretation of Cultures.* New York: Basic Books.

Geller, Peter. 1996. "'Hudson's Bay Company Indians': Images of Native People and the Red River Pageant, 1920." In S. Elizabeth Bird, ed., *Dressing in Feathers: The Construction of the Indian in American Popular Culture*: 65–77. Boulder, CO: Westview Press.

Gibbons, Roy W. 1980. "'La Grande Gigue Simple' and 'The Red River Jig': A Comparative Study of Two Regional Styles of a Traditional Fiddle Tune." *Canadian Journal for Traditional Music* 8: 40–48.

Goertzen, Chris. 1996. "Balancing Local and National Approaches at American Fiddle Contests." *American Music* 14/3: 352–81.

Goffman, Erving. 1967. *Interaction Ritual: Essays on Face-to-Face Behavior.* Chicago: Aldine.

———. 1974. *Frame Analysis: An Essay on the Organization of Experience.* New York: Harper & Row.

Goodenough, Caroline Leonard. 1931. *High Lights on Hymnists and their Hymns.* New Bedford, MA: The author.

Green, Richard. "DeJarlis, Andy." In *The Encyclopedia of Music in Canada.* Web ed. <http://www.thecanadianencyclopedia.com/index.cfm?PgNm=EMCSubjects&Params=U2> (accessed 12 April 2006).

Greenhill, Pauline. 1999. "Backyard World/Canadian Culture: Looking at Festival Agendas." *Canadian University Music Review* 19/2: 37–46.

Gross, Lawrence L. 2002. "The Comic Vision of Anishinaabe Culture and Religion." *American Indian Quarterly* 26/3: 436–59.

[Guettel, Alan]. 1979. Liner notes to Don Messer et al., *The Good Old Days*, sound recording, produced by Alan Guettel and David Pritchard, directed by Scott Edwards. Apex TVLP 79052 – 1979. Toronto: MCA.

Habermas, Jürgen. 1989. *The Structural Transformation of the Public Sphere: An Inquiry into a Category of Bourgeois Society.* Translated by Thomas Berger. Cambridge, MA: MIT Press.

Hallowell, A. I. 1955. *Culture and Experience.* Philadelphia: Pennsylvania University Press.

———. 1992. *The Ojibwa of Berens River: Ethnography into History.* Edited with a preface and afterword by Jennifer S. H. Brown. Fort Worth, TX: Harcourt Bruce Jovanovich College.

Hanchard, Michael. 2000 [1998]. "Jody." In *Intimacy: A Special Issue*, edited by Lauren Berlant: 193–217. Chicago: University of Chicago Press.

Harrison, Klisala. 2002. "The Kwagiulth Dancers: Addressing Intellectual Property Issues at Victoria's First People's Festival." *World of Music* 44/1: 137–51.

Hasty, Jennifer. 2005. "Sympathetic Magic/Contagious Corruption: Sociality, Democracy, and the Press in Ghana." *Public Culture* 17/3: 339–69.

Hebdige, Dick. 1979. *Subculture: The Meaning of Style.* London: Routledge.

Hertz, Robert. 1960 [1907]. "A Contribution to the Study of the Collective Representation of Death." In *Death and the Right Hand*, translated by Rodney and Claudia Needham and with an introduction by E. E. Evans-Pritchard: 27–86. Glencoe, Ill.: Free Press.

Herzfeld, Michael. 1997. *Cultural Intimacy: Social Poetics in the Nation-State.* New York: Routledge.

Hickerson, Harold. 1967. "Some Implications of the Theory of the Particularity, or 'Atomism,' of Northern Algonkians." With comments by several respondents and a reply by the author. *Current Anthropology* 8/4: 313–43.

Hiebert, Daniel. 1991. "Class, Ethnicity, and Residential Structure: The Social Geography of Winnipeg, 1901–1921." *Journal of Historical Geography* 17/1: 56–86.

Hilger, Sister M. Inez. 1944. "Chippewa Burial and Mourning Customs." *American Anthropologist* 46/4: 564–68.

Hirschkind, Charles. 2006. *The Ethical Soundscape: Cassette Sermons and Islamic Counterpublics.* New York: Columbia University Press.

Hoefnagels, Anna. 2002. "Powwow Songs: Traveling Songs and Changing Protocol." *World of Music* 44/1: 127–36.

Hohmann, Walter H., and Lester Hostetler, eds. 1959 [1940]. *The Mennonite Hymnary.* Berne, IN: Mennonite Book Concern; Newton, KS: Mennonite Publication Office.

Horden, John, compiler. 1889. *A Collection of Psalms and Hymns, in the Language of the Cree Indians of North-West America.* London: Society for Promoting Christian Knowledge.

———, compiler. 1890. *A Collection of Psalms and Hymns, in the Language of the Cree Indians of North-West America.* London: Printed for the Society for Promoting Christian Knowledge.

———, compiler. 1949. *A Collection of Psalms and Hymns in the Language of the Cree Indians of North-West America.* Revised ed. with appendix. Toronto: Thorn Press.

Horden, John, and John Sanders. 1879. *Moosonee Hymnal.* Translated into the Ojibbeway language by the Bishop of Moosonee and John Sanders. London: Society for Promoting Christian Knowledge.

Howard, James H. 1955. "Pan-Indian Culture of Oklahoma." *Scientific Monthly* 81/5: 215–20.

Jenness, Diamond. 1935. *The Ojibwa Indians of Parry Island: Their Social and Religious Life.* Canada Department of Mines Bulletin No. 78. Ottawa: National Museum of Canada.

Johnston, Patrick. 1983. *Native Children and the Child Welfare System.* Toronto: Canadian Council on Social Development in association with James Lorimer and Company.

Johnston, Thos., and Frederick Genthon. N.d. *The Red River Jig, Published by Authority of the Old Timers' Association of Manitoba, Canada.* In two versions, the first credited to "Thos. Johnstone (Version) Transposed by W. E. Delaney," the second credited to "Frederick Genthon (Version)." A version of "Tapatoe" and dance instructions are also included. Old Timers' Association of Manitoba, Canada. Photocopy of a photocopy found in the "Red River Jig" file in the Provincial Library of Manitoba, 2003.

Julian, John, ed. 1925. *A Dictionary of Hymnology Setting Forth the Origin and History of Christian Hymns of All Ages and Nations.* Revised ed. with new supplement. London: John Murray.

"Kē Kē Pā Sakihitin." N.d. Author unknown. One of the songs in the Sinclair binder (see below).

Keil, Charles. 1987. "Participatory Discrepancies and the Power of Music." *Cultural Anthropology* 2/3: 275–83.

Keillor, Elaine. 2002. "Amerindians at the Rodeos and their Music." *World of Music* 44/1: 75–94.

Kelly, John D. 1995. "Diaspora and World War, Blood and Nation in Fiji and Hawai'i." *Public Culture* 7/3: 475–97.

Kipnis, Laura. 2000 [1998]. "Adultery." In *Intimacy: A Special Issue*, edited by Lauren Berlant: 9–47. Chicago: University of Chicago Press.

Kolinski, Mieczyslaw. 1973. "A Cross-Cultural Approach to Metro-Rhythmic Patterns." *Ethnomusicology* 17/3: 494–506.

Krims, Adam. 2000. *Rap Music and the Poetics of Identity.* Cambridge: Cambridge University Press.

Krotz, Larry. 1980. *Urban Indians: The Strangers in Canada's Cities.* Photographs by John Paskievich. Edmonton: Hurtig.

Kruzenga, Len. 2001. "Pauingassi Artifacts Spirited into U.S. by Three Fires Society: Community Demands Immediate Return of sacred items." *The Drum*, September 2001.

[Lacombe, A.]. 1886. *Katolik Ayamihewimasinahigan Nehiyawewinik: Livre de prières en langue crise.* [Montreal: C. O. Beauchemin.]

Landes, Ruth. 1968. *Ojibwa Religion and the Midéwiwin.* Madison: University of Wisconsin Press.

Lassiter, Luke Eric, Clyde Ellis, and Ralph Kotay. 2002. *The Jesus Road: Kiowas, Christianity, and Indian Hymns.* Lincoln: University of Nebraska Press.

Lederman, Anne. 1987. Liner notes to *Old Native and Métis Fiddling in Western Manitoba/Ka Été Nagamunan Ká~Kakkwékkiciwąnk*, Vol. 1: *Ebb and Flow, Bacon Ridge, Eddystone and Kinosota.* Toronto: Falcon Productions. 33⅓ disc FP–187.

———. 1988. "Old Indian and Métis Fiddling in Manitoba: Origins, Structure and Question of Syncretism." *Canadian Journal of Native Studies* 8/2: 205–30.

———. 2001. "Métis." In *The Garland Encyclopedia of World Music. Vol. 3: The United States and Canada*, edited by Ellen Koskoff: 404–11. New York: Garland.

———. 2003. CD booklet for *Old Native and Métis Fiddling in Western Manitoba*. Falcon Productions FPCD-387.

———. 2006. "Metis Fiddling: Found or Lost?" Version of conference paper sent in personal correspondence.

Lerdahl, Fred, and Ray Jackendoff. 1983. *A Generative Theory of Tonal Music*. Cambridge, MA: MIT Press.

London, Justin. 2004. *Hearing in Time: Psychological Aspects of Musical Meter*. New York: Oxford University Press.

Lysaght, Patricia. 1997. "'Caoineadh os Cionn Coirp': The Lament for the Dead in Ireland." *Folklore* 108: 65–82.

MacAndrew, Craig, and Robert B. Edgerton. 1969. *Drunken Comportment: A Social Explanation*. Chicago: Aldine.

Mackay, J. A., compiler and trans. 1927 [1891]. *Psalms and Hymns in the Language of the Cree Indians of the Diocese of Saskatchewan, North-West America*. London: Society for Promoting Christian Knowledge.

Manitoba. 1956. Acts of the Legislature of the Province of Manitoba 1956: Passed in the Session Held in the Fourth and Fifth Years of the Reign of Her Majesty Queen Elizabeth the Second, and being the Third Session of the Twenty-Fourth Legislature Begun and Holden at Winnipeg, on the Thirty-First Day of January, 1956 and closed by Prorogation on the Twenty-Third Day of April, 1956. Winnipeg: Printed by the Queen's Printer for [the] Province of Manitoba.

Mason, Leonard. 1967. *The Swampy Cree: A Study in Acculturation*. Ottawa: National Museum of Canada, Department of the Secretary of State.

Mass-Observation. 1987 [1943]. *The Pub and the People: A Worktown Study by Mass-Observation*. Introduction by Godfrey Smith. London: Cresset Library.

Mauss, Marcel. 1990 [1950]. *The Gift: The Form and Reason for Exchange in Archaic Societies*. Translated by W. D. Halls. Foreword by Mary Douglas. New York: W. W. Norton.

McCreless, Patrick. 1991. "Syntagmatics and Paradigmatics: Some Ramifications for the Analysis of Chromaticism in Tonal Music." *Music Theory Spectrum* 13: 146–79.

McCulloh, Judith. 1967. "Hillbilly Records and Tune Transcriptions." *Western Folklore* 26/4: 225–44.

McIvor, Olga. 2003. Notes taken during an Ojibwe elders' group meeting, on the afternoon of April 24, 2003. The meeting was one activity conducted during the Provincial Elders Gathering sponsored by the Manitoba First Nations Education Resource Centre.

McNally, Michael D. 2000. *Ojibwe Singers: Hymns, Grief, and a Native Culture in Motion*. Oxford: Oxford University Press.

———. 2009. *Honoring Elders: Aging, Authority, and Ojibwe Religion*. New York: Columbia University Press.

Messer, Don. 1981. *The Don Messer Anthology of Favorite Fiddle Tunes* [posthumous anthology]. Toronto: Gordon V. Thompson.

Metcalf, Peter, and Richard Huntington. 1991. *Celebrations of Death: The Anthropology of Mortuary Ritual*. 2nd ed. Cambridge: Cambridge University Press.

[Methodist Church (Canada)]. 1917. *The New Canadian Hymnal: A Collection of Hymns and Music for Sunday Schools, Young People's Societies, Prayer and Praise Meetings, Family Circles*. Toronto: William Briggs.

Michaels, Eric. 1994. *Bad Aboriginal Art: Tradition, Media, and Technological Horizons*. Foreword by Dick Hebdige. Introduction by Marcia Langton. Minneapolis: University of Minnesota Press.

Miller, J. R. 1996. *Shingwauk's Vision: A History of Native Residential Schools*. Toronto: University of Toronto Press.

———. 2000. *Skyscrapers Hide the Heavens: A History of Indian-White Relations in Canada*. 3d ed. Toronto: University of Toronto Press.

Mishler, Craig. 1993. *The Crooked Stovepipe: Athapaskan Fiddle Music and Square Dancing in Northeast Alaska and Northwest Canada*. Urbana: University of Illinois Press.

Monson, Ingrid. 1996. *Saying Something: Jazz Improvisation and Interaction*. Chicago: University of Chicago Press.

Morrison, Sheila Jones. 1995. *Rotten to the Core: The Politics of the Manitoba Métis Federation*. [Winnipeg]: J. Gordon Shillingford.

Neal, Jocelyn R. 2009. *The Songs of Jimmie Rodgers: A Legacy in Country Music*. Bloomington: Indiana University Press.

Nelson, Terrance. 2002a. "Singleton Report" [Letter to the Premier of Manitoba, January 8, 2002]. *Winnipeg Free Press*.

———. 2002b. "Our Grandfathers are NOT Artifacts." *Grassroots News* July 2002.

Nettl, Bruno. 1983. *The Study of Ethnomusicology: Twenty-nine Issues and Concepts*. Urbana: University of Illinois Press.

———. 2005. *The Study of Ethnomusicology: Thirty-one Issues and Concepts*. 2d ed. Urbana: University of Illinois Press.

———. 2008. "Native American Music." In Philip V. Bohlman, Bruno Nettl, and Tom Turino, *Excursions in World Music*: 336–61. 5th ed. Upper Saddle River, NJ: Pearson Prentice-Hall.

[Northern Canada Evangelical Mission]. 1977. *Coastal Cree Gospel Songs*. Prince Albert, Sask.: Northern Canada Evangelical Mission.

———. 1979. *Moose Cree Gospel Songs*. Prince Albert, Sask.: Northern Canada Evangelical Mission.

———. 1980. *Cree Hymns*. Prince Albert, Sask.: Northern Canada Evangelical Mission.

Pappas, Nikos. 2007. "'This is one of the most crooked tunes I ever did hear. But once you understand it, then it's alright to play': Crookedness in Oldtime American Fiddle Tune Repertories.' Paper presented 11 July 2007 at the 39th World Conference of the International Council for Traditional Music, Vienna.

Parmentier, Richard J. 1994. *Signs in Society: Studies in Semiotic Anthropology*. Bloomington: Indiana University Press.

Peirce, Charles Sanders. 1960. *Collected Papers*. Vols. 1 and 2: *Principles of Philosophy* and *Elements of Logic*. Edited by Charles Hartshorne and Paul Weiss. Cambridge, MA: Belknap Press of Harvard University Press.

Pettipas, Katherine. 1994. *Severing the Ties that Bind: Government Repression of Indigenous Religious Ceremonies on the Prairies*. Winnipeg: University of Manitoba Press.

Poloma, Margaret M. 1997. "The 'Toronto Blessing': Charisma, Institutionalization, and Revival." *Journal for the Scientific Study of Religion* 36/2: 257–71.

Povinelli, Elizabeth. 1998. "The State of Shame: Australian Multiculturalism and the Crisis of Indigenous Citizenship." *Critical Inquiry* 24: 575–610.

———. 1999. "Settler Modernity and the Quest for Indigenous Traditions." *Public Culture* 11/1: 19–47.

Powers, William K. 1990. *War Dance: Plains Indian Musical Performance*. Tucson: University of Arizona Press.

Preston, Richard J. 1985. "Transformations musicales et culturelles chez les Cris de l'est." Translated from the English by Nicole Beaudry and Évelyne Cossette. *Recherches Amérindiennes au Québec* 15/4: 19–28.

Provart, John. 2003. "Reforming the Indian Act: First Nations Governance and Aboriginal Policy in Canada." *Indigenous Law Journal* 2: 117–69.

Quick, Sarah. 2008. "The Social Poetics of the Red River Jig in Alberta and Beyond: Meaningful Heritage and Emerging Performance." *Ethnologies* 30/1: 77–101.

———. 2009. "Performing Heritage: Métis Music, Dance, and Identity in a Multicultural State." Ph.D. diss., Indiana University.

———. 2012. "'Frontstage' and 'Backstage' in Heritage Performance: What Ethnography Reveals." *Canadian Theatre Review*: 151: 24–29.

Radano, Ronald, and Philip V. Bohlman. 2000. "Music and Race: Their Past, Their Presence." In *Music and the Racial Imagination*, edited by Ronald Radano and Philip V. Bohlman. Chicago: University of Chicago Press.

Rice, Brian. 2002. "Repatriating War Trophies from Museums and Universities." *Grassroots News*, March 2002.

Rockwell, Joti. 2009a [2007]. "Listening along the Crooked Road: Meter in Old-Time Country and Bluegrass Music." Version of paper presented 11 July 2007 at the 39th World Conference of the International Council for Traditional Music, Vienna.

———. 2009b. "The Rhythm of Roots: Temporal Symmetries in Early Country and Blues Recordings." Paper given at the 2009 Meeting of the Society for Ethnomusicology, Mexico City.

———. 2011. "Time on the Crooked Road: Isochrony, Meter, and Disruption in Old-Time Country and Bluegrass Music." *Ethnomusicology* 55/1: 55–76.

Rogers, Edward S. 1962. "The Round Lake Ojibwa." Occasional Paper 5, Art and Archaeology Division, Royal Ontario Museum, University of Toronto. Toronto: Ontario Department of Lands and Forests, for the Royal Ontario Museum.

[Roman Catholic Diocese of Keewatin–The Pas]. 1998. *Ayamihewi-Nikamowina Masinahikan: Roman Catholic Cree Hymnbook (1998–Western Cree)*. The Pas, Man.: Roman Catholic Diocese of Keewatin–The Pas.

Saggers, Sherry, and Dennis Gray. 1998. *Dealing with Alcohol: Indigenous Usage in Australia, New Zealand and Canada*. Cambridge: Cambridge University Press.

Saindon, J. Emile. 1934. "Two Cree Songs from James Bay." *Primitive Man* 7/1: 6–7.

Samuels, David W. 2004. *Putting a Song on Top of It: Expression and Identity on the San Carlos Apache Reservation*. Tucson: University of Arizona Press.

———. 2009. "Singing Indian Country." In *Music of the First Nations: Tradition and Innovation in Native North America*, edited by Tara Browner: 141–159. Urbana: University of Illinois Press.

Sawchuk, Joe. 2001. "Negotiating an Identity: Métis Political Organizations, the Canadian Government, and Competing Concepts of Aboriginality." *American Indian Quarterly* 25/1: 73–92.

Scales, Christopher. 2002. "The Politics and Aesthetics of Recording: A Comparative Canadian Case Study of Powwow and Contemporary Native American Music." *The World of Music* 44/1: 41–59.

———. 2004. "Powwow Music and the Aboriginal Recording Industry on the Northern Plains: Media, Technology, and Native American Music in the Late Twentieth Century." Ph.D. diss., University of Illinois at Urbana–Champaign.

———. 2007. "Powwows, Intertribalism, and the Value of Competition." *Ethnomusicology* 51/1: 1–29.

———. 2012. *Recording Culture: Powwow Music and the Aboriginal Recording Industry on the Northern Plains*. Durham, NC: Duke University Press.

Schneider, David M., and Raymond T. Smith. 1973. *Class Differences and Sex Roles in American Kinship and Family Structure*. Englewood Cliffs, NJ: Prentice-Hall.

Silver, Jim, Cyril Keeper, and Michael MacKenzie. 2005. "'A Very Hostile System in Which to Live': Aboriginal Electoral Participation in Winnipeg's Inner City." Report for the Canadian Centre for Policy Alternatives. <http://www.policyalternatives.ca/documents/Manitoba_Pubs/2005/aboriginal_electoral_participation.pdf> (accessed 1 September 2009).

Silverstein, Michael. 1993. "Metapragmatic Discourse and Metapragmatic Function." In *Reflexive Language: Reported Speech and Metapragmatics*, edited by John A. Lucy: 33–58. Cambridge: Cambridge University Press.

———. 1997. "The Improvisational Performance of Culture in Realtime Discursive Practice." In *Creativity in Performance*, edited by Keith R. Sawyer: 265–312. Greenwich, CT: Ablex.

———. 2004. "'Cultural' Concepts and the Language-Culture Nexus." *Current Anthropology* 45/5: 621–52.

Silverstein, Michael, and Greg Urban, eds. 1996. *Natural Histories of Discourse*. Chicago: University of Chicago Press.

[Sinclair binder]. 2003. Song binder owned by Kendra and Mary Sinclair, two of my Winnipeg consultants.

Singleton, Jon. 2002. *Investigation of Missing Artifacts at the Anthropology Museum of the University of Winnipeg*. Winnipeg: Office of the Auditor General [of Manitoba].

Skinner, Alanson. 1911. *Notes on the Eastern Cree and Northern Saulteaux.* Anthropological Papers of the American Museum of Natural History, Vol. 9, Part 1. New York: Published by Order of the Trustees.

Smith, Christina. 2007. "Crooked as the Road to Branch: Asymmetry in Newfoundland Dance Music." *Newfoundland and Labrador Studies* 22/1: 139–64.

Spivak, Gayatri Chakravorty. "Can the Subaltern Speak?" In *Colonial Discourse and Post-Colonial Theory: A Reader,* edited by Patrick Williams and Laura Chrisman: 66–111.

Statistics Canada. 2003. "Aboriginal Identity (8), Age Groups (11B) and Sex (3) for Population, for Canada, Provinces, Territories, Census Metropolitan Areas and Census Agglomerations, 2001 Census—20% Sample Data." Catalogue no. 97F0011XCB01002. Ottawa: Statistics Canada January 21, 2003.

———. 2007. "Portrait of the Canadian Population 2006, 2006 Census: Population and Dwelling Counts, 2006 Census." Catalogue no. 97-550-XIE. Ottawa: Published by authority of the Minister responsible for Statistics Canada. <http://www12.statcan.gc.ca/english/census06/analysis/popdwell/pdf/97-550-XIE2006001.pdf> (accessed 1 September 2009).

———. "Aboriginal Peoples in Canada in 2006: Inuit, Métis and First Nations, 2006 Census: Aboriginal Peoples, 2006 Census." Catalogue no. 97-558-XIE. Ottawa: Published by authority of the Minister responsible for Statistics Canada. <http://www12.statcan.ca/english/census06/analysis/aboriginal/pdf/97-558-XIE2006001.pdf> (accessed 1 September 2009).

Stokes, Martin. 2002. "Marx, Money, and Musicians." In *Music and Marx: Ideas, Practice, Politics,* edited by Regula Burkhardt Qureshi: 139–66. New York: Routledge.

———. 2010. *The Republic of Love: Cultural Intimacy in Turkish Popular Music.* Chicago: University of Chicago Press.

Stokes, Martin, ed. 1994. *Ethnicity, Identity, and Music: The Musical Construction of Place.* Oxford: Berg.

Strathern, Marilyn. 1988. *The Gender of the Gift: Problems with Women and Problems with Society in Melanesia.* Berkeley and Los Angeles: University of California Press.

Taussig, Michael. 1993. *Mimesis and Alterity: A Particular History of the Senses.* London: Routledge.

Taylor, Gordon. 1989. *Companion to the Song Book of the Salvation Army.* St. Albans: Campfield Press.

Thatcher, Richard W. 2004. *Fighting Firewater Fictions: Moving Beyond the Disease Model of Alcoholism in First Nations.* Toronto: University of Toronto Press.

Tichi, Celia. 1994. *High Lonesome: The American Culture of Country Music.* Chapel Hill: University of North Carolina Press.

Titley, E. Brian. 1986. *A Narrow Vision: Duncan Campbell Scott and the Administration of Indian Affairs in Canada.* Vancouver: University of British Columbia Press.

Turino, Thomas. 1999. "Signs of Imagination, Identity, and Experience: A Peircian Semiotic Theory for Music." *Ethnomusicology* 43/2: 221–55.

———. 2008. *Music as Social Life: The Politics of Participation.* Chicago: University of Chicago Press.

Turner, Victor. 1969. *The Ritual Process: Structure and Anti-Structure.* Chicago: Aldine.

United Church of Canada. 1958. *The United Church of Canada Cree Hymn Book.* Enlarged republished ed. Translated from the United Church Hymnary by Rev. F. G. Stevens. Toronto: Board of Home Missions.

[United Church of Canada]. 1971. *Cree-English Hymnbook.* [Winnipeg] Manitoba Conference Home Missions Committee, United Church of Canada.

UMASC (University of Manitoba Archives and Special Collections). [1953]. "Ending Costly Nonsense." *Winnipeg Tribune* Newsclipping Collection. File: "Indians 1943–57."

van Gennep, Arnold. 1960 [1909]. *The Rites of Passage.* Translated by Monika B. Vizedom and Gabrielle L. Caffee. Introduction by Solon T. Kimball. Chicago: University of Chicago Press.

Wallis, Wilson. 1947. *The Canadian Dakota.* Anthropological Papers of the American Museum of Natural History 41, Part 1. New York: American Museum of Natural History.

Warner, Michael. 2002. *Publics and Counterpublics.* New York: Zone Books.

Waterman, Christopher. 1990. *Jùjú: A Social History and Ethnography of an African Popular Music.* Chicago: University of Chicago Press.

Wenger, Etienne. 1998. *Communities of Practice: Learning, Meaning, and Identity.* Cambridge: Cambridge University Press.

Whidden, Lynn. 1985. "Les hymnes, une anomalie parmi les chants traditionnels des Cris du nord." Translated from the English by Nicole Beaudry. *Recherches amérindiennes au Québec* 15/4: 29–36.

———. 2007. *Essential Song: Three Decades of Northern Cree Music.* Aboriginal Studies Series. Waterloo, Ont.: Wilfrid Laurier University Press.

Recordings

Beach, Chris. 2002a. *Opportunity.* Produced by Craig Fotheringham. Recorded at Dreamland [Studios Winnipeg] and published by Man-U-Sun. Privately distributed compact disc.

———. 2002b. "My Soap Opera Woman." On Beach 2002a.

———. 2004a. *Maano.* Recorded at Apple Blossom Studios, Winnipeg, and published by Man-U-Sun. Privately distributed compact disc CB2004CD2.

———. 2004b. "#1 on NCI." On Beach 2004a.

———. 2004c. *A New Life with Jesus—A Special Christmas Edition.* Recorded at Apple Blossom Studios, Winnipeg, and published by Man-U-Sun. Privately distributed compact disc.

Byrd, Tracy. 1998. "I'm from the Country (Single Version)." On *I'm from the Country.* Song written by Marty Brown, Richard Young, and Stan Webb. UMG Recordings. AAC audio file, downloaded 6 June 2012 from iTunes store.

C-Weed Band [Errol Ranville]. 1983. "Pick Up Truck Cowboy." On *Going the Distance* EP. AAC audio file, downloaded 27 May 2012 from iTunes store.

———.1995. *The Cowboy Code.* Album of AAC audio files, downloaded 27 May 2012 from iTunes store.

———. 2000. "Run as One." On *Run as One.* Song credited to "Errol Ranville" in CD booklet and to "Errol Ranville/Mike Bruyere" on cover. Recorded at the Recording Studio, Edmonton. Self-produced and -distributed compact disc.

De Jarlis, Andy. [1961]. *Andy De Jarlis and His Early Settlers.* [Montreal]: London Records. 33⅓ disc EB 44.

———. 2000. "Red River Jig." On *Fiddle Legends: Andy De Jarlis, Marcel Meilleur, Reg Bouvette, Eugene Laderoute.* Winnipeg: Sunshine Records. Compact disc SSCD 506.

Drops of Brandy. 2001. Saskatoon: Gabriel Dumont Institute. Compact disc GDI001.

Haggard, Merle. 1991. "Okie from Muskogee." On *Country Pride.* Cema Special Markets. Compact disc CDL-57420.

Hamelin, Bill. 2002. *Warriors in Chains.* Winnipeg: Cherish Records (Sunshine Records). Compact disc CRCD 6036.

Labbé, Gabriel. 1997. *100 ans de musique traditionelle québécoise d'après les recherches de Gabriel Labbé: Première époque: 1900 à 1940.* Research and selection by Gabriel Labbé. Produced by Lorraine Chalifoux. Transit Productions Sonores TRCD 9504/5.

Little, Joe, and Juliet Little. N.d. *The Old Rugged Cross: Cree Songs.* Cassette tapeN.p: n.d.

Maytwayashing, Cliff. N.d. *Flaming Arrow.* Winnipeg: Sunshine Records. Cassette tape SSCT 479.

———. N.d. *Native Fiddling Fever.* Winnipeg: Sunshine Records. Cassette tape SSBCT 443.

———. 2005a. *Skiffle Fiddle.* Winnipeg: Sunshine Records. Compact disc SSCD-524.

———. 2005b. "Big John McNeil." On Maytwayashing 2005a.

McGraw, Tim. 2001. "Cowboy In Me." On *Set This Circus Down.* Song written by Jeffrey Steele [LeVasseur], Al Anderson, and Craig Wiseman. Curb Records. AAC audio file, downloaded 6 June 2012 from iTunes store.

Messer, Don, and His Islanders. 1979. *The Good Old Days.* 33⅓ disc. Apex TVLP 79052.

Old Native and Métis Fiddling in Western Manitoba/Les violoneux autochtones et métis de l'ouest du Manitoba. 2003 [1987]. 2d ed. Toronto: Falcon Productions. Compact disc FPCD-387.

Prince. 1984. "Purple Rain." On *Purple Rain.* Warner Brothers. Compact disc 9 25110-2

Ranville, Errol. *See* C-Weed.

Richard, Cal, and the Big Stone Band. N.d. "Family Tree." On *Family Tree.* Winnipeg: Apple Blossom Studios. Compact disc.

Rimes, Lee Ann. 1998. "Purple Rain." On *Sittin' on Top of the World*. Curb Records. AAC audio file, downloaded 9 November 2007 from iTunes store.

Roberts, Julie. 2003. "Break Down Here." On *Julie Roberts*. Mercury Records. AAC audio file, downloaded ca. 10 August 2005 from iTunes store.

St. Germain, Ray. 2003. *My Many Moods*. Liner notes by St. Germain. Winnipeg: Arbor Records AR-12032. Compact disc.

Shannacappo, Les. 2007. "Never Be a Cheatin' Heart." On *Sounds Like... NCI FM*. Song written by Philip Sinclair. Winnipeg: [NCI FM?]. Compact disc NR-6607.

Spence, Emile. Ca. 2001 [1975]. *Emile Spence's Reel*. Canada Disc and Tape. Privately distributed compact disc GR2001D.

Thomas, Hubert. 2002a. *Cree Hymns by Hubert Thomas*, Vol. 1. Winnipeg: Cherish Records. Compact disc CRCD 6038.

———. 2002b. "Son [*sic*] of My Soul" ["Keya Oopimachihiwāo"]. On Thomas 2002a.

———. 2002c. *Cree Hymns by Hubert Thomas*, Vol. 2. Winnipeg: Cherish Records. Compact disc CRCD 6039.

Williams Hank, Jr. 1993. "Family Tradition." On *Hank Williams Jr.'s Greatest Hits*. Curb Records. Compact disc D2-77638.

Wood that Sings: Indian Fiddle Music of the Americas. 1997. Smithsonian Folkways Recordings. Compact disc SF 40472.

Interviews

Audy, Albert. Winnipeg, August 9, 2008.

Bulycz, Danny. Winnipeg, November 2, 2002.

Courchene, Victor and Laureen Courchene. Winnipeg, August 17, 2003.

———. Winnipeg, August 26, 2003.

Guiboche, Edward and Audrey Guiboche. Winnipeg, July 22, 2003.

———. Winnipeg, July 30, 2003.

Marsden, Emery. Winnipeg, August 30, 2003.

Maytwayashing, Cliff. August 12, 2008.

McLeod, David. Winnipeg, July 24, 2003.

———. Winnipeg, July 15, 2006.

Menow, Nelson. Winnipeg, August 15, 2003.

———. Winnipeg, August 10, 2008.

Michaels, Ness. Winnipeg, October 10, 2002.

Moneas, Morris. Black Island, August 1, 2003.

Monias, Ernest. Winnipeg, November 13, 2002.

Ranville, Errol. Near Ste. Anne, Manitoba, September 21, 2002.

Ranville, Stirling. Winnipeg, August 12, 2003.

Sinclair, Kendra and Mary Sinclair. Winnipeg, January 23, 2003.

Websites

The Cyberhymnal. <http://www.cyberhymnal.org/>.

Frontier Fiddlers. <http://www.frontierfiddlers.ca/> (accessed 26 April 2006, 6 June 2006).

Frontier School Division. <http://www.frontiersd.mb.ca/> (accessed 15 May 2006).

GuideStar. <http://www.guidestar.org/> (accessed 22 May 2008).

Indian and Northern Affairs Canada. <http://www.ainc-inac.gc.ca/> (accessed 21 June 2006).

IRS Exempt Organizations Select Check. <http://apps.irs.gov/app/eos/> (accessed 22 August 2012).

John Arcand Fiddle Fest. <http://www.johnarcandfiddlefest.com/> (accessed 6 June 2006).

Manitoba Conservation [department of Government of Manitoba] document on "First Nation hunting, trapping and fishing rights and responsibilities." <http://www.gov.mb.ca/conservation/firstnations/hunting-fishing-jan03.pdf> (accessed 20 June 2006).

Manitoba Hydro. 2009. <http://www.hydro.mb.ca/about_us/history/history_timeline.html> (accessed 2009).

Manitoba Education Citizenship and Youth [department of Government of Manitoba]. *Frontier School Division Map.* <http://www.edu.gov.mb.ca/ks4/schools/schoooldivmap.html> (accessed 2004).

NCI FM Aboriginal Music Hall of Fame: Errol Ranville. <http://www.ncifm.com/aboriginal-music-hall-of-fame/errol-ranville.html> (accessed 14 November 2007).

Peguis First Nation. 2012. <http://www.peguisfirstnation.ca/> (accessed 9 August 2012).

Sanderson, Daryl. 2006. Blog entry dated November 8, 2006. <http://derrylsanderson.blogspot.com/2006_11_01_archive.html> (accessed 29 November 2007).

Tehaliwaskenhas (Bob Kennedy). 2004. "Guilty! Grand Chief IS a Grand Thief . . . Misappropriated More than $60,000 of First Nations Funds in Manitoba." Turtle Island Native Network News, March. <http://www.turtleisland.org/discussion/viewtopic.php?p=2547> (accessed 13 July 2012).

Three Fires Midewiwin Lodge. <http://www.threefires.net/tfn/> (accessed 22 May 2008, 22 August 2012).

Films

Canadian Broadcasting Corporation. 1958. "The Newcomer." *Explorations* series. <http://www.cbc.ca/manitoba/features/originalcitizens/index_flash.html> (accessed 1 May 2002).

Loukinen, Michael. 1991. *Medicine Fiddle.* Northern Michigan University, Up North Films. <http://www.folkstreams.net/film>, 178 (accessed 15 January 2010).

Rodgers, Bob, dir. 1980. *The Fiddlers of James Bay.* National Film Board of Canada. VHS tape.

Index